Land Records of
Sussex County
Delaware

Various Dates

1693-1698, 1715-1717, 1782-1792, 1802-1805

Mary Marshall Brewer

HERITAGE BOOKS
2008

HERITAGE BOOKS

AN IMPRINT OF HERITAGE BOOKS, INC.

Books, CDs, and more—Worldwide

For our listing of thousands of titles see our website
at
www.HeritageBooks.com

Published 2008 by
HERITAGE BOOKS, INC.
Publishing Division
100 Railroad Ave. #104
Westminster, Maryland 21157

Other books by the author:

Kent County, Delaware, Land Records, Volumes 1 through 8
Land Records of Sussex County, Delaware, 1681-1725
Land Records of Sussex County, Delaware, 1763-1769
Land Records of Sussex County, Delaware, 1753-1763
Philadelphia County, Pennsylvania, Land Records 1706-1713

International Standard Book Numbers
Paperbound: 978-1-58549-028-8
Clothbound: 978-0-7884-7124-7

CONTENTS

INTRODUCTION

Few records of the Swedish Colony (1638-1655) have survived. From 1655 to 1664 and from 1673 to 1674, the Dutch West India Company and the City of Amsterdam were proprietors of the land which became Delaware (ignoring claims by the Calverts of Maryland). The surviving records are held by the Archives of New York at Albany.

The Duke of York was proprietor from 1664 to 1673 and from 1674 to 1682. These land records are also held at Albany. *Original Land Titles in Delaware, commonly known as The Duke of York Record, 1646-1679,* was printed by order of the General Assembly of the State of Delaware (1899), reprinted by Family Line Publications in 1989.

The southernmost portions of Sussex County were once treated as part of Somerset County, Maryland. Somerset County ws created n 1666 with the Atlantic Ocean and Chesapeak Bay its eastern and western boundaries, and its northern boundary - which today lies well inside Sussex County, Delaware - the Nanticoke River. Worcester County, Maryland, was formed out of Somerset in 1742; at that time the northern boundary of Worcester was set at "Broad Creek Bridge," the present location of the town of Laurel, Delaware. In 1769 the new line, established by Charles Mason and Jeremiah Dixon, was offically accepted. Prior to 1769 all records of the residents of land south of the Nanticoke and Indian Rivers should be sought in Maryland record books. When in doubt check records on both states.

Those records from 1681 through 1725 which were found in Liber A were published in an earlier volume. All records of Liber A which pertained to later years and all records of Liber B regardless of years, are included here. Liber B appears to pick up some of the records for 1693-1698 that were not covered in Liber A. Some of the records found in Liber A pertained to transactions between 1764 and 1805; these were abstracted into 12 pages and are included here. At the end of each entry in parens is the Liber followed by the original page number.

F. Edward Wright
Westminster, Maryland
1998

v

ABBREVIATIONS

ackn - acknowledged
adj - adjoining
adminr - administrator or
administratrix
afsd - aforesaid
atty - attorney
a. - acres
co - county
cr - creek
dau(s) - daughter(s)
decd - deceased
e - east
ft - feet
Hund - Hundred

mi - miles
MD - Maryland
n - north
PA - Pennsylvania
pt/o - part of
purch - purchased
rd - road
s - south
Suss - Sussex
tr - tract
uxor - wife
w - west
wit - witness
w/o - wife of

DORCHESTER CO

SUSSEX CO

Nanticoke R.

Indian R

NANTICOKE 100

BALTIMORE 100

S O M E R S E T   C O

WICOMICO 100

MONIE 100

POCOMOKE 100

BOGETENORTEN 100

MANOKIN 100

MATTAPANY 100

ANNEMESSEX 100

ACCOMACK CO

Somerset County MD
in 1724, based on a
map from *The National
Genealogical Society
Quarterly.*

IN 1742, WORCESTER COUNTY, MD, WAS CREATED FROM SOMERSET
COUNTY. In setting the northern boundary at 'Broad Creek Bridge', site of
present day Laurel, Lord Baltimore reaffirmed his claim to Sussex County lands
even though, in 1732, he had signed an agreement in which he ceded them to Wm
Penn. *A word of caution: information derived from the above map should be
interpreted very broadly, based as it is on vague descriptions of Lord Baltimore's
boundaries which often conflict with maps from the period. Surviving maps, in
fact, often conflict with one another, and even bear obvious inaccuracies like the
transposition of Somerset and Worcester Counties.*

1

SUSSEX CO DEED RECORD
Volume B2

5 Sep 1694. Power of Atty. THOMAS JONES of Suss Co planter
appoint my loving friend JOHN BARKER of same co planter my atty to
convey my pt/o a tr of land sw side of Middle Cr as by pattent unto
WILLIAM BURTON of Accamack VA gent. Wit: ROBERT BURTON,
THOMAS WEST. Proved 5 Sep 1694. Attest: NEHEMIAH FIELD
clerk. (B:pg 1)

5 Sep 1694. Deed. JOHN JONES als GOLLEDGE and THOMAS
JONES als GOLLEDGE of Suss Co PA planters for 55 pounds sold to
WILLIAM BURTON of Accamack VA gent ... a tr of land called the
Brothers Portion s side of Middle Cr granted unto the said JOHN and
THOMAS JONES als GOLLEDGE by virtue of a warrent confirmed by
patten by WILLIAM PENN proprietary of PA ... on Herring Cr als
Goldsmiths Cr adj GEORGE YOUNG ... 600 a. Wit: PETER WAPLES,
JOHN STUCHBURY, ROGER CORBETT. Ackn 5 Sep 1694 by JOHN
BARKER by vertue of a power of atty [above] from THOMAS JONES
togather with his brother JOHN JONES als GOLLEDGE. (B:pg 1)

4 Sep 1694. Deed. CORNELUS WILTBANCK of Lewes Suss Co PA
yeoman for 8 pounds sold to JOHN GIBB late of Piscattaway New
England marriner ... a lott of ground in Front Street of the Town of
Lewes between JOHN MIERS hatter and ISAAC BOWDES decd 60 ft
in breadth and 200 ft in length. Wit: [blank]. Ackn 6 Dec 1694. Attest
NEHEMIAH FIELD clerk. (B:pg 4)

29 Jul 1692. Deed. WILLIAM BRADFORD of Accamack Co VA for 105
pounds sold to WILLIAM SWEATNAM, PETER RAYMAN and
ROGER CORBETT ... a tr of land called Bradford Hall s side of
Rehoboth Cr of Rehoboth Bay granted unto NETHANIEL BRADFORD
by vertue of a warrent 25 Mar 1676 confirmed by letter of pattent by
the commissioners of WILLIAM PENN esqr absolute proprietary and
governor of PA ... 1200 a. Wit: WM CLARK, ALBERTUS JACOBS, AD
JOHNSON. Ackn 29 Jul 1692. Attest: THO PEMBERTON clerk. (B:pg
5)

8 Aug 1694. Power of Atty. PETER RAYMAN of Suss Co PA marriner
appoint my loving friend ALBURTUS JACOBS my atty to ackn unto
RICHARD PAYNTER Junr adminr of WILLIAM SWEATNAM decd

1/3 pt/o 1200 a. of land upon Loves Cr, and ROGER CORBETT another pt/o said tr, and also be cearfull that I have my own proper 400 a. where I have built and emproved .... Wit: LEAR STRECTHER, NEHEMIAH FIELD. Proved 5 Sep 1694. (B:pg 7)

4 Sep 1694. Deed. PETER RAYMAN and ROGER CORBETT both of Suss Co PA for mortallity sake and prevention of future inconveniencies convey unto RICHARD PAYNTER and JANE his wife adminrs of WILLIAM SWEATNAM late of same co decd ... a tr of land [see above] ... 400 a. Wit: HENRY STRETCHER, JOHN AMERY, PETER LEWES. Ackn 5 Sep 1694. Attest: NEHEMIAH FIELD clerk. (B:pg 8)

7 Dec 1694. Deed. ROGER CORBETT of Suss Co PA for 13 pounds 10 shillings sold to RICHARD PAYNTER Junr of same co ... a tr of land pt/o a tr purch of WILLIAM BRADFORD of Accamack VA by the said ROGER CORBETT adj the line parting the land of the said PAYNTER and CORBETT on Loves Cr of Rehoboth Bay ne side of Angola Neck ... 150 a. Wit: HENRY STRETCHER, SARAH STRETCHER. Ackn 6 Dec 169-. Attest: NEHEMIAH FIELD clerk. (B:pg 10)

4 Sep 1694. Deed. PETER RAYMAN and RICHARD PAYNTER for himself and JANE his wife adminrs of WILLIAM SWEATNAM decd all of Suss Co for mortality sake and prevention of future inconveniencies conveyed unto ROGER CORBETT of same co ... a tr of land [see above] ... 400 a. Wit: LEAR STRECTHER, JOHN AMERY, PETER LEWES. Ackn 5 Sep 1694 PETER RAYMAN. (B:pg 11)

4 Sep 1694. Deed. ROGER CORBETT of Suss Co PA and RICHARD PAYNTER for himself and JANE his wife adminrs of WILLIAM SWEATNAM late of Suss Co decd for mortallity sake and the prevention of future inconveniancies conveyed to PETER RAYMAN of same co ... a tr of land [see above] ... 400 a. Wit: LEAR STRECTHER, JOHN AMERY, PETER LEWIS. Ackn 5 Sep 1694. (B:pg 13)

5 Dec 1694. Deed. JOSEPH BOOTH justice of Suss Co PA for 70 pounds sold to PETER GOYTE a tr of land s side of Muspillion Cr adj ART JOHNSON VERKIRK and land called Little Graves End, laid out by warrant of ROBERT HUDSON for 475 a. and by ROBERT HUDSON sold 4 Jun 1693 unto HENRY BOWMAN now decd, and 200 a. thereof conveyed unto JOSEPH BOOTH 6 Sep year afsd, adj land called Hills Content and Little Cr ... 200 a. Wit: WILLIAM ORR, AUTHOR STARR. Ackn 6 Dec 1694. (B:pg 14)

4 Sep 1694. Deed of Gift. LUKE WATSON of Suss Co PA gent for love and effection and 50 pounds give unto my eldest son LUKE WATSON Junr ... pt/o a 600 a. tr of land called Fairfield s side of Prime Hook Neck bounded by HENRY SMITH decd and JOHN and WILLIAM BELLAMY, surveyed 5 Mar 1684 upon warrant bearing date 5 Jul 1683 and confirmed unto me by pattent on 1 Jun 1684 ... 200 a. Wit: ALBURTUS JACOBS, WM CLARK. Ackn 5 Sep 1694. (B:pg 16)

5 Dec 1694. Deed. JOSEPH BOOTH of Suss Co PA adminr of the estate of WILLIAM COWTHRY late of same co decd for 7000 pounds of tobacco in right of his late wife the dau of Major WILLIAM SPENCER decd and adminr of his estate sold to THOMAS MAY of same co ... a 500 a. tr of land, whereas WILLIAM COWTHRY was in his life time possessed as proper estate of inheritance of a tr of land formerly called Joseys Choice and now Spencers Hall n side of Ceder Cr bounded by ROBERT HART and ART JOHNSON VANKIRK ... which WILLIAM COWTHRY in his life time sold unto Major WILLIAM SPENCER and received of him 5000 pounds of tobacco pt/o the purch moneys being 12,000 pounds of tobacco. Wit: LUKE WATSON, THOMAS OLDMAN. Ackn 6 Dec 1694. (B:pg 18)

2 Dec 1693. Deed. HENRY BOWMAN Senr of Suss Co PA planter for 35 pounds sold to JOSEPH HICKMAN of same co planter ... a tr of land called Hickmans Field pt/o a tr called Bowmans Farms in Slaughter Neck adj land of HENRY PENNINGTON, in TROILLEY's line, surveyed 5 Apr last past ... 200 a. Wit: JOSEPH BOOTH, ARTHUR VERKIRKE. JOHN HILL ackn 2nd day this instant by virtue of a power of atty from HENRY BOWMAN. (B:pg 20)

2 Sep 1693. Deed. HENRY BOWMAN Senr of Suss Co PA for 36 pounds sold to HENRY SKIDMORE of same co planter ... a tr of land called Skidmores Choice pt/o a tr called Bowmans Farms in Slaughter Neck adj land of LUKE WATSON Junr ... 200 a. Wit: JOSEPH BOOTH, ARTHUR VERKIRKE. JOHN HILL ackn 7 Sep 1693 by virtue of a power of atty from HENRY BOWMAN. (B:pg 22)

1 Dec 1693. Deed. HENRY BOWMAN Senr of Suss Co PA for 18 pounds sold to WILLIAM STAPLEFORD of same co planter ... a tr of land called Staplefords Field pt/o a tr called Bowmans Farms in Slaughter Neck adj HENRY SKIDMORE's land ... 100 a. survey bearing date 8 Apr last past. Wit: JOSEPH BOOTH, AUTHUR VERKERKE. JOHN HILL ackn 7 Dec 1693 by virtue of a power of atty from HENRY BOWMAN. (B:pg 23)

1 Dec 1693. Deed. HENRY BOWMAN Senr of Suss Co PA for 20 pounds sold to HENDRICK AHASUERUS (HENRICK ASSUERUS) (AHASURUS) of same co cordwayner ... a tr of land called Sushans Pallice pt/o a tr called Bowmans Farms in Slaughter Neck adj ALEXANDER DRAPER and THOMAS TILTON ... 100 a. survey bearing date 12 Apr last past. Wit: JOSEPH BOOTH, AUTHUR VERKERKE. JOHN HILL ackn 7 Dec 1693 by virtue of a power of atty. (B:pg 25)

1 Dec 1693. Deed. WILLIAM CLARK of Lewes Suss Co PA for 46 pounds sold to OBEDIAH DAWSON of Dorsett Co MD planter and FRANCES WILLIS of Dorsett Co widow ... a tr of land, whereas JAMES CLAYPOOLE and ROBERT TURNER, two of the commissioners appointed by WILLIAM PENN esqr proprietary of PA to grant warrants and pattents, on 29 Sep 1686 granted unto JAMES GRAY a 1000 a. tr of land s side of Broad Cr called Millford bounded

4

by HENRY BOWMAN, and JAMES GRAY for 20 pounds on 6 Dec 1687 conveyed it unto WILLIAM CLARK ... 1000 a. Wit: LUKE WATTSON Junr, CORNELUS WILTBANCK, THOMAS KLAMAN[?]. Ackn 7 Dec instant. (B:pg 27)

6 Mar 1693/4. Deed. ALEXANDER MOLLISTON (MOLESTON) of Suss Co PA planter for 7 pounds sold to SAMUEL DICKASON of same co planter ... a tr of land near the town of Lewes pt/o a tr whereon the said ALEXANDER MOLLISTON now lives called [blank] beginning near Oyster Shell Point on Lewes Cr ... 40 a. Wit: THO PEMBERTON, JOHN BARON. Ackn 8 Mar 1693/4 by HENRY MOLESTON by vertue of a power of atty from his father ALEXANDER MOLESTON [below]. (B:pg 29)

6 Mar 1693/4. Power of Atty. ALEXANDER MOLESTON of Suss Co PA appoint my beloved son HENRY MOLESTON my atty to ackn the [above] deed in open court. Wit: THO PEMBERTON, JOHN BARON. Proved 8 Mar 1693/4. Attest: NEHEMIAH FIELD clerk. (B:pg 30)

1 Mar 1694. Deed. JACOB WARING of Suss Co PA planter for 50 pounds sold to JOHN HAYNES of same co planter ... a tr of land, whereas JAMES CLAYPOOLE and ROBERT TURNER, two of the commissioners appointed by WILLIAM PENN proprietor of PA to grant warrants and pattents, on 2 Apr 1686 granted unto ABRAHAM POTTER of same co planter a 300 a. tr of land called Abrahams Lott nw side of Cold Spring Br of the Great Cr beginning at land of CORNELUS JOHNSON ... which the said ABRAHAM POTTER on 4 Sep 1686 conveyed unto the said JACOB WARING ... 300 a. Wit: WM CLARK, RICHARD PARR. Ackn 5 Sep 1694. (B:pg 30)

5 Mar 1694. Deed. WILLIAM CLARK of Lewes Suss Co PA for 200 peaces of eight sold to JAMES JOHNSON of same place merchant ... a tr of land at Ceder Cr se side of Muspillion Cr by Long Love Br adj BENJAMAN COWDRY and RICHARD HILL, whereas 500 a. of land was conveyed unto GEORGE CULLIN 27 May 1680 and by him conveyed unto JOHN EDMONDSON of Talbutt Co MD on 13 Dec 1693, and he on 5 Jan 1693 conveyed it unto the said WILLIAM CLARK, except 100 a. which JOHN WILLIAMS was to have for seating the said land, WILLIAM MARKHAM, ROBERT TURNER and JOHN GOODSON three of the commissioners appointed by WILLIAM PENN proprietor of PA on 16 Feb 1693/4 confirmed the 500 a. unto the said WILLIAM CLARK except 100 a. afsd ... 400 a. to the only proper use and behoofe of JAMES JOHNSON during the term of his naturall life ... to the said WILLIAM CLARK from JOHN EDMONDSON and for and during the naturall life of the w/o the said JAMES JOHNSON if ever he shall have any and after the decease of the said JAMES JOHNSON and his wife and the longest liver of them, then to the heirs of JAMES JOHNSON, or shall return to WILLIAM CLARK. Wit: THOMAS FISHER, MARGERY FISHER, RICHARD THOMAS, PETER LUCAS. Ackn 8 Mar 1694. (B:pg 32)

4 Sep 1693. Deed. ALEXANDER MOLESTON of Suss Co PA yeoman

for 160 pounds sold to PETER LEWIS (LEWES) of same co gent ... a
tr of land called [blank] pt/o a tr where the said HENRY MOLESTON
now liveth near Lewes Town by Pagan Br ... 476 a. royall mines
excepted. Wit: THO PEMBERTON, WILL RODENEY. By commission
from his excellency BENJAMAN FLETCHER capt gent and governor
in cheafe ackn in open court on 6&7 Sep 1693. (B:pg 34)

1 Dec 1693. Deed. WILLIAM CLARK of Lewes Suss Co PA merchant
for 14 pounds and 5000 pounds of tobacco with cask sold to JOHN
BARKER of same co ... a tr of land, whereas WILLIAM MARKHAM,
ROBERT TURNER and JOHN GOODSON three of the commissioners
appointed by WILLIAM PENN esqr proprietor of PA on 26 Nov 1690
granted unto the said WILLIAM CLARK a tr of land on sw br of
Indian River adj land called Cattle Delight and on Barking Cr ... 800 a.
Wit: [blank]. Ackn -- Dec 1693. (B:pg 36)

12 Sep 1693. Deed. WILLIAM CLARK of Lewis Suss Co PA merchant
for 60 pounds sold to ABRAHAM POTTER of same co planter ... a tr
of land, whereas WILLIAM MARKHAM and JOHN GOODSON two of
the commissioners appointed by WILLIAM PENN esqr proprietor of
PA on 14 May 1687 granted unto the said CORNELUS JOHNSON a
tr of land called Johnsons Bay s side of Broad Cr bounded by JOHN
KIRK, HENRY HARMON and RICHARD PATTE ... 400 a. which
CORNELUS JOHNSON sold unto the said WILLIAM CLARK on 3
Feb 1687. Wit: JOHN STOCKLY, JA SANGSTER, AD JOHNSON.
Ackn 7 Dec 1693. (B:pg 37)

7 Dec 1693. Deed. SAMUEL PRESTON of Suss Co PA for 150 pounds
sold to JAMES PETERKIN of same co ... a plantation or tr of land
called Tower Hill near Lewes Town 400 a. adj Pagans Cr and
EDWARD SOUTHREN. Wit: THO PEMBERTON, WILL RODENEY,
JOHN HILL. Ackn 7 Dec 1693. (B:pg 39)

24 Jan 1693. Deed. President WILLIAM CLARK and justice THOMAS
OLDMAN both of the town of Lewis PA for 200 pounds sold to
ALBURTUS JACOBS of same co ... a tr of land, whereas WILLIAM
MARKHAM, ROBERT TURNER and JOHN GOODSON three of the
commissioners appointed by WILLIAM PENN esqr proprietor of PA
hath granted unto the said THOMAS OLDMAN and WILLIAM
CLARK on 26 Nov 1690 a tr of land adj Pothooks Cr, Whorekill, JOHN
VINES and ALEXANDER MOLLISTON ... 920 a. Wit: ROBERT
CLIFTON, SAM GRAY. Ackn 6 Feb 1693/4. (B:pg 40)

13 Apr 1693. Deed. ALEXANDER MOLESTON (MOLESTINE) of
Suss Co PA for 45 shillings sold to JACOB KOLLOCK of same place
cooper ... a single front lott in the town of Lewes pt/o the plantation
whereon the said ALEXANDER MOLESTON now liveth adj THOMAS
CLIFTON. Wit: WM RODENEY, WM DYRE. Ackn 7 Sep 1693. (B:pg
42)

17 Feb 1685. Deed. NICHOLAS BARTLETT of Kent Co PA planter for
100 pounds sold to FRADRICK PHILLIPS of NY marchant ... pt/o a tr

of land, whereas WILLIAM PENN proprietary and governor of PA by his letters pattons bearing date 7 Nov 1683, granted unto the said NICHOLAS BARTLETT a 948 a. tr of land called Bartletts Lott in Kent Co n side of Mother Cr and s side of Dover River by Mill Br ... NICHOLAS BARTLETT hath conveyed 300 a. unto JOHN RICHARDSON Senr adminr of the estate of EDWARD WILLIAMS late of Kent Co decd and 100 a. unto JOHN NEWALL of Kent Co planter. Wit: WM CLARK, GEORGE MARTIN, ALBURTUS JACOBS. Ackn 18 Feb 1685 in Kent Co Court. Attest: JOHN BRINCKLOE clerk. (B:pg 43)

22 Dec 1685. Deed. WILLIAM CARTER of Lewis Suss Co PA bricklayer for 5000 pounds of tobacco with cask sold to JACOB WARING (WARRIN) of same co turner ... a plantation house with 100 a. of land s side of Pothooks Cr pt/o a tr of land that was granted by pattent by the late governor of NY unto OTTO WOOLGAST (WOOLLGAST) and ABRAHAM CLEMMENT and by the will of the said OTTO WOOLGAST bearing date 26 Apr 1681 declared that if the said WILLIAM CARTER should pay the said 100 a. of land and plantation that his will was that he should have it, it doth appear that the said WILLIAM CARTER hath paid for the same for the satisfying of the said OTTO WOOLGAST debts. Wit: WM CLARK, JOHN ROADS. Ackn at court held 9,10,11 and 12 Mar 1686. Attest: NORTON CLAYPOOLE clk. (B:pg 45)

11 Nov 1684. Deed. JOHN PYE of Lewes Town PA sold unto WILLIAM EMMOTT of same place one parcell of land 300 a. being in a devident of land of ABRAHAM POTTER at Indian River as by my masters will ... . Wit: THOMAS HODGKINGS, THOMAS ALLETT. Ackn 16 Jun 1685. Attest: JOHN KIPHAVEN. (B:pg 46)

14 Sep 1686. Deed. HENRY PENNINGTON (PENINGTON) of Suss Co planter for 7200 pounds of tobacco sold to WILLIAM CLARK of Lewis same co ... a tr of land surveyed and laid out to the said HENRY PENNINGTON by virtue of a grant and warrant obtained 12 Jan 1679 s side of Ceder Cr adj ALEXANDER DRAPER and JOHN OUTON ... 425 a. called Callis Land [rest of page blank]. (B:pg 46)

5 Sep 1693. Deed. ANDRIES DIRRECKSON of Suss Co PA gent by his atty PETER LEWES for 84 pounds sold to ROBERT BURTON of same co ... a tr of land called Kannings Adventure on Rehoboth Bay adj Middle Cr ... 400 a. royall mines excepted. Wit: WILL RODENEY, MARY DYRE. Ackn at court held 6&7 Sep 1693. (B:pg 48)

5 Dec 1693. Deed. JOHN BARKER of Suss Co PA planter for 140 pounds sold to ANDRIES DIRECKSON of same co mariner ... a 1000 a. tr of land, whereas JOHN BARKER by virtue of a commission granted by WILLIAM PENN propriator and governor of PA unto WILLIAM MARKHAM secretary, THOMAS ELLIS, JOHN GOODSON or any two of them for granting of land, did obtain a pattent dated at Phila 10 Jan 1689 for a tr of land s side of Indian River adj land formerly serveyed and laid out for JOHN OAKEY called Mollattoe Hall

... whereas the said JOHN BARKER purch 800 a. from ALEXANDER MOLLISTON formerly appertaining to JOHN OAKEY on Black Water Run Cr called Mollattoe Hall on 5 Dec 1693 ... and also 400 a. of the afsd 800 a. tr on Fishing Cr to road over the beaverdam to Assawaman, the other 1/2 sold by the said JOHN BARKER unto THOMAS WEST, the two trs, 1400 a., now called Fairfield. Wit: WM DYRE, JAMES THOMAS, JOHN BARON. Ackn 7 Dec 1693. (B:pg 49)

2 Apr 1686 at Phila. Confirmation of Pattent. THOMAS LLOYD, JAMES CLAYPOOLE, ROBERT TURNER being appointed commissioners by WILLIAM PENN proprietary and governor of PA to grant warrants and pattents, whereas there is a tr of land between Coolespring Br and Mill Cr ... 500 a. granted by patent 6 Mar 1684 and resurveyed 5 Mar 1686 unto WILLIAM CLARK ... we confirm the same pattent unto WILLIAM CLARK. (B:pg 52)

21 Nov 1717. HONOUR BEDWELL gentlewoman executrix of the will of WILLIAM CLARK gent late of Suss Co decd assign over all my right to the [above] pattent unto PRESERVED COGGESHALL of said co. Wit: SIMON KOLLOCK, JAMES SIMSON, ELIAS FISHER. Proved 28 Jun 1723. Attest: PHILL RUSSELL dep rolls. (B:pg 54)

19 Nov 1717. Deed. HONNOR BEDWELL sometime relict and widow of WILLIAM CLARK gent late of Suss Co decd gent for 50 pounds paid to WILLIAM CLARK gent sold to PRESERVED COGGESHALL yeoman ... a messuage tr of land between Coolespring Br and Mill Cr ... 500 a. [same as above] ... HONNOR BEDWELL appoint my trusty friend JAMES SIMSON inholder of the town of Lewes my atty to ackn this deed in open court. Wit: SIMON KOLLOCK, JAMES SIMSON, ELIAS FISHER. Ackn 4 Feb 1717. Attest: ROGER CORBETT clerk. Proved 28 Jun 1723. Attest: PHILL RUSSELL dep rolls. (B:pg 54)

20 Jul 1724. Deed of Gift. WILLIAM GREAR (GRERR) of Suss Co for love, goodwill and effection give to my loving granson GREAR (GRERR) BISHOP of same place ... 1 parcell of land s side of Bowmans Br in Ceder Cr Hund ... 200 a. called William Burdge with all the rest of my moveable estate when be pleas God to call me out of this world. Wit: JOHN HINMAN, MARY HINMAN. Recorded 20 Jul 1724. Attest: PRESERVD COGGESHALL clerk. (B:pg 57)

10 Aug 1698. Deed. WILLIAM PILES of Suss Co PA for 20 pounds sold to CALEB CIRWITHIN (KIRWITHIN) of same co weaver ... the residue of a tr of land, whereas WILLIAM MARKHAM secretary and JOHN GOOD(SON) commissioners appointed by WILLIAM PENN proprietary and governor of PA to grant pattents, at Phila 17 May 1698 granted unto JOHN and SAMUEL WATSON a 600 a. tr of land n side of Primehook which said JOHN and SAMUEL WATSON at a court held 5,6,7,8 Jun 1698 made over unto the said WILLIAM PILES, and for a valuable consideration he made over 300 a. of the 600 a. unto LUKE WATSON Junr adj WILLIAM BELLAMEY ... 300 a. Wit: HENRY STRETCHER, NEHEMIAH FIELD. Ackn 7 Sep 1698. (B:pg 58)

10 Aug 1698. Deed. WILLIAM PILES of Suss Co PA yeoman for 30
pounds sold to CALEB CIRWITHIN (KIRWITHIN) of same co ... 2
parcells of meadow als marsh pt/o a tr of land called Watsons Marshes
serveyed -- Feb 1684 by virtue of a special warrant unto LUKE
WATSON Senr of same co gent by pattent bearing date 5 Mar 1683
and by him at a court held 5,6,7,8 Jun 1688 conveyed unto the afsd
WILLIAM PILES ... one parcel begins at JOHN BELAMEY's
(BELLAMAY) land to Slaughter Cr, the other parcell begins at land
the said LUKE WATSON Senr lived upon to Cypriss Swamp, to land
then belonging unto JOHN and SAMUEL WATSON ... 150 a.
WILLIAM PILES on 4 Mar 1695 made over unto LUKE WATSON
Junr yeoman 75 a. pt/o the said marsh ... 75 a. Wit: HENRY
STRETCHER, NEHEMIAH FIELD. Ackn 7 Sep 1698. (B:pg 60)

8 Feb 1675. Agreement. PETER BAWCOMBE and JOHN BRIDGE
(BRIGS) have contracted between each other and give to each other to
save one parcell of land, the said JOHN BRIDGE gives unto PETER
BAWCOMBE the tr near Bawcombbridge Cr adj PETER BAWCOMBE
his land, for which consideration the said PETER BAWCOMBE doth
give an equall quantity of land being at JOHN BRIDGE's side of said
br unto the said JOHN BRIDGE. Wit: CORNELUS VERHOOFE,
EDMUND REYLE. Recorded 23 Feb 1675/6. (B:pg 62)

10 Nov 1676. WILLIAM DAVIS of Whorekill planter ackn to assign
and sett over to ROBERT TRALE of same place planter all my right to
a parcell of land n side of Great Kill called Rose Hill and to make over
the pattent within 1 year. Wit: EDWARD SOUTHRIN, ALEX
MOLESTONE. Ackn 21 Nov 1676. (B:pg 62)

7 Mar 1677/8. Deed. SAMUEL STYLES and ROBERT TRAYLY
(TRAYLEY) of Whorekill NY planters for a valuable consideration sold
to JOHN SHARKLEY and RUNNER WILLIAMS of NY marchants ...
whereas his royall highness JAMES Duke of York and Albaney on 29
Sep 1677 did grant unto the said SAMUEL STYLES and ROBERT
TRAYLY a parcell of land called Styles Delight n side of Mispann Cr ...
740 a. Wit: HALM WILTBANCK, EDWARD SOUTHRIN. Ackn at
Whorekill 12-15 Mar 1677/8. Attest: CORNELUS VERHOOFE clark.
(B:pg 63)

21 Sep 1681. HALMANIAS WILTBANCK aged 47 years or
thereabouts being examined and say that this deponant was witness to
[above] deed and presedent of the court [above] said and saw the
acknowledgment thereof. 26 Sep 1681 sworn before WM CLARK. (B:pg
64)

10 Sep 1677. Deed. EDWARD SOUTHRIN of Whorekill and MARY his
wife for 4000 pounds of tobacco sold to LUKE WATSON of same place
... a tr of land, whereas his royall highness by his grant under the seal
of NY on 24 Jun 1676 did grant unto EDWARD SOUTHRIN of
Whorekill gent a parcell of land called Saint Gileses about 1 mile from
Pagan Cr adj DANIEL BROWN ... 196 a. Wit: HALM WILTBANCK,
PAUL MARSH. Ackn 12 Sep 1677. Attest: CORNELUS VERHOOFE

clark. (B:pg 66)

15 Jan 1675. Confirmation of Patent. EDMOND ANDROS esqr
seigneior of Sasmorere, leaftenant and governor generall under his
royall highness JAMES Duke of York and Albeney ... whereas there is
a tr of land upon the Whorekill by virtue of a warrant hath been laid
out for WILLIAM TOM being formerly the land of PETER ALDVICKS
by the side of Pagan Cr bounded by HALMANIAS WILTBANCK and
ALEXANDER MOLISTON ... 132 a. as by the survey by Capt
EDMOND CANTWELL surveyer ... by virtue of the authority unto me
given confirm unto the said WILLIAM TOM the afsd recited tr of land
and premises. Examined by MATHIAS NICOLLS serv and entered
upon record 22 Sep 1681. Attest: WM CLARK. (B:pg 67)

8 Nov 1677 at New Castle. Deed of Mortgage. WILLIAM TOM of New
Castle gent for 5000 pounds of tobacco to be paid by LUKE WATSON,
3000 pounds in 1677 and the remaining 2000 pounds in 1678, sold to
LUKE WATSON of Whorekill the [above] patton land and premisses.
Wit: ED CANTWELL, EPHR HARMON. Recorded at New Castle per
EPHR HARMON. Entered upon record 22 Sep 1681 per WM CLARK.
(B:pg 68)

2 Feb 1681. Articles of Agreement. OTTO WOOLGAST gent and
WILLIAM BUTLER (BUTLAR) planter both of Whorekill alias Deal
Co, OTTO WOOLGAST agree to farm lett unto WILLIAM BUTLER 1
parcell of land 400 a. on Mill Cr near the afsd Deal for the term of 5
years, the said OTTO WOOLGAST to put upon the land 3 milch cowes
with calves and a bull of which cowes increas the said WILLIAM
BUTLER is to have the equal 1/3 calfe and to manage and attend said
cowes and increase during the term and at the expiriation of term to
return the princible stock of cattle and 2 equall 1/3 pt/o the encrease
thereof unto OTTO WOOLGAST, the said OTTO to putt on the land 6
sowes and a boore of which the said parties each to have 1/2 increase,
the said WILLIAM BUTLER to manage and attend them, at the end of
said term the just 1/2 increase and the whole principale unto the said
OTTO WOOLGAST, WILLIAM BUTLER is to build upon the land one
20 ft new dwelling house but OTTO WOOLGAST to find nailes to the
said house, the said WILLIAM BUTLER is to pay yearly as rent 1
capen or cock to the said OTTO or order and to surender at the
expiration of the lease the land plantation to the said OTTO
WOOLGAST. Wit: LUKE WATSON, CORNELUS VERHOOFE.
Recorded 30 Sep 1681. Attest: WM CLARK. (B:pg 69)

13 May 1679. Deed. LUKE WATSON (WATTSON) of Whorekill for
3000 pounds of tobacco sold to SAMUEL GRAY of same place ... 1/2 n
pt/o a tr of land, whereas his royall highness of NY on 24 Jun 1676 did
grant unto EDWARD SOUTHRIN of Whorekill gent a parcell of land
called Saint Gileses which the said LUKE WATSON having purch from
the said EDWARD SOUTHRIN w of Whorekill about 1 mi from Pagan
Cr adj DANIEL BROWN ... 196 a. Wit: JOHN AVERY, JAMES
WELLES. Recorded 10 Oct 1681. Attest: WM CLARK. (B:pg 70)

10

1 Jun 1681. Quit Claim. JOHN CREW of Deal Co planter quit claim
unto ROBERT HIGNETT of same co planter all manner of actions,
suits, bills, bonds, debts, sums of money, tobacco, lands, judgments and
demands whatsoever against the said ROBERT HIGNETT which I
have from the beginning of the world ... . Wit: WM CLARK servr,
ALEXANDER DRAPER. (B:pg 72)

14 Mar 1676/7 at Whorekill. Indian Deed. WATER WRITTE KING
SAUEGAIHU (SAUGASHIS) ackn I have sold a parcell of land called
Mispen to JOHN BRIGS and received satisfaction therefore to the full.
Wit: HALMANIS WILTBANCK. (B:pg 73)

8 Feb 1681. Articles of Agreement. PETER BAWCOMBE and JOHN
BRIGS have contracted and agreed between each other and give to
each other one parcell of land, the said JOHN BRIGS gives unto
PETER BAWCOMBE a tr of land near Bawcombe Bridge Cr adj
PETER BAWCOMBE's land for which consideration the said PETER
BAWCOMBE doth give 1 equall quantity of land in lew of the same
point of land afsd at JOHN BRIGSes side of br unto the said JOHN
BRIGS. Wit: CORNELUS VERHOOFE, EDMOND REYLE. (B:pg 73)

-- -- 1678. Deed. JOHN BRIGS of Whorekill NY planter and MARY his
wife for 9000 pounds of tobacco sold to JOHN CURTIES of MD
planter ... a tr of land, whereas his royall highness JAMES Duke of
York hath granted 400 a. of land unto JOHN BRIGS planter s side of
Baucom Briges Cr ... 400 a. Wit: FRANCIS WHETWELL, GRIFF
JONES. Ackn 8 Jun 1680. Attest: CORNELUS VERHOOFE clerk.
(B:pg 73)

11 Oct 1678 at NY. Letter. Gentlemen. There was a peace of land laid
out for Capt NETHANIEL WALKER by CORNELUS VERHOOFE 11
May 1677 called Ceder Neck sw of Rehoboth Bay 680 a., it is the
governors order that he shall have the said land after its having been
certified by your court that it is not already granted or possessed by
any other upon the return whereof he may have a patton for the same,
there is one thing more about a peace of land at the Whorekill possest
between Capt NETHANIEL WALKER and Capt JOHN WINDER of
Summerset Co MD for which there is a patton in the name of
ROBERT WINDER instead of JOHN WINDER, which is to be
rectifyed, called Winders Neck by Broad Cr between the said kill and
Primehook 1000 a., and a certain island at the bottom of the land 100
a. which one HENRY STRETCHER having a grant for 600 a. in no
certain place, hath pitch upon this 100 a. island as pt/o his complement,
it is the governor pleasure that the said island shall belong to the said
Capt WINDER's patton and said STRETCHER is to take up his land in
some place altogather not by parcells or peace meals. (signed)
MATHIAS NICHOLS. (B:pg 75)

27 Nov 1677. Deed. JAMES CRAFORD of DEL Co province of Albaney
and JUDETH his wife for a valuable consideration sold to FRANCIS
WHETWELL carpenter of same place ... a parcell of land called
Whetwell His Delight sw of St. Jones Cr beginning at Mulbery Point

binding on Murder Cr and land of CHARLES HUCHINS (HUCHENS) at Little Cr now called Mill Cr ... 450 a. in DEL Co. Wit: JOHN BRINKLOE, JOHN WALKER. (B:pg 76)

27 Nov 1677. Bond. JAMES CRAFORD of DEL Co province of Albaney am firmly bound unto FRANCIS WHETWELL of same place in the sum of 20,000 pounds of tabacco with cask to be paid on demand ... the condition of this obligation is such that if JAMES CRAFORD doe well and truly keep and perform such articles and clauses held fourth by a deed of sale bearing date 27 Nov 1677 then this obligation to be void and of none effect otherwise to stand in full force. Wit: [blank] BRINCKLOE, [blank] WALKER. Recorded by WM CLARK. (B:pg 78)

22 Jan 1679. Deed. PETER BAWCOMBE of Whorekill Co NY planter for 4000 pounds of tobacco and cask and with the consent of JOHN (JOHNIS) RICHARDSON of Dorchester Co MD planter sold to JOHN GLOVER of Dorchester Co MD carpenter ... a plantation tr of land late in the tenor of the said PETER BAWCOMBE adj the plantation of JOHN BRIGS beginning at Bawcombe Brigs Cr ... for the onely proper use of JOHN RICHARDSON and SUSANAH his wife during the term of her naturall life and the life of the longest liver of them and after their decease then to the use and behoofe of JAMES SHARKLADY son of the said SUSANAH begotten by JAMES SHARKLADY her former husband decd, and to the heirs of JAMES SHARKLADY the younger, and for default of such issue to the use of SUSANAH SHARKLADY dau of the said SUSANAH w/o the said JOHN RICHARDSON and to her heirs, and for default of such issue then to the use and behoofe of JOHN RICHARDSON son of the said JOHN RICHARDSON the elder and to his heirs, and for default of such issue then to the use and behoofe of SARAH RICHARDSON dau of the said JOHN RICHARDSON the elder and to her heirs, and for default of such issue then to the use and behoofe of heirs of the said JOHN RICHARDSON party to these presents. Wit: WM SMITHSON, GRIFF JONES, SIGNNUI PDRIS. (B:pg 79)

19 Jan 1680 1/2. Articles of Agreement. HENRY SMITH doe give unto his dau MARGREY w/o LUKE WATSON for her life time 300 a. of land and to her issue, but if MARGREY should die before her husband without issue then the said LUKE WATSON is to have that 300 a. made up the quantety of 500 a. paying unto the said HENRY SMITH 15,000 pounds of tobacco and cask, in Primehook near unto Deal alias Whorekill on Slaughter Cr, to the performance whereof HENRY SMITH binds himself to the penall sum of 30,000 pounds of tobacco and cask. Wit: THOMAS MORGAN, ELIZABETH DAVIDS. (B:pg 82)

20 Sep 1676. Deed. PETOROQUE Indian called amongst the English CHRISTIAN having received 8 bottles of rum, 3 match coates, 4 yards of frize and 1/2 the buttons and thread to the vallue of 2 of them and 1 match coat more to be paid to me the said PETOROQUE MEHORY my brother sold unto JOHN RICHARDSON of Dorchester Co MD planter a tr of land s side of Dock Cr 2000 a. of English measure, further I do ingage to assist and help the said JOHN RICHARDSON or

any one that doth belong to him that liveth upon the said land if either his or their hogs or cattle shall run a stray in the woods to use the best of my indeavers to drive them to his plantation, upon his or their request .... Wit: THOMAS CRAMPTON, CHARLES GUINDY, THOMAS WILLIAMS. Ackn 10 Dec 1679. Proved by WILLIAM WATTSON. Attest: CORNELUS VERHOOFE clerk. (B:pg 83)

25 Mar 1676 at NY. Confirmation of Patent. EDMOND ANDROS esqr seigneur of Sausmore leaftanent and governor generall under his royall highness JAMES Duke of York and Albaney ... whereas there is a tr of land upon the Whorekill by virtue of a warrant hath been laid out for ABRAHAM CLEMENT and OTTO WOOLGAST on Pothox Cr bounded by Whorekill, Pagan Cr and ALEXANDER MOLISTON ... 600 a. surveyed by Capt EDMOND CANTWELL surveyer ... by virtue of the authority unto me given have confirmed and granted unto the said ABRAHAM CLEMENT and OTTO WOOLGAST the afsd recited tr of land and premisses. Examined by MATHIAS NICHOLS servr. (B:pg 84)

22 Jun 1680. Deed. BRYANT ROWLES of Whorekill percints and BARTREE his wife the relix of ABRAHAM CLEMENTS decd for 5700 pounds of tobacco sold to WILLIAM CLARK of same place merchant ... pt/o a tr of land [same as above] ... 300 a. Wit: LUKE WATTSON, JOHN ROADES, JOHN KIPHAVEN, OTTO WOOLGAST. Ackn 22 June 1680. Attest: CORNELUS VERHOOFE clerk. Recorded 4 Mar 1682 per WM CLARK. (B:pg 85)

30 Nov 1681. Deed. WILLIAM CLARK of Deal merchant and HONOUR (HONNOR) his wife for 13,500 pounds of tobacco sold to WILLIAM DARVALL of the City of NY merchant ... [same as above] ... 300 a. Wit: EDWARD WILLIAMS, EDMOND GIBBON, JOHN VINES, LUKE WATTSON, JOHN KIPHAVEN. (B:pg 87)

14 Mar 1680 1/2. Arbitration Award. LUKE WATTSON and EDWARD WILLIAMS were men indefferantly appointed arbitrators by ALEXANDER DRAPER and HENRY BOWMAN to vew papers concerning a title of land on Slaughter Cr between the said DRAPER and the said BOWMAN ... our award being the lands that was in defferance is properly the lands of BOWMAN ... the said DRAPER shall have the liberty to plant 2 years upon the said land and no longer .... (B:pg 89)

15 Jan 1675 at NY. Confirmation of Patent. EDMOND ANDROS esqr seignear of Sasmore leaftenant and governor generall under his royall highness JAMES Duke of York and Albaney ... there is a tr of land unto the Whorekill called Youngs Hope by virtue of a warrant hath been laid out for GEORGE YOUNG ... 300 a. serveyed by Capt EDMOND CANTWELL serveryer ... by virtue of the authority unto me given confirm and grant unto the said GEORGE YOUNG the afsd land and premisses. Examined by MATHIAS NICHOLLS servr. (B:pg 90)

11 Sep 1677. Assignment. GEORGE YOUNG of Whorekill precints

carpenter assign all my right of the [above] patton unto JAMES
WELLES of same place planter .... Wit: CORNELUS VERHOOFE,
ALEX MOLISTON. (B:pg 91)

1 Jan 1680. Assignment. The [above] patton and land was assigned
over unto ALEXANDER DRAPER by JAMES WELLES and MARY his
wife. Attest: WM CLARK. (B:pg 91)

14 Nov 1682. Deed. ALEXANDER DRAPER of Whorekill als New Deal
Co planter for 12,000 pounds of tobacco sold to JOHN SIMONS and
WILLIAM LOWING of St. Martons MD planters ... a tr of land [same
as above]. Wit: WM CLARK, JOHN VINES. (B:pg 91)

14 Nov 1682. Mortgage. It is agreed that if the within named JOHN
SIMONS and WILLIAM LOWING do not pay unto the said
ALEXANDER DRAPER 12,000 pounds of tobacco, that is 4000 pounds
on 1 Apr next ensuing, 4000 pounds more on 1 Apr 1684, and 4000
resedue on 1 Apr 1685, that then it shall be lawfull for the said
ALEXANDER DRAPER to enter upon the [above] mentioned land and
possess and enjoy the same forever ... 300 a. Wit: WM CLARK, JOHN
VINES. (B:pg 93)

13 Feb 1682. Deed. WILLIAM LOWING of Sumerset Co MD planter
for 6000 pounds of tobacco sold to WILLIAM DARVALL of Lewis Suss
Co merchant ... 1/2 pt/o a 300 a. tr of land called Youngs Hope between
the land of JOHN ROADES and WILLIAM ROADES near Whorekill
Cr [same as above] .... Wit: WM CLARK, JOHN HILL. (B:pg 94)

5 May 1683. Articles of Agreement. Docter GERRARDUS VESSELL
(WESSELL) of Boston New England merchant and REYNIER
VANDER COLEN of New Castle PA merchant by mutall and vollintary
agreement do contract and agree for the term of 7 years that
whatsoever estate of moveables and unmoveables that either party afsd
possess being by this presents firmly joyntly in copartnership, only the
said Docter GERRARDUS WESSELLS excepting 1 house and lott in
the City of Boston belonging to his wife but yearly rent and benifitt
thereof shall be to the joynt copartnership, also the said REYNIER
VANDER COLEN excepting 1 lott with 2 houses at New Castle
between the church and EPHRAM HARMON's which he say be
belonging unto his wife, but the yearly rent and benefitt thereof shall
be of the joynt copartnership ... 300 a. further that all debts of either
or both parties to be paid, if either of the parties doth refuse, neglect,
defraud and delinquence his utmost to endeavour, help and assistance
in the good management of the 300 a. afsd, shall forfitt to the party
wronged the just sum of 500 pounds .... Wit: CORNELIOUS
VERHOOFE, ANTONEY HEVERLY, WM CLARK. (B:pg 96)

Feb 1681/2. JOHN OAKEY of Deal Co NY sold 1 parcell of land 300 a.
binding upon HENRY SMITH or the land which was formerly
WILLIAM CAINE's binding upon SAMUEL GRAY unto JOHN
KIPHAVEN and ALEXANDER MOLISTON, Mr. KIPHAVEN and Mr.
MOLISTON to pay for the servey and patton in my name and also for

14

the Indian right and I JOHN OAKEY bind myself when paid to give a draught of the said land unto the said KIPHAVEN and MOLISTON ... . Wit: HARMON CORNELISON, WM EMMOTT. (B:pg 97)

13 Feb 1682. Deed. LUKE WATTSON of Suss Co formerly called Whorekill gent for 30 pounds sold to SAMUEL GRAY of same co ... a tr of land, whereas JAMES Duke of York by his grant under the great seal of NY on 24 Jun 1676 did grant unto EDWARD SOUTHRIN of the Whorekill gent a parcell of land called St. Giles w of Whorekill about 1 mi from Pagan Cr beginning at land of DANIEL BROWN to the Beaver Dam ... 196 a. which parcell of land the said EDWARD SOUTHRIN did on 10 Sep 1677 sell unto the above named LUKE WATTSON. Wit: WILLIAM CLARK, HERCULUS SHEPARD, NORTON CLAYPOOLE. (B:pg 98)

10 Dec 1677. Deed. JOHN AVERY of the Whorekill precints and SARAH his wife for 4000 pounds of tobacco sold to JOHN DEPREE of same place ... a tr of land, whereas JAMES Duke of York by his grant under the great seal of NY on 15 Jan 1675 did grant unto JOHN AVERY of the Whorekill precints gent a parcell of land called Averys Rest near the Whorekill upon Rehoboth Bay adj JOHN KING and the Forked Neck where one JOHN GRAY made a setlement for JOHN AVERY's use ... 200 a. pt/o 800 a. [surveyed] by WILLIAM TAYLOR. Wit: CORNELUS VERHOOFE, JOHN VINES. (B:pg 99)

21 Dec 1681. Deed. WILLIAM COWDRY (COWDRAY) (COWTHRY) of Ceder Cr St. Jones Co sold to ARTHUR JOHNSON VANKIRK 300 a. pt/o a tr formerly belonging to my brother JOSIAS COWDRY and the afsd VANKIRKE is to have the land where his now dweeling house is adj to a parcell of land HENRY BOWMAN bought of THOMAS MORE and THOMAS WILLIAMS, for the true performance hereof I do bind myself in the penall sum of 100 pounds to give assurance from all claim to be made by last of May next for which I have received full statisfaction. Wit: HENRY BOWMAN, MARY BOWMAN. Proved 13 Aug 1684. Attest: NORTON CLAYPOOLE clerk. (B:pg 101)

17 Sep 1685. Deed. WILLIAM KANIN (KANINGE) (KAINING) of Suss Co PA in consideration of a bill for 2000 pounds of tobacco bearing date with this presents, sold unto GEORGE YOUNG of same co a parcell of land on South River formerly called the Indian River adj land of GEORGE YOUNG where he now liveth ... 300 a. Wit: WM EMMOTT, HENRY PULLIN. Ackn at court held 14-16 Sep 1686. Attest: NORTON CLAYPOOLE cleark. (B:pg 102)

30 Oct 1682. Articles of Agreement between Capt NETHLL WALKER and STEPHEN WHETTMAN both of Deal Co ... STEPHEN WHETTMAN doth agree and dispose and possess Capt NATH WALKER with the just right and 1/2 pt/o a 500 a. parcell of land the said STEPHEN hath purch from one JOHN LIMING s side of Pottocks Cr now seated by the said STEPHEN WHETTMAN, lately surveyed by CORNELUS VERHOOFE ... . Wit: CORNELUS VERHOOFE, EDWARD SOUTHRIN. (B:pg 104)

30 Oct 1682. Capt NATH WALKER doth further engage himself to the
said STEPHEN WHETTMAN (WHITTMAN) to take in full and ample
possession the next spring insuing 1 cow and calf which the said
STEPHEN WHETTMAN shall be pleased to make choice of out of the
stock of Capt NATHANIEL WALKER already intrusted to the said
STEPHEN WHETTMAN ... in part consideration of the premisses
[above] mentioned. Wit: CORNELUS VERHOOFE, EDWARD
SOUTHRIN. (B:pg 105)

7 Mar 1693/4. Power of Atty. THOMAS GILLETT of Sumerset Co MD
do appoint my trusty friend THOMAS PEMBERTON of Lewes Suss
Co PA my atty to ackn in open court 300 a. of land and 150 a. of land
in Angola Neck unto WILLIAM ROBINSON of Summerset Co
according to the conveyance bearing date 6 Mar 1693. Wit: CEAS
GODWIN, WILLIAM WHITE. Proved 8 Mar 1693/4. Attest:
NEHEMIAH FIELD clerk. (B:pg 105)

6 May 1694. Deposition. DANIEL BROWN of Kent Co PA gent an
antient inhabitant of Suss Co saith that he was personally present at
the first survey of the land called Winders Neck and since called
Walkers Purch n side of Broad alias Great Cr and further saith that
the very first tree that ever was marked of the said WINDER's land
above mentioned FRANCIS JENKINS surveyer stand on the
lowermost point next to land formerly seated and cleared by BRYANT
ROWLES and sence inhabitted by ROBERT MURDOCK, and upon the
e most end of said point near the marsh, which said tree this deponant
upon the said point to look for, but could not find by reason by some
means or other it was fallen made use of or rotted away ... . Taken
before THOMAS OLDMAN justice of the peace. Wit: JOHN MIERS,
CORNELUS WILTBANCK, NEHEMIAH FIELD clerk. (B:pg 105)

19 May 1694. Power of Atty. WILLIAM CARTER (CARTOR) of Dorset
Co MD bricklayer did formerly give unto my son in law WILLIAM
WARGENT of said co planter 500 a. of land n side of Broad Kill near
South Bridge which land I am given to understand, that he hath for a
valuable consideration sold unto HENRY STRETCHER of Lewes Suss
Co PA and oblidged himself by bond to confirm the same ... I hereby
appoint my loving friends PHILLP RUSSEL or CORNELUS
WILTBANCK or both to confirm the said 500 a. of land unto HENRY
STRETCHER and ackn the deed in court. Wit: THOMAS HICKS,
JOHN MIERS. Proved 6 Jun 1694. [written in subject, deed to be
conveyed to JAMES STANDFIELD and JAMES THOMAS]. (B:pg 106)

6 Mar 1693. Deed. THOMAS GILLETT of Summerset Co MD planter
for 15,000 pounds of tobacco sold to WILLIAM ROBINSON of same co
farmer ... a tr of land called Robert His Fortune w side of Rehoboth
Bay about 10 mi distant from Lewes formerly called the Whorekills as
by pattent of the Honorable EDMOND ANDROS esqr bearing date 9
Sep 1677 300 a. and also 150 a. adj, being 1/2 of a 300 a. tr on Middle
Cr or Fishing Cr, it being formerly the land of RICHARD BRAYCEY,
in the whole 450 a. Wit: CEASER GODWIN, FRANCIS WILLIAMS,
RICHARD HOLLAWAY. Ackn 8 Mar 1693 by Capt THOMAS

PEMBERTON by virtue of a power of atty from THOMAS GILLETT. (B:pg 107)

6 Mar 1693/4. Deed. JOHN HILL of Suss Co PA atty of GRIFFITH JONES of Phila merchant by a power bearing date 9 May 1693 for 60 odd pounds sold unto HENRY STRETCHER of Lewes inholdr ... a tr of land about 2 mi distant from the town of Lewes adj the land of ALEXANDER MOLESTON, which was formerly belonging unto OTTO WOOLGAST called the Flatt Lands 350 a. as by the pattent bearing date 9 Dec 1690. Wit: WM CLARK, ALBURTUS JACOBS, LUKE WATTSON. Ackn 8 Mar 1693/4. (B:pg 109)

2 Jul 1690. Deed. WILLIAM CLARK of Lewes Suss Co PA for 35 pounds sold to RICHARD PATTE of same co ... a tr of land called Cornbury s side of the Back Cr adj unto land FRANCIS WILLIAMS live upon ... 400 a. surveyed and laid out for the said FRANCIS WILLIAMS and sold by him unto EDWARD BENBRICK and by him sold unto JOHN MILLINGTON and by MORRIS EDWARDS of same co adminr of the estate of the said JOHN MILLINGTON conveyed unto the said WILLIAM CLARK on 2 Jun 1690. Wit: ALBURTUS JACOBS, LUKE WATTSON Junr. Ackn 5 Sep 1694 by WILLIAM CLARK unto JOHN PATTE son & heir of the afsd RICHARD PATTE decd. Attest: NEHEMIAH FIELD clerk. (B:pg 111)

28 Nov 1694. Deed. JOHN CROUTCH (CROUTCHE) of Lewis Suss Co PA gent for 23 pounds sold unto CHARLES HAYNES of same place chirurgeion ... a house and 3 lotts in the town of Lewis in Second Street formerly granted unto ALBURTUS JACOBS of same co gent and by him on 7 Sep 1693 ackn unto CHARLES HAYNES, bounded on North Street, ackn and made over in open court 8 Mar last past by deed of sale from the said CHARLES HAYNES unto JOHN CROUTCH afsd. Wit: THO PEMBERTON, NEHEMIAH FIELD. Ackn 6 -- 1694. (B:pg 113)

28 Nov 1694. Deed. CHARLES HAYNES for 57 pounds 10 shillings sold to THOMAS FENWICK of Summerset Co MD gent ... my dwelling house and land whereon it stands within the town of Lewis se side of Middle Street and n side of Pagan Cr ... 8 a. ... and have made my loving wife JANE my atty to deliver these presents in open court. Wit: JOHN RICHARDS COOPER, WM EMMOTT. Ackn 6 Dec 1694. (B:pg 114)

26 Nov 1694. Deed. THOMAS JONES of Suss Co PA planter for 35 pounds sold to his brother JOHN JONES of same co planter ... pt/o a 1200 a. tr of land s side of Long Love Br adj LUKE WATTSON and ROBERT BRACEE (BRACEY), confirmed unto RICHARD BUNDICK formerly of this co now decd by pattent bearing date at Phila 1 Mar 1684 which he sold 500 a. unto NORTON CLAYPOOLE and 700 a. unto the afsd JOHN and THOMAS JONES on 4 Sep 1686 ... 350 a. my brother JOHN's own part ... THOMAS JONES have made my friend JOHN BARKER my atty to ackn these presents in open court. Wit: JONATHAN WYNNE, CHARLES TINDALL. Ackn 6 Dec 1694. (B:pg

116)

7 Dec 1694. Deed. ARTHUR STARR of Suss Co PA cordwayner for 60 pounds sold to ROBERT CADE of Summerset Co MD tannear ... a parcell of land, 5 lotts in Second Street of the town of Lewis, 2 a. of sevanah land where the said ARTHUR STARR now dwells and 6 a. backward on Pagan Cr. Wit: THO PEMBERTON, ROGER CORBETT. Ackn 6 Dec 1694. (B:pg 118)

10 Nov 1692. Deed. JOHN BARKER of Suss Co PA planter for 4500 pounds ot tobacco sold to PETER WAPLES late of Summersett Co MD and now of Suss Co planter ... a 300 a. tr of land, whereas WILLIAM MARKHAM, ROBERT TURNER and JOHN GOODSON three of the commissioners appointed by WILLIAM PENN proprietor of PA on 25 Sep 1691 granted unto RICHARD PATTE late of Suss Co decd a 300 a. tr of land s side of Indian River at Pine Neck which JOHN PATTE son and heir of afsd RICHARD PATTE did on 3 Aug 1692 for 2000 pounds of tobacco owen unto the said JOHN BARKER by the said RICHARD PATTE decd, convey unto the said JOHN BARKER the 300 a. Wit: WM CLARK, ALBURTUS JACOBS. Ackn 5 Sep 1694. (B:pg 120)

5 Sep 1693. Deed. WILLIAM CLARK of Lewis Suss Co PA merchant for 4300 pounds of tobacco with cask sold to PETER WAPLES of same co planter ... a 400 a. tr of land, whereas WILLIAM MARKHAM, ROBERT TURNER and JOHN GOODSON three of the commissioners appointed by WILLIAM PENN proprietor of PA on 25 Sep 1691 granted unto WILLIAM CLARK a 400 a. tr of land s side of Indian River adj RICHARD PATTE and JOHN BARKER. Wit: ALBURTUS JACOBS, LUKE WATTSON Junr. Ackn 5 Sep 1694. (B:pg 122)

10 Jun 1695. Bond. ROBERT BRACEE and ANN BRACEE (BRACEY) both of Suss Co are firmly bound each to the either in the sum of 200 pounds ... the condition of this obligation is such that if ROBERT BRACEE and ANN BRACEE shall abide the determination and award of THOMAS FISHER and JONATHAN WYNNE both of this co, being indefferently chosen to make a full end of all the contraversies that are now touching the estate of ROBERT BRACEY decd, provided the said arbitrators signifye their award in writing within 3 days, then this obligation to be void and of no effect, otherwise to stand and remain in full force and virtue. Wit: JOHN GREAVE, ANTONEY INLOYCE. A true copy per NEH FIELD dpt rotulorum. (B:pg 123)

-- Jun 1695. Arbitration Award. THOMAS FISHER and JONATHAN WYNNE arbitrators being indefferently chosen by ROBERT BRACEE and ANN BRACEE touching all differances betwixt them relating to the estate of ROBERT BRACEE decd ... we having considered both parties so nigh as wee can doe make these our finall end and award that the said ANN BRACEE shall have 1/2 of the clear ground on that side the plantation next the Indian River and 2 pts/o the orchard and 1/2 of the housing, she always keeping her pt/o the housing and fencing in good repair and to keep her pt/o the orchard well trimmed and the said ANN BRACEE to have 1/2 of the personall estate shee paying 1/2 of the debts and the said ANN shall nott committ any waste on the plantation but shall behave herself lovingly towards the said ROBERT BRACEE, and all the remainder of the estate shall be the said ROBERT BRACEY forever, and at her death the housing land and orchard shall emmediately return unto the said ROBERT BRACEY. (B:pg 124)

5 Mar 1694. Deed. HENRY STRETCHER of Lewis Suss Co PA carpenter for 17 pounds sold to THOMAS STANDFIELD and JAMES THOMAS of Phila merchants ... a tr of land called Stretchers Hall s side of Cypress Br of Primehook ... 500 a. Wit: JOHN HILL, NEHEMIAH FIELD. Ackn 6 Mar 1694. (B:pg 125)

16 Apr 1695. Deed. JAMES JOHNSON of Musmillion Suss Co PA gent for 30 pounds sold to THOMAS CLIFTON of Suss Co carpenter ... a tr of land, whereas WILLIAM MARKHAM, ROBERT TURNER and JOHN GOODSON three of the commissioners appointed by WILLIAM PENN esqr absolute proprietor of PA on 16 Feb 1693/4 granted unto WILLIAM CLARK a 500 a. tr of land s side of Musmillion Cr beginning at Long Loved Br adj land of BENJAMAN COWDRY (COUTHRY) and RICHARD HILL ... WILLIAM CLARK on 5 Mar 1694/5 made over unto JAMES JOHNSON 200 a. pt/o the afsd land lying next to where JOSEPH BOOTH now is seated ... 200 a. JAMES JOHNSON appoint my worthy friend JOHN HILL of Suss Co gent my atty to ackn this deed in open court. Wit: DANIEL ITHELL, SAMUEL WEBSTER. Ackn 4 Jan 1695. (B:pg 127)

2 Dec 1695. Deed. JOHN HAYNES of Suss Co PA planter for 60 pounds sold to ROBERT CADE of Lewis same co cordwaynr ... a tr of land, whereas JAMES CLAYPOOLE and ROBERT TURNER two of the commissioners appointed by WILLIAM PENN proprietor of PA on 2 Apr 1686 granted unto ABRAHAM POTTER of same co planter a 300 a. tr of land called Abrahams Lott nw side of Coldspring Br of the Great Cr adj CORNELUS JOHNSON, the said ABRAHAM POTTER on 4 Sep 1686 conveyed it unto JACOB WARING (WARRON) of same co turner, and JACOB WARING by his conveyance bearing date 1 Mar 1694 and ackn in open court held 5 Sep year next afsd for 50 pounds made over the land unto the afsd JOHN HAYNES ... 300 a. Wit: THOMAS FISHER, NEHEMIAH FIELD. Ackn 3 Dec 1695. (B:pg 129)

13 Nov 1695. Deed. JOHN YOUNG of Suss Co PA for 40 pounds sold to JOHN WILLIAMS of same co ... a tr of land near the town of Lewis near Beaverdam Br adj MICHALL CHAMBERS ... . Wit: SAM PRESTON, MICHALL CHAMBERS. Ackn 8 Jan 1695. (B:pg 131)

15 Sep 1694. Deed. WILLIAM CLARK of Lewis Suss Co PA for 55 pounds sold to JOSEPH ALLIFF of same co planter ... a tr of land, whereas WILLIAM MARKHAM, ROBERT TURNER and JOHN GOODSON three of the commissioners appointed by WILLIAM PENN esqr proprietor of PA on 16 Feb 1693/4 granted unto the said WILLIAM CLARK a peace of marsh and upland w side of Rehoboth

Bay in Angola Neck bounded by land called Benefield being the land that the said WILLIAM CLARK purch of JOHN STREET ... 107 a. called Horse Island. Wit: SAM PRESTON, JACOB WARRING. Ackn 6 Dec 1694. (B:pg 132)

20 Jan 1695. Deed. WILLIAM WOOLFE of Suss Co PA planter for 20 pounds paid unto WILLIAM CLARK for the proper debt of the said WILLIAM WOOLFE, sold to JOHN HAYNES of same co planter ... a 200 a. tr of land, whereas JAMES CLAYPOOLE and ROBERT TURNER two of the commissioners appointed by WILLIAM PENN proprietor and cheaf governor of PA on 14 Apr 1687 granted unto RICHARD PATTE late of Suss Co planter a 200 a. tr of land w side of Mill Cr adj unto the land that was WILLIAM WARGENT's and land of CORNELUS WILTBANCK ... JOHN PATTE son and heir of the said RICHARD PATTE decd for a valuable consideration paid unto him by BABTIST NEWCOMBE decd late husband of ANN NEWCOMBE did on 6 Feb 1693 convey unto ANNE NEWCOMBE the afsd 200 a., and she for 10 pounds due and oweing unto WILLIAM CLARK by the afsd BAPTIST NEWCOMBE did on 6 Feb 1693 convey it unto WILLIAM CLARK, and WILLIAM CLARK for 20 pounds conveyed it unto the said WILLIAM WOOLFE. Wit: THO PEMBERTON, THO OLDMAN. Ackn 2 Jun 1696. (B:pg 134)

5 Jun 1696. Deed. PETER LEWES (LEWIS) and GRACE his wife for 20 pounds sold to JACOB KOLLOCK all of Suss Co PA ... a corner street lott in the town of Lewis adj the lotts formerly belonging unto ARTHUR STARR 60 ft in breadth and 200 ft in length with a brick house thereon, was by WILLIAM CARTER bricklayer owner thereof mortgaged unto WILLIAM ANDERSON of Accamack VA gent and by him by deed of gift bearing date 18 Jul 1692 and by THOMAS PEMBERTON his atty made over in open court on 6 Dec 1694 unto GRACE LEWES. Wit: SAM PRESTON, JOHN BARKER, SARAH STRETCHER. Ackn 2 Jun 1696. (B:pg 136)

1 Jun 1696. Bond of Warranty. PETER and GRACE LEWIS of Suss Co PA are firmly bounden and stand justly indebted unto JACOB KOLLOCK of the town of Lewis cooper in the sum of 100 pounds ... the condition of this obligation is such that whereas PETER LEWIS and GRACE his wife hath bargained and sold unto JACOB KOLLOCK their brick house and lott in the town of Lewis [see above], if the said house and lott bee clearly discharged of and from all manner of former and other gifts, grants, leases, bargains, sales, jointures, dowers, rights and incomberances whatsoever, then this obligation to be void and of none effect or else to stand and remain in full fource and virtue. Wit: SAM PRESTON, JOHN BARKER, SARAH STRETCHER. (B:pg 138)

30 Nov 1695. Deed. MICHALL CHAMBERS of Suss Co PA for 6 pounds sold to EDWARD CRAGUE of same co ... a tr of land near unto the town of Lewis adj JOHN YOUNG and MICHALL CHAMBERS ... 100 a. Wit: SAM PRESTON, (JO)HN WILLIAMS. Ackn 8 Jan 1695. (B:pg 139)

20

4 Mar 1695. Deed. ROBERT CADE of Suss Co PA cordwaynr for 23 pounds sold to JOHN PAYNTER of same place blacksmith ... two lotts of land in Second Street of the town of Lewis and 2 a. of sevanna land, where the said ROBERT CADE dweels and 3 a. backwards in the said town on Pagan Cr which said premisses were formerly purch by the said ROBERT CADE of ARTHUR STARR on 7 Dec 1694. Wit: THOMAS BESENT, ROGER CORBETT. Ackn 4 Mar 1695. (B:pg 140)

27 Feb 1695/6. Power of Atty. ADAM BURCH of Phila appoint my well beloved friend JOHN HILL of Suss Co gent my atty to ackn and make over in open court 1 lott of land and 1 house upon it in the town of Lewis unto WILLIAM ORR ... . Wit: JNO GODFREY, ROBT WEBB. Proved at Phila 29 Feb 1695/6 before ANTONEY MORRIS justice. (B:pg 142)

28 Aug 1696. Deed. JOHN HILL of Lewis Suss Co PA gent atty of ADAM BURCH inholdr of Phila for 40 pounds sold to WILLIAM ORR of the town of Lewis merchant ... a house and lott in the town of Lewis in the front Banck or Strand Street 60 ft in breadth and 200 ft in length adj lotts of the said JOHN HILL formerly belonging unto ARTHUR STARR, did properly belong unto JACOB KOLLOCK of the town of Lewis cooper and for 30 pounds JACOB KOLLOCK on 9 Mar 169- made over unto the said ADAM BURCH. Wit: WM CLARK, LUKE WATTSON. Ackn 2 Sep 1696. (B:pg 143)

20 May 1696. Deed. CHARLES BRIGHT of Suss Co PA planter for 46 pounds sold to ABRAHAM POTTER of same co ... a 150 a. tr of land, whereas WILLIAM MARKHAM and ROBERT TURNER two of the commissioners appointed by WILLIAM PENN proprietor and cheafe governor of PA on 5 Nov 1690 granted unto ROBERT MURDOCK now or late of Suss Co a 150 a. parcell of land n side of Broad Cr beginning at HENRY STRETCHER's island, and the said ROBERT MURDOCK did convey the land unto WILLIAM CLARK, and WILLIAM CLARK on 6 Sep 1692 did convey it unto the said CHARLES BRIGHT ... CHARLES BRIGHT do appoint THOMAS FISHER to be my atty to ackn in court this conveyance. Wit: WM CLARK, WILLIAM FISHER. Ackn -- Sep 1696. (B:pg 145)

1 May 1695. Deed. WILLIAM CLARK of Lewis Suss Co PA for 16 pounds sold to EDWARD PAGE of same co planter ... pt/o a tr of land, whereas ALEXANDER MOLLISTON of same co by his deed bearing date 17 May 1694 sold unto the said WILLIAM CLARK 64 a. of land n side of the Flatt Lands adj the lands of ABRAHAM CLEMENT, OTTO WOOLGAST, ALBURTUS JACOBS, HENRY STRETCHER, PETER LEWIS and the said ALEXANDER MOLLISTON, on Pothooks Cr or Br and Pagan Cr or Br ... 32 a. Wit: JONATHAN BAILY, CORNELUS WILTBANCK. Ackn 3 Sep 1696. (B:pg 147)

1 Jun 1696. Deed. JOHN HILL of Suss Co PA sheriff by virtue of my authority sold to WILLIAM CLAMPETT of same co cordwayner ... a tr of land, whereas WILLIAM CLAMPITT on 13 Jun last past recoverd a judgment of court against STEPHEN SARGENT by default of

appearance upon a bond for the sum of 28 pounds 16 shillings with condition for the payment of 14 pounds 8 shillings like money, also whereas there is a parcell of land s side of Middle Cr of Rehoboth Bay adj the land of FRANCIS WILLIAMS called Cornbury ... 300 a. called Blacksmiths Hall which being the proper estate of the said SARGENT and for his onely proper debt, appraised by 12 men and at a court held 4 Mar last past brought to publick sale, whereas the plantiff WILLIAM CLAMPITT afsd is oblidged to accept the same being 5 pounds for each 100 a. Wit: WILLIAM FISHER, N FIELD. Ackn 2 Jun 1696. (B:pg 148)

18 Jul 1695. Deed. WILLIAM CLARK of Lewis Suss Co PA adminr of the estate of HENRY BOWMAN late of same co decd for 4 pounds sold to JOSEPH BOOTH of same co gent ... pt/o a 2000 a. tr of land called Mill Rang, whereas WILLIAM MARKHAM and JOHN GOODSON two of the commissioners appointed by WILLIAM PENN proprietor of PA granted unto the said HENRY BOWMAN a 2000 a. tr of land in Kent Co and Suss Co on the Three Runs of Muspillion Cr at Clarks Brook in the line of the proprietors mannour, as by the pattent bearing date 5 Aug 1687, and HENRY BOWMAN dyed intestate and WILLIAM CLARK att the request of MARY BOWMAN widow of HENRY BOWMAN on 13 Jul 1694 being princable creaditor adminr upon his estate, as the said HENRY BOWMAN in his life time and at the time of his death stood indebted unto severall persons to the vallue of 600 or 700 pounds and left very little besides lands to satisfye and pay his just debts, the laws provide that the land to be sold ... 50 a. on Herring Br ... WILLIAM CLARK doe hereby appoint my trusty and loving friend JOHN HILL high sheriff of Suss Co my atty to ackn this conveyance in open court Wit: DANIEL ITHELL, JOHN ARISKINE. Ackn -- Sep 1695. (B:pg 150)

4 Mar 1695/6. Deed. ELIZABETH WYNNE and WILLIAM CLARK both of Lewis Suss Co PA adminrs of WILLIAM EMMATT late of same co decd for 50 pounds sold to WILLIAM FISHER of Phila cordwaynder ... plantation land s side of Ceder Cr pt/o a dividend of land belonging to the estate of ALEXANDER DRAPER decd called Little Button in the line of Bowmans Farmes surveyed and laid outt by order of the said ALEXANDER DRAPER 10 Aug 1687 for the said WILLIAM EMMATT pursuant to his articles of agreement bearing date 12 Nov 1686 ... 300 a. which the said ALEXANDER DRAPER did bind himself to convey unto the said WILLIAM EMMATT in penalty of 120 pounds when the said WILLIAM EMMATT paid 60 pounds and HENRY MOLISTON and REBECKAH DRAPER adminrs of the estate of the said ALEXANDER DRAPER decd for 60 pounds paid to ALEXANDER DRAPER in his life time and 60 pounds paid to them did grant unto the said WILLIAM EMMATT the recited land on 1 Dec 1691, which the said WILLIAM EMMATT became in his life time vested in the said plantation and dyed intestate and that letters of administration was on 7 Feb 1695 granted unto the said ELIZABETH WYNNE and WILLIAM CLARK, as WILLIAM EMMATT in his life time and att the time of his death stood justly indebted to severall persons to the value of 100 pounds and left very little besides the

plantation land afsd, the land to be sold to satisfie and pay his just debts. Wit: ELIZABETH HAYNES, THO FISHER. Ackn 2 Jun 1696. (B:pg 154)

2 Jun --. Power of Atty. ELIZABETH WYNNE doe hereby appoint my son in law CORNELUS WILTBANCK to be my atty to ackn the [above] conveyance in open court. Wit: THO FISHER, ELIZABETH HAYNES. (B:pg 157)

1 Jun 1696. Deed. JOHN HILL of Suss Co PA sheriff by vertue of my authority for 21 pounds 6 shillings sold to WILLIAM FISHER of same co merchant ... a house and front lott in the town of Lewis 60 ft breadth and 200 ft length between presedent WILLIAM CLARK and JOHN MIERS and the same that did belong unto JOHN BAKER TAYLOR and THOMAS CRAMER of Lewis carpentr and for their proper debt unto THOMAS OLDMAN, the said house and lott executed att the suit of the said THOMAS OLDMAN and brought to publick sale. Wit: [blank] FISHER, N FIELD. Ackn 2 Jun 1696. (B:pg 157)

5 Mar 1696/7. Deed of Gift. LUKE WATTSON Senr of Lewis Suss Co PA esqr for the naturall love and affection give to my son SAMUEL WATTSON of Suss ... a 200 a. tr of land in Primehook Neck where my son SAMUEL now dwells on Green Br bounded by JOHN BELLAMEY and HENRY SMITH. Wit: WILLIAM ORR, RICHARD HOLLOWAY, ROGER CORBETT. Ackn 5 Mar 1696. (B:pg 159)

1 Jun 1697. Deed. WILLIAM CLARK of Suss Co PA merchant adminr of the estate of HENRY BOWMAN late of same co decd for paying and discharging of the just debts of the said HENRY BOWMAN decd and for 130 pounds sold to THOMAS DAVIDS of same co yeoman ... a tr of land called Bowmans Farmes n side of Slaughter Cr on Indian Br bounded by JOHN NUTTER, ALEX DRAPER, HENRY ASUERUS and WILLIAM STAPLETON ... 800 a. Wit: LUKE WATTSON, JOHN HILL, THOMAS OLDMAN. Ackn -- -- 1697. (B:pg 161)

1 Jun 1697. Deed. WILLIAM CLARK of Suss Co PA merchant adminr of the estate of HENRY BOWMAN late of same co decd for paying and discharging of the just debts of the said HENRY BOWMAN decd and 170 pounds sold to JOHN NUTTER of same co yeoman ... a tr of land called Nutters Farme n side of Slaughter Cr on Barnwells Br bounded by THOMAS PRICE, Indian Br & THOMAS DAVIDS ... 1 [blank]. Wit: LUKE WATTSON, JNO HILL, THOS OLDMAN. Ackn 2 J-- 1697. (B:pg 164)

1 Jun --. Deed. WILLIAM CLARK of Suss Co PA merchant adminr of the estate of HENRY BOWMAN late of same co decd for paying and discharging of the just debts of the said HENRY BOWMAN decd and for 32 pounds sold to JAMES CARPENTER of same co planter ... a parcell of land called Carpenters Field pt/o a tr called Bowmans Farme s side of Slaughter Neck bounded by LUKE WATTSON Junr, HENRY SKIDMORE, WILLIAM STAPLETON and THOMAS TILTON ... 200

a. Wit: LUKE WATTSON, JOHN HILL. Ackn 2 Jun 169-. (B:pg 168)

1 Jun 1697. Deed. THOMAS PRICE son, heir and executor of THOMAS PRICE of Slaughter Neck Suss Co PA gent decd for 70 pounds unto my said father and myself fully paid sold to THOMAS TILTON of same co yeoman ... a parcell of land called Thomas His Field and pt/o my own tr since the decease of my father called Price His Hall and Citty on Slaughter Cr bounded by LUKE WATTSON Junr ... 2 [blank] a. Wit: JONATHAN BAILY, JAMES SEATTOUN, N FIELD. Ackn 2 J- --. (B:pg 171)

4 Mar 169-. Deed. WILLIAM CLARK of Lewis Suss Co PA for 20 pounds sold to MATHEW OZBORNE of same co ... pt/o a 800 a. tr of land nw side of Coldspring Br bounded by Abrahams Lott, Little Field and Mill Cr called the Mill Plantation granted by pattent by JAMES CLAYPOOLE and ROBERT TURNER, two of the commissioners appointed by WILLIAM PENN proprietor and governor of PA, on 2 Apr 1686 unto the said WILLIAM CLARK ... 200 a. the rents and services due to the proprietor from 21 Jan 1692 only excepted. Wit: THOMAS FISHER, NATHANIEL STARR, JAMES FISHER. Ackn -- Mar 1696. (B:pg 173)

10 -- 1696. Deed. BRYANT ROWLES of Suss Co PA planter for 30 pounds sold to HENRY SMITH of same co planter ... a tr of land n side of Broad Cr bounded by BRYANT ROWLES ... 50 a. Wit: [blank] WILLIAMS, (NE)HEMIAH FIELD. Ackn 3 Mar 1696. (B:pg 175)

2 Mar 169-. Deed. JOHN STUTCHBURY of Suss Co PA yeoman for 50 pounds sold to JOHN PRITTYMAN (PRETTYMAN) of same co yeoman ... pt/o a 400 a. tr of land called Hooknorton n side of the South Indian River ... 250 a. on Middle Br bounded by TH[blank] SHOTTENS hill. Wit: [blank] OLDMAN, [blank] HORTT, [blank] CORBETT. Ackn 4 Mar 1696. (B:pg 177)

8 Aug 169-. Deed. JOHN PAYNTER of Suss Co PA blacksmith for a valuable [blank] give unto my y[blank] brother RICHARD PAYNTER of same co husband(man) ... my double part and share by right of inheritance unto the lands and housen and personall estate of my said fathers estate, whereas RICHARD PAYNTER late of same co taylor decd father of the afsd JOHN and RICHARD PAYNTER died intestate having at the time of his death sundry lands and houses becometh due and payable unto JOHN by right of inheritance as eldest (son), our mothers life in the said real estate only excepted. Wit: [blank] MIERS, [blank] LEWIS, (NEHEMI)AH FIELD. Ackn 3 Mar 1696. (B:pg 179)

3 Mar MDCCLXX. DAVID HALL and JACOB KOLLOCK Junr being appointed by the Honourable House of Assembly to inspect the ancient defaced records and to have them transcribed, do hereby certify that the within book marked B is a true copy which we submit to the Honourable House of Assembly. (B:pg 181)

25 Jan 1783 at Phila. This certifies that the bearer, Serjeant WILLIAM

REDDON of DEL, having been examined by me is found to be unfit for any further duty either in the field or in garrison from a wound he had received in the service of the US which also appears by a certificate lodged in my office signed by his colonel and the surgeon of his regiment, he is, at his own request, recommended to his excellency the Commander in Chief, for a discharge agreeable to a resolution of Congress of 23 Apr 1782. (signed) WALTER STEWART colo inspector Northn Army. (B:pg 182)

25 Jan 1783 at War Office. Serjeant WILLIAM REDDON of DEL being from various causes assigned in a certificate under the hand of inspector general of the Army of the US unfit for any further duty and having applied for a discharge I do hereby discharge him from the service of the US and do certify that he is intitled to the provision made by Congress in such cases, agreable to their act of 23 Apr 1782. (signed) W. JACKSON assist secr at war. (B:pg 182)

27 Jun 1785 at Suss Co DEL. WILLIAM REDDON personally applyed to the subscribers two of the justices of peace of said co approving of his discharge and having knowledge that he is a citizen of said state do make this our order to pay him the sum of $5 per month during his natural life. (signed) JOSEPH HAZZARD, RAME MARTIN. Recorded 27 Jun 1785 per JNO RUSSEL recorder. (B:pg 182)

21 Jun 1687. Certificate. Doctr JOSEPH HALL do hereby certify that WILLIAM REDDEN an invalid of the co appeared before me and produced sufficient testimony of his receiving a wound in the service of the US for which he was discharged as unfit for any further duty either in the field or garrison, and that upon examination of the said invalid, am of the opinion that he is intitled of 1 pound 17 shillings 6 pence per month. (B:pg 183)

23 Jun 1687. Affidavit. WILLIAM REDING (REDDEN) came before HENRY NEILL justice of Suss Co and made oath that he was examined by doctr JOSEPH HALL appointed by the general assembly of DEL for that purpose, obtained a certificate setting fourth that he had served in the DEL redgment, that he was disabled by a wound and that he now lives in Suss Co DEL. (B:pg 183)

30 Jun 1787. Certificate. Doct JOSEPH HALL do hereby certify that JOHN CLIFTON an invalid of Suss Co appeared before me and produced sufficient testimony of his receiving his disability in the service of the US for which he was discharged as unfit for any further duty either in the field or garrison and that upon examination of him, am of the opinion that he is intitled to 1 pound 17 shillings 6 pence per month. (B:pg 183)

30 Jun 1787. Affidavit. JOHN CLIFTON came before HENRY NEILL justice of Suss Co and made oath that he was examined by Doctr JOSEPH HALL & obtained a certificate sitting forth that he had served in the DEL redgment and that he was disabled by a wound and that he now lives in Suss Co DEL. (B:pg 183)

4 Jul 1787. Certificate. Doctr JOSEPH HALL do hereby certify that
HAMILTON O'NEILL an invalid of Suss Co appeared before me and
produced sufficient testimony of his receiving a wound in the service of
the US on 16 Aug 1780 by which he is rendered incapable of procuring
a livelyhood and that upon examination of the said invalid am of
opinion that he is intitled to 1 pound 15 shillings per month. (B:pg 184)

4 Jul 1787. Affidavit. HAMILTON O'NEILL came before HENRY
NEILL justice for Suss Co and made oath that he was examined by
Doctr JOSEPH HALL & obtained a certificate setting forth that he
had served in the DEL redgment and that he was disabled by a wound
and that he now lives in Suss Co DEL. (B:pg 184)

7 Aug --. Certificate. Doctr JOSEPH HALL do hereby certify that
TIMOTHY SAYFIELD an invalid of Suss Co appeared before me and
produced sufficient testimony of his receiving a wound in his left leg in
the service of the US by which he is rendered incapable of procuring a
livelyhood and that upon examination of him am of the opinion that he
is entitled to 1 pound 2 shillings 6 pence per month. Counter signed by
JOSEPH HALL 5 May 1788. (B:pg 184)

9 Aug 1787. Affidavit. TIMOTHY SAYFIELD came before SIMON
KOLLOCK justice for Suss Co and made oath that he was examined by
Dr JOSEPH HALL & obtained a certificate setting forth that he had
served in the DEL regt and that he was disabled by a wound at the
Battle of Camdon wilst in the said regt and that he now lives in Broad
Cr Hund Suss Co. (B:pg 185)

5 May 1788. Affidavit. TIMOTHY SAYFIELD came before RHOADS
SHANKLAND justice for Suss Co and made oath that he was
examined by doctr JOSEPH HALL & obtained a certificate seting forth
that he had served in the DEL regment and that he was disabled by a
wound at the Battle of Camdon whilst in the said regt and that he now
lives in Broadkill Hund Suss Co and he is intitled to 1 pound 2 shillings
6 pence per mo. (B:pg 185)

23 Jun 1788. Certificate. Doctr JOSEPH HALL having examined
JOHN CLIFTON late a common soldier in the DEL rigiment do find
him still disabled from a wound he received in the service of the US
and entitled to 1 pound 17 shillings 6 pence per month. (B:pg 185)

23 Jun 1788. Affidavit. JOHN CLIFTON came before RHOADS
SHANKLAND justice for Suss Co and made oath that he was
examined by Doctr JOSEPH HALL appointed by the general assemby
of DEL for that purpose & obtained a certificate that he doth find him
still disabled from a wound he received in the service of the US, and
intitled to 1 pound 17 shillings 6 pence per month. (B:pg 185)

23 Jun 1788. Affidavit. WILLIAM REDING (REDEN) came before
RHOADS SHANKLAND justice for Suss Co and made oath that he
was examined by doctr JOSEPH HALL appointed by the general
assembly of DEL for that purpose, obtained a certificate setting forth

that he had served in the DEL regiment, that he was disabled by a wound, and that he now lives in Suss Co DEL. (B:pg 186)

4 Sep 1787. Deed of Mortgage. HENRY FLOWER of Suss Co bricklayer for 49 pounds 9 shillings 4 pence sold to JOHN BAYNARD of Kent Co yeoman ... a tr of land in NW Fork Hund pt/o a tr called Cannons Regulation ... 96 a. with the saw mill ... if HENRY FLOWER shall well and truly pay unto the said JOHN BAYNARD the sum of 49 pounds 9 shillings 4 pence with interest on or before 4 Jun next ensuing, then this instrument of writing and sale shall be void and of none effect. Wit: JOHN TENNENT, JOSHUA OBUR. (B:pg 186)

28 Jul 1788. HENRY FLOWER am justly indebted to JOHN BAYNARD in the sum of 35 pounds 4 shillings 8 pence and do agree that the above mortgage is equally binding for this sum of money, and shall be considered as so much added to the same which makes the whole amount 84 pounds 14 shillings exclusive of the interest that is now due on the same. Attest: CHARLES MOORE. (B:pg 187)

6 Nov 1788. Affidavit. THOMAS HOLSTON appeared before NATHANIEL WAPLES justice of the peace for Suss Co & made oath that he was examined by Docter JOSEPH HALL & obtained a certificate setting fourth that he had served in the DEL regiment in the service of the US & that he was disabled at the Battle of Cow Penns in SC by a wound he received in his arm & that he now lives in Suss Co. (B:pg 187)

10 Jun 1789. Affidavit. TIMOTHY SAYFIELD came before RHOADS SHANKLAND justice of the peace of Suss Co and made oath that he was examined by Docter JOSEPH HALL & obtained a certificate seting forth he had served in the DEL regment and that he was disabled by a wound at the Battle of Camden whilst in the said regt and that he now lives in Broad Cr Hund Suss Co. (B:pg 187)

20 Mar 1789. Certificate. Docter JOSEPH HALL do hereby certify that WILLIAM REDDEN an invalid of Suss Co appeared before me and upon examination of him am of the opinion that he is intitled to 1 pound 17 shillings 6 pence per month. (B:pg 188)

20 Mar 1789. Affidavit. NATHANIEL WAPLES justice of the peace for Suss Co do certify that WILLIAM REDEN who was then a soildger in the DEL regment & received a wound at the Battle of Campden having this day obtained a certificate from Docter JOSEPH HALL, that WILLIAM REDDEN is a invalid and resident of this co. (B:pg 188)

9 Apr 1790. Certificate. Docter JOS HALL do hereby certify that having reexamined TIMOTHY SAYFIELD late a common soldier in the DEL regiment, find him still disabled by a wound which he received in the service of the US and entitled to 1 pound 2 shillings 6 pence per month. Wit: GEORGE BUSH esqr. (B:pg 188)

9 Apr 1790. Affidavit. TIMOTHY SAYFIELD came before RHOADS

SHANKLAND justice of the peace of Suss Co and made oath that he was examined by Doctr JOS HALL, obtained a certificate seting forth he had served in the DEL regiment and that he was disabled by a wound which he received in the service of the US. (B:pg 188)

7 Feb 1792. Certificate. Doctr JOS HALL do hereby certify that having examined JOHN CLIFTON late a private soldier in the DEL regiment do find him still disabled from a wound he received in the service of the US and intitled to 1 pound 17 shillings 6 pence per month. (B:pg 188)

7 Feb 1792. Affidavit. JOHN CLIFTON came before ROBERT HOUSTON justice of the peace for Suss Co and made oath that he is the same JOHN CLIFTON to whom the original certificate now in his possession was given [see above]. (B:pg 189)

9 Feb 17--. Bond of Conveyance. JOSEPH MARSHOLL (MERSHOL) of Worcester Co (MD) blacksmith am firmly bound unto OBID OUTON ship carpenter in the sum of 300 pounds ... the condition of this obligation is such that if JOSEPH MARSHOLL shall transfer and make over unto OBID OUTON a saw mill & grice mill together with 50 a. of land on 1 Mar ensuing date hereof, then this obligation to be void else to remain in full force & virtue in law. Wit: JNO SCARBROUGH Junr, SHADRACH CLAYWELL. (B:pg 189)

OBID OUTTIN assign all my right of the [above] bond to JONATHAN DOLBEY. Wit: JOSEPH BOYCE. (B:pg 189)

22 Oct 1760 at Worcester. JONATHAN DOLBEE of Worcester Co MD do assign over all my rights of the [above] bond unto RICHARD CROCKET SAWER of same place. Wit: MARY DOLBEE, JOHN DOLBEE. (B:pg 189)

18 Apr 1730. Deed. ALEXANDER DRAPER of Suss Co merchant for 20 pounds sold to HENRY DRAPER of same co yeoman ... a parcel of land pt/o a 400 a. tr laid out for EDWARD FURLONG (FURLOUNG) called My Fortune in Slaughter Neck granted by pattent unto ye said EDWARD FURLONG from EDMOND ADROS esqr governour of NY 29 Sep 1677 on Loghouse Br and Long Point Gutt ... 124 a. Wit: THOS GORDEN, THOS DAVIS Junr, JAS WHITE. Ackn 21 Apr 1730. (B:pg 190)

26 Jul 1704. Deed. THOMAS DAVIS of Slaughter Neck Suss Co planter for 25 pounds sold to MARK MANLOVE of Kent Co gent ... the remaining pt/o a tr of land, whereas HENRY BOWMAN Senr of same co in his lifetime by indenture of sale made 10 May 1685 and ackn in court 12 May did convey unto GRIFFITH JONES of Phila merchant a 500 a. tr of land & plantation which he had purch of JOHN OUTHAM of Summersit Co MD, sw side of Cedar Cr adj ye land of ALEXANDER DRAPER and land formerly laid out for HENRY PEDDINGTON, the said GRIFFITH JONES by his atty SAMUEL PRESTON on 6 Mar 1699 did assign the 500 a. unto HENRY

BOWMAN eldest son of the said HENRY BOWMAN Senr decd,
HENRY BOWMAN Junr since decd, by his will proved 19 Aug 1700 did
give unto ye child that MARY his wife then went with the 1/2 of said
land and plantation, MARY now the w/o THOMAS DAVIS and the said
child in its infancy long since decd ... 373 a., 127 a. already made over
unto THOMAS TILTON 3 Nov 1702. Wit: JAMES SEATOUN, YEATS
CONWELL, NEHEMIAH FIELD. Ackn 1 Aug 1704. (B:pg 191)

20 Apr 1730. Deed. ALEXANDER DRAPER of Suss Co marchant for
25 pounds sold to HENRY DRAPER of same co yeoman ... a percel of
land pt/o a 100 a. percel made over by deed of sale from THOMAS
DAVIS to ALEXANDER DRAPER ... adj land of ALEXANDER
DRAPER, land that was GABRIEL HENRY's, HENRY DRAPER and
LUKE DAVIS ... 50 a. Wit: THOS GORDEN, JAMES FINWICK, JAS
WHITE. Ackn 21 Apr 1730. (B:pg 193)

2 Jan 1709/10. Quit Claim. MORRIS SHEPARD of Accomack Co VA
eldest son of JOHN SHEPARD late of Northampton Co VA decd for 10
pounds quit claim unto JAMES DRAKE of Suss Co PA ... all the estate
right in 300 a. of land between 2 crs at the head of Rehoboth .... Wit:
JNO WASHBOURNE, (THO)MAS COPE. Ackn Feb Court 1711. (B:pg
194)

5 Jan 1693. Deed. JOHN EDMONSON of Talbott Co MD gent for
8000 pounds of tobacco due and owen unto WILLIAM CLARK by
RICHARD MITCHEL late of Kent Co decd to whose estate JOHN
EDMONSON is adminr sold to WILLIAM CLARK of Lewis Suss Co
PA ... a 500 a. tr of land se side of Mispillion Cr between the land
THOMAS MAY now or late lived on and the land that JOSEPH
BOOTH is now seated upon, which land was formerly surveyed and
laid out for GEORGE CULLIN now of Kent Co planter, and GEORGE
CULLIN on 30 Dec last conveyed it unto the said JOHN EDMONSON,
except 100 a. that JOHN WILLIAMS was to have for seating the tr ...
JOHN EDMONSON impower THOMAS PEMBERTON and THOMAS
FISHER or either of them to be my atty to ackn this indenture in open
court. Wit: JOHN MORROGH, PDNE PUKE, JAMES JAHAER.
Proved and Ackn 6 Feb 1693/4. (B:pg 195)

20 Jan 1701. Deed. WILLIAM FUTCHER of Suss Co planter for 11
pounds paid unto JONAS GREENWOOD of Kent Co for the debt and
proper account of the said WILLIAM FUTCHER sold to JOHN
DEPREE of same co planter ... a tr of land, whereas there hath been
several differances depending between the father of the said WILLIAM
FUTCHER & ye father of the said JOHN DEPREE both decd as well
as between the said WILLIAM FUTCHER and the said JOHN
DEPREE about the bounds and limits of the land they live upon, for
the avoiding and puting an end of all differances about the bounds and
limits of the land granted by patent from Sir EDMUND ANDROS late
governor of NY unto WILLIAM FUTCHER decd bearing date 25 Mar
1676 ... e side of Kings Cr of Rehoboth Bay ... 200 a. Wit: GEORGE
THOUNSON, PETER LEWIS. Ackn 6 Feb 1701. (B:pg 196)

1 Jun 1696. Deed. THOMAS CLIFTON of Lewis Suss Co PA carpenter
for 40 pounds sold to HENRY MOLLESTON of same co yeoman ... a tr
of land, whereas WILLIAM MARKHAM, ROBERT TURNER and
JOHN GOODSON three of the commissioners appointed by WILLIAM
PENN esqr absolute proprietary of PA granted unto WILLIAM
CLARK a 500 a. tr of land s side of Muspillion Cr, WILLIAM CLARK
on 6 Mar 1694 conveyed unto JAMES JOHNSON late of Suss Co
merchant 200 a. pt/o the afsd tr bounded by JOSEPH BOOTH, and
JAMES JOHNSON on 4 Jun 1695 by his atty JOHN HILL did make
over unto the afsd THOMAS CLIFTON the 200 a. Wit: WM CLARK,
THOMAS PEMBERTON. Ackn 2 Jun 1696. (B:pg 197)

13 Feb 1682. Deed. ANDREW DEPREE of Suss Co planter for 5000
pounds of tobacco sold to JOHN DEPREE of same co cooper ... 400 a.
of land bounded by JOHN AVERY as by patten signed by Sir
EDMOND ANDROS bearing date 31 Aug 1679. Wit: WM DARVAL,
ROBERT HART, WM CLARK. (B:pg 199)

8 Oct 1686. Deed. JOHN STREET of Suss Co PA planter for 20
pounds sold to WILLIAM CLARK of Lewis same co merchant ... a tr of
land, whereas JAMES CLAYPOLE and ROBERT TURNER
commissioners on 29 Sep 1686 granted unto the said JOHN STREET a
tr of land called Swan Hill s side of the Great Cr bounded by THOMAS
HALL ... 400 a. Wit: JOHN ROADES, SAMUEL GRAY, [?]. Ackn 9
Nov 1686. (B:pg 200)

15 Feb 1686. Deed. GEORGE MARTIN of Kent Co for [blank] pounds
sold to WILLIAM CLARK of Lewis Suss Co ... a 600 a. tr of land,
whereas JAMES CLAYPOOLE & ROBERT TURNER commissioners
appointed by WILLIAM PENN proprietary & governer on 29 Sep 1686
granted unto ye said GEORGE MARTIN a 600 a. tr of land called
Springford s side of the Great Cr bounded by land of HALMANUS
WILTBANK decd. Wit: ADAM JOHNSON, HENRY MOLLESTON.
Ackn at court held 8,9 & 10 [blank]. Attest: NORTON CLAYPOOL.
(B:pg 201)

1 Feb 1742/3. Deed of Gift. CHRISTOPHER TOPHAM of Lewis Suss
Co merchant for the advancement of religion quit claim 6 a. of land
pt/o a 600 a. tr granted by WILLIAM PENN esqr to WILLIAM
CLARK by patent bearing date 1 Aug 1684 which land on the backside
of said pattent was assigned over by said WILLIAM CLARK unto a
certain ARTHER COOK which said COOK left severall children who
impowered a certain THOMAS CADE to recover or sell the same,
which said THOMAS CADE assigned over unto afsd CHRISTOPHER
TOPHAM the 600 a. on 18 Sep 1731 ... bounded by land of
HARMANUS WILTBANK now called Piles Lane ... unto the Friends
commonly called Quakers being specially given for the use of a meeting
place. Wit: JOHN MIERS, JOS FISHER. Ackn 2 Feb 1742. Attest
SHEPARD KOLLOCK dep prothonotary. (B:pg 203)

2 Apr 1687 at Phila. Confirmation of Patent. THOMAS LOYD, JAMES
CLAYPOOLE, ROBERT TURNER commissioners appointed by

WILLIAM PENN proprietary and governor of PA ... whereas there is a tr of land called Greenfield on Couldspring Br of Broad Cr bounded by land of Capt PAUL MARSH, Beaver Dam, SAMUEL GRAY, town meadows and Kimballs Neck ... 100 a. of marsh land granted by warrant bearing date 10 Oct 1685 and laid out 10 Jun 1686 unto FRANCIS CORNWELL renter ... we confirm by pattent unto FRANCIS CORNWELL the afsd 100 a. (B:pg 204)

8 Sep 1697. Power of Atty. JOHN HAYNES of Suss Co planter sold 1/8 pt/o a tr of land to JONATHAN BAYLY carpenter and 7/8 pt/o the tr of land to RICHARD WILLIAMS planter both of Suss Co ... which 200 a. I bought of WILLIAM CLARK ... whereas I am removing myself and family into MD and cannott so well personally attend ye confirmation of said titles, I appoint my loving friend NEHEMIAH FIELD of Suss Co clerk my atty to convey and ackn in open court the said land. Wit: THO OLDMAN, WM DYRE. Proved. (B:pg 205)

9 Nov 1697. Deed. NEHEMIAH FIELD of Suss Co PA clerk and atty of JOHN HAYNES late of same co planter by virtue of a power unto me given [see above] for [blank] money sold unto RICHARD WILLIAMS a tr of land granted by patent unto RICHARD PATTEE (PATEY) and by JOHN PATEY son and heir of said RICHARD PATTEE decd sold unto ANN NEWCOMB widow and executrix of BAPTIST NEWCOMB late of Suss Co and by her sold unto WILLIAM CLARK, and by him sold unto WILLIAM WOOLF of Suss Co planter, and by him for 20 pounds sold to afsd JOHN HAYNES on 20 Feb 1695 as by the pattent bearing date 14 Apr 1687 200 a. except out of this present bargain 25 a. which I have sold unto JONATHAN BAILY. Wit: THO OLDMAN, JOSEPH BOOTH. Ackn 8 Dec 1697. (B:pg 205)

4 Aug 1684 at Phila. Confirmation of Patent. Whereas there is a tr of land called Batchellers Lott n side of South River bounded by WILLIAM KANING Junr ... 650 a. granted 8 Mar 1681 & laid out by the surveyor on 7 Sep 1681 unto EDWARD SOUTHERN & he on 6 May 1684 conveyed ye same unto GRIFFITH JONES ... WILLIAM PENN proprietary & governer of PA grant and confirm unto GRIFFITH JONES ye 650 a. (B:pg 207)

7 May 1717. Deed. JOHN NUTTER of Suss Co yeoman for 300 pounds sold to CHRISTOPHER NUTTER of same co yeoman ... a tr of land on Barnwell Br in Slaughter Neck pt/o a larger tr called Nutters Farms bounded by MATHEW PARKER, Slaughter Cr and JOHN NUTTER ... 428 a. Wit: DEURE VUIET[?], ELIAS FISHER, PHIL RUSSEL Junr. Ackn 7 May 1717. Attest: ROGER CORBETT clerk. (B:pg 208)

10 Dec 1717. Deed. CHRISTOPHER NUTTER of Suss Co yeoman for 125 pounds sold to ALEXANDER DRAPER of same co yeoman ... a tr of land s side of land called Bowmans or Nutters Farms binding on Barnwells Br, Slaughter Cr, his brother JOHN NUTTER's part and MATTHEW PARKER ... 428 a. Wit: MATTHEW PARKER, ISAAC WALTION, THOMAS GORDON Junr. Ackn 4 Feb 1717. Attest: ROGER CORBETT clerk. (B:pg 209)

27 Oct 1768. Deed. DANIEL DINGEE marriner of Suss Co and
ESTHER his wife for 31 pounds 15 shillings sold to JOHN DRAPER
carpenter of same co ... a parcel of land in Cedar Cr Neck ne side of
the County Road near the land called Timber Neck, the land that
BENJAMIN RILEY bought of JAMES FISHER, about 22 mi from the
town of Lewis and with the original lines of HENRY SCIDMORE's 800
a. pattent on the e ... 31 3/4 a. pt/o a larger tr called Farmers Delight
near HART's 700 a. tr, adj land of THOMAS STAPLEFORD and
GEORGE RILEY decd ... by sundry conveyances became the property
of the afsd DANIEL DINGEE & ESTHER his wife ... we impower
JONATHAN MAY & RHOADS SHANKLAND our attys to ackn this
deed in open court. Wit: JACOB COVINGTON, THOMAS CAREY
Junr. Proved and Ackn 2 Nov 1768. Attest: JNO RUSSEL dep
prothonotary. (B:pg 211)

1 Feb 1763. Quit Claim. WILLIAM LANE of Suss Co yeoman for 40
shillings quit claim unto ISAAC JONES of same co yeoman ... all his
right in the land his grandfather died seized in, whereas a certain
JOHN JONES of same co, grandfather to the afsd WILLIAM LANE,
died intestate being seized with sundry lands and his several heirs
never making any legal division thereof the afsd WILLIAM LANE
became an heir at law to pt/o the afsd lands. Wit: JOHN CLOWES
Junr, JOB SMITH. Ackn 1 Feb 1763. Attest: JNO RODNEY dep
prothonotary. (B:pg 213)

31 Dec 1781. Bond. THOMAS MARTIN of Lewis Suss Co labourer am
firmly bound unto ELIZABETH SIMPSON of same place spinster in
the sum of 50 pounds ... the condition of this obligation is such that if
THOMAS MARTIN shall abide and truly perform the award
determination and judgment of JOHN WILTBANCK, JOHN RODNEY
and JOHN RUSSEL of same co gent arbitrators indefferently chosen
by the said THOMAS MARTIN on behalf of the afsd ELIZABETH
SIMPSON to arbitrate concerning the making division between the
said parties of 2 lotts of land in Lewes town binding with Ship
Carpenters Street being the same lott of land which a certain JAMES
SIMPSON by his will devised to his 2 daus the afsd ELIZABETH and
MARGARET SIMPSON which said THOMAS MARTIN is assignee of
SARAH BIGGS dau and heires of the said MARGARET provided the
said award given up in writing unto the said parties on or before 10
Jan next ensuing, then this obligation to be void. Wit: SARAH WHITE,
JNO RUSSEL. (B:pg 214)

31 Dec 1781. Bond. ELIZABETH SIMPSON of Lewis Suss Co spinster
am firmly bound unto THOMAS MARTIN of same place labourer in
the sum of 50 pounds ... [same as above]. Wit: SARAH WHITE, JNO
RUSSEL. (B:pg 214)

31 Dec 1781. Award. JOHN WILTBANCK, JOHN RODNEY and
JOHN RUSSEL of Suss Co gent arbitrators ... [see above] first we
have alloted unto the said THOMAS MARTIN assignee of SARAH
BIGGS all that part of the lotts of land ne side of THOMAS MARTIN's
house parallel with Second Street and Ship Carpenters Street ...

32

secondly we have alloted unto the said ELIZABETH SIMPSON all that
parcel of the 2 lotts sw side of Second Street, adj THOMAS MARTIN's
lott afsd ... . (B:pg 215)

7 Aug 1716. Quit Claim. JOHN COE of Kent Co esqr for 18 pounds
quit claim unto JOHN JACOBS of Suss Co yeoman ... all the estate
right I have in pt/o land & marsh in Kickout Neck nw side of Lewes Cr
which is mentioned in the bounds of 600 a. of land called Martins
Vineyard granted unto HENRY STRETCHER decd by pattent bearing
date 25 Mar 1767 [sic] and was by EDWARD STRETCHER, son and
heir of the said HENRY STRETCHER decd, on -- May 1716 sold unto
ye afsd JNO COE. Wit: FRANCIS BAGWELL, PHIL RUSSEL Junr.
Ackn 7 Aug 1716. Attest: ROGER CORBETT clerk. (B:pg 217)

7 May 1717. Deed. CHRISTOPHER NUTTER of Suss Co yeoman for
300 pounds sold to JOHN NUTTER of same co ... 392 a. of land
bounded by THO PRICE, Barnwells Br, CHRISTOPHER's part,
JOHN's fence, Black Walnutt Hamock or Island, Hogg Island, Oyster
Inlett, Indian Br or Cr & THOMAS WILLSON's 50 a., and also 86 a.
of marsh s side of Slaughter Gutt or Pond adj Nutters Farms in
Slaughter Neck. Wit: PHILIP RUSSELL, THO GEAR, ROBERT
CLIFTON, PHIL RUSSEL Junr. Ackn 7 May --. Attest: W WHITE
clerk as per minits taken by ye decd clerk ROGER CORBETT. (B:pg
217)

6 Aug 1772. Deed. JOSHUA JONES of Suss Co yeoman for 30 pounds
sold to MARK DAVIS of same co yeoman ... pt/o a tr of land s side of
Bridge or Beverdam Br of Prime Hook Cr in Cedar Cr Hund which tr
by virtue of a warrant was surveyed for a certain JAMES JONES and
JAMES JONES by his will did bequeath to the afsd JOSHUA JONES
the whole tr ... 90 1/2 a. Wit: JNO RUSSEL, WILLIAM BURTON.
Ackn 6 Aug 1772. Attest: JACOB KOLLOCK prothonotary. (B:pg 219)

3 Feb 1680/1. Deed. ANTHONY ENLOSS (ANTHONEY ENLESS) of
New Deal NY for 3000 pounds of tobacco in caske, & 1 cow with calfe
or calfe by her side with a heifer of 2 year old this next Spring after
the date for the said cowe the said ANTHONY to have the choyce out
of the stock, sold unto JOHN KIPHAVEN (KIPSHAVEN) ... a tr of
land with plantation on Whorekill als Deale Cr in NY called Kickin 150
a. ... JOHN KIPHAVEN to pay the patten of said land and ANTHONY
ENLOSS to have priviledge if he please to stay 1 year ... . Wit: JOHN
VINES, CORNELUS VERHOOFE. Ackn 8 Feb 1680/1. (B:pg 221)

23 Oct 1780. Deed. WHITE BROWN of Suss Co for 5 shillings sold to
HUMPHRESS BROWN, WILLIAM ROSS (of JAMES), JOHN
FLOWERS, HENRY SMITH (of GEORGE), THOMAS LAYTON,
ELIJAH ADDAMS and SPENCER HITCH all of co afsd and THOMAS
WHITE and EDWARD WHITE of Kent Co trustees ... pt/o a tr of land
called Canaan Improved ... 1 a. upon special trust and confidence and
to the intent and express purpose of building a preaching house or
chapel thereon for the use of the Methodist preacher or the friendly
clergey of the Church of England, WHITE BROWN hereby appoint

JOHN RUSSELL of the town of Lewis Suss Co his atty to ackn this
deed in open court ... . Wit: CURTIS SMITH, SAMUEL HANDY.
Proved and Ackn 7 Feb 1782. Attest: JOS HALL dep prothy. (B:pg
221)

30 Jun 1782. Power of Atty. THOMAS MARTIN of Lewes Suss Co
yeoman appoint my dear and well beloved wife MARTHA MARTIN my
atty to contract and sell a 60 a. tr of land in Accomack Co VA which
my said wifes late honoured father JOHN JENEFOR OZBURN by his
will devised to his dau PATIENCE DAVIS and the heirs of her body,
and in case of her death without such issue, that then the lands should
revert to my said wife MARTHA, which contingency happened by the
death of the said PATIENCE DAVIS without such issue. Wit: JNO
RUSSEL, PHILLIP RUSSEL. Proved 8 Aug 1782. (B:pg 223)

4 Mar 1779. Receipt. WILLIAM MERIDETH received of JOHN
HEMMONS the sum of 53 pounds 6 shillings 4 pence 1/2 penny being
the sum of money arising from share of the lands of THOMAS
HEMMONS decd. Attest: ELI PARKER. (B:pg 224)

11 Mar 1779. Receipt. BETTY HEMMONS received of JOHN
HEMMONS the sum of 53 pounds 6 shillings 4 pence 1/2 penny being
the sum of money arising from my share of the present division of the
lands of THOMAS HEMMONS decd. Wit: ELI PARKER. (B:pg 224)

1 Nov 1779. Receipt. SOLOMON TAYLOR received of JOHN
HAMMONS the sum of 53 pounds 6 shillings 4 pence 1/2 penny upon
the account of THOMAS HEMMONS decd land. (B:pg 224)

4 Aug 1715. Deed. JOHN PETTYJOHN Senr of Suss Co yeoman for
20 pounds sold to JOHN PETTYJOHN Junr of same co ... a tr of land
s side of Love Long Br of Rehoboth Bay 340 a. pt/o a 1200 a. tr
formerly belonging to RICHARD BUNDICK late of this co decd and by
ye said BUNDICK sould to THOMAS JONES & JOHN JONES both
late of said co decd, whereas the said THOMAS JONES did sell his
right to ye land to ye said JOHN JONES, JEAN JONES widow relict
& adminr by virtue of an order of court qualified to dispose of 240 a. of
the afsd 340 a. of ye heirs of said JOHN JONES, RUTH DIXON alls
JONES being interest in ye other hund a. by virtue of her heirship did
sell to JNO PETTYJOHN Senr the afsd 340 a. bounded by one
RICHARD BRACEY. Wit: JOHN WALKOR, W(NA?) WHITE. Ackn 4
Aug 1715. Attest: ROGER CORBETT clerk. (B:pg 224)

5 Aug 1718. Deed. JOHN PETTYJOHN Junr of Suss Co yeoman for
55 pounds sold to JOHN ALLEN of same co yeoman ... pt/o a 340 a. tr
of land ... 240 a. [same as above]. Wit: EDW PARKER, ROBERT
SHANKLAND. Ackn 5 Aug 1718. (B:pg 225)

25 Jan 1722. Deed. RICHARD BUNDICK (BUNDOCK) (BUNDUCK)
of Accomack Co VA planter and SUANNA his wife for 20 pounds sold
to JOHN ALLEN of Suss Co yeoman ... a tr of land s side of Love
Long or Long Love Br pt/o a 1200 a. tr formerly taken up by RICHD

34

BUNDICK father of afsd RICHARD BUNDICK ... 500 a. RICHARD
BUNDICK do hereby appoint JOHN CHAMBERS of Suss Co
wheelright to ackn this presents in open court. Wit: JOHN FOORD,
RICHARD BUNDUCK, WILLIAM ROSS. Ackn Feb 1722. Attest:
PRESERVD COGGSHALL clerk. (B:pg 227)

26 Jan 1722 at Accomack Co. Came before TULLY ROBINSON justice
of the peace for Accomack Co, JOHN FOORD & RICHARD
BUNDUCK Junr both of said co and made oath that they saw the
[above] RICHARD BUNDUCK & SUANNA his wife sign seal & deliver
the [above] deed of saile and also that they saw WILLIAM ROSS sign
as a wit to the same. (B:pg 228)

14 Jul 1783. Power of Atty. JAMES SHOCKLEY of Pittsylvania Co VA
appoint my son CHALTON SHOCKLEY of same place my atty to sell a
tr of land near the head of Nantus River 150 a., was granted unto me
20 Dec 1741, also to recover all sums of money that may be due me
from my father DAVID SHOCKLEY decd either by will or otherwise.
Wit: SAML CALLANDE, THOS BLACK, [?]. Proved at Pittsylvania Co
VA 15 Jul 1783. Attest: WILL TUNSTALL. Recorded 7 Nov 1783 per
JNO RUSSEL recorder. (B:pg 228)

21 Jan 1782. Power of Atty. DAVID RANKIN of Westmoreland Co PA
do appoint my trusty friends WILLIAM PERRY esqr and JAMES
MARTIN gent of Suss Co my attys to recover or receive monies from
all persons indebted to me within the co of Suss .... Wit: ROBERT
MCKEE, JAMES KING. Proved and ackn 25 Jan 1782 before JOHN
GOTHRIE justice of the peace of Westmoreland Co. (B:pg 229)

1 Feb 1782. at Westmoreland Co PA. JOHN GOETHRY esqr at the
time of taking and subscribing the same and now is one of the justices
of peace for co afsd in PA. (signed) MICHAEL HUFFNAGLE esqr
prothonotary for Westmoreland & also clerk of the Court of General
Quarter Sessions. (B:pg 2nd 228)

3 Feb 1784. Bond. CORD HAZZARD esq high sheriff of Suss Co and
WILLIAM PERRY and JAMES THOMPSON both of same co are
firmly bound unto DEL state in the sum of 700 pounds ... the condition
of this obligation is such that if CORD HAZZARD shall well and
faithfully execute the office of sheriff and perform in every thing the
duty and trust in him reposed then this obligation to be void. Wit:
JOHN LITTLE, THOMAS COULTER. (B:pg 2nd 228)

16 Jul 1783. Bond of Release. ELIZABETH HOLLAND widow of Suss
Co am firmly bound unto ISRALL & BENJAMIN HOLLAND both of
same co in the sum of 1000 pounds of good & lawfull passing gold &
silver money ... the condition of this obligation is such that if
ELIZABETH HOLLAND shall relinquish & quit all her right and claim
of her dower unto several trs of land in Baltimore Hund late the
property of WILLIAM HOLLAND decd namly Fair Meadow, Morgans
Chance, Friendship, Hollands Purch, Bair Trap Ridge, Hollands
Addition and Woodmans Folly, all which trs WILLIAM HOLLAND afsd

was in his lifetime seized & possessed being husband to the said
ELIZABETH HOLLAND, then this obligation to be void and of non
effect or else to stand and remain in full force and virtue in law. Wit:
MARY HAZZARD, JOHN EVANS. Proved 2 Oct 1783 before DAVID
HALL prothonotary. (B:pg 2nd 229)

30 Aug 1783. Deed of Release. WILLIAM HOMEY and HANNAH his
wife, JOHN HOMEY and MARY his wife, JOHN CHIPMAN and
PARIS CHIPMAN Junr all of Gilford Co NC release unto JOHN
CLOWES of Suss Co ... a tr of land, whereas PARIS CHIPMAN father
to the afsd HANNAH, MARY, JOHN and PARIS did sell to the afsd
JOHN CLOWES a parcell of land pt/o the estate of ELNATHAN
INCLE and whereas the said CLOWES has paid to PARIS CHIPMAN
the elder the purch money we WILLIAM HOMEY & HANNAH his
wife, JOHN HOMEY and MARY his wife, JOHN CHIPMAN and
PARIS CHIPMAN Junr have released to the afsd JOHN CLOWES all
our rights to the afsd land. Wit: WM MANLOVE, JAMES
CALDWELL. Ackn 2 Oct 1783. Attest: DAVID HALL prothonotary of
Suss Co. (B:pg 2nd 229)

18 Aug 1783. Power of Atty. MANLOVE WHEELOR, JONATHAN
WHEELOR and MARGARET WHEELOR of Gilford Co NC do appoint
our trusty uncle WILLIAM MANLOVE of this place (but late of Kent
Co) our atty to sell our land, pt/o the land whereon our father did live,
now in the possession of the representatives of JOHN PLOWMAN
decd. Wit: PARIS CHIPMAN, JAMES CALDWELL. Proved 2 Oct 1783
before DAVID HALL prothonotary of Suss Co. (B:pg 230)

19 Aug 1782 at NC. Order. Whereas WILLIAM WHEELOR who
formerly lived in Cedar Cr Neck and removed from there some years
ago with his father JOHN WHEELOR, did before he died appoint
JOHN WHEELOR and JAMES CALDWELL to have the care of his
children, we do request and desire that the executors or adminrs of
JOHN PLOWMAN decd do pay into the hands of WILLIAM
MANLOVE of Kent Co that pt/o the value of the land which KEZIA
WHEELOR late of Suss Co died intestate of, which to the said
WILLIAM WHEELOR did belong, and this instrument of writing with
his receipt thereon shall be a sufficient discharge for the same. Attest:
PARIS CHIPMAN, JONATHAN WHEELOR. Proved 2 Oct 1783
before DAVID HALL prothonotary. (B:pg 230)

26 Jan 1769. Bond. JOHN MCCULLAH (MACKOULLAH) of Suss Co
yeoman am firmly bound unto JACOB WALKER of same co farmer in
the sum of 272 pounds ... the condition of this obligation is such that if
JOHN MCCULLAH by deed within 1 whole year conveys his right of a
tr of land being the right and property of his decd father ALEXANDER
MACCULLAH at his death in Broadkill Hund and adj land of JAMES
& DAVID MCELVAIN decd, GEORGE WEST, SAMUEL COULTER &
others, to the afsd JACOB WALKER, then this obligation to be void &
of none effect otherwise to remain in full force. Wit: GEORGE
WALKER, RHOADS SHANKLAND. Proved 24 Nov 1783. (B:pg 231)

24 Nov 1783. Deed. JAMES SHOCKLEY of Pittsylvania Co VA yeoman, by his son CHALTON SHOCKLEY of same place his atty, for 90 pounds sold to ELSEY SPICER of Suss Co yeoman ... a parcell of land originally granted by pattent bearing date 20 Dec 1741 by the proprietor of MD to the said JAMES SHOCKLEY called James's Chance formerly in MD but now in Suss Co in Nanticoke Hund adj DAVID SHOCKLEY's plantation ... 150 a. Wit: WILLIAM BEVINS, JNO RUSSEL. Ackn 4 Nov 1783. (B:pg 231)

24 Nov 1783. Deposition. EBENEZER CALLAWAY aged 32 years or there abouts and being solemnly sworn deposeth that in 1774 he saw WILLIAM BEVINS Senr now decd sign, seal and deliver a bond to ISAAC JONES for the conveyance of 90 1/2 a. of land pt/o a tr called Hap Hazzard whereon the said ISAAC JONES now lives, and that this deponant subscribed the said bond as a wit and also saw RACHEL BEVINS now decd subscribe the same as a wit to the same bond, which bond he this deponant is informed by the said ISAAC JONES, is now by some means lost; and this deponant further saith by reason of his indisposition of body, he is not able to appear in the Court of Common Pleas at Lewis and make this deposition. Sworn before CHA MOORE. (B:pg 233)

24 Nov 1783. Deposition. WILLIAM BEVINS of Little Cr Hund Suss Co yeoman aged 37 years or thereabouts, who is acting executor of the will of his father WILLIAM BEVINS late decd and being solemnly sworn deposeth that ISAAC JONES of same place planter applyed to him for the conveyance of 90 1/2 a. of land which he in the lifetime of the said WILLIAM BEVINS had purch of him being pt/o a tr of land called Hap Hazzard, for the conveyance of which land, the said WILLIAM BEVINS decd in his lifetime, as this deponant thinks and believes, had given his bond to the said ISAAC JONES ... at the house of WILLIAM BRERETON the said ISAAC JONES delivered him the bond to look at, who when he saw the bond believed it to be executed by his father ... the witnesses to the bond were RACHEL BEVINS his sister now decd and EBENEZER CALLAWAY ... which bond together with a pocket book and some money therein the said ISAAC JONES afterwards informed this deponant he had lost. Sworn before JOHN WILTBANK esqr and his associates justices. (B:pg 233)

24 Nov 1783. Deposition. JOHN RUSSEL of Lewis Suss Co aged 47 years or thereabouts and being solemnly sworn deposeth that ISAAC JONES of Little Cr Hund Suss Co planter, some time last summer applyed to him to write a deed for the conveyance of land which the said ISAAC JONES told him he had purch of WILLIAM BEVINS Senr then decd and at the same time delivered him a bond, purporting to be a bond from the said WILLIAM BEVINS to the said ISAAC JONES dated 18 Feb 1774 conditioned for the conveyance of 90 1/2 a. of land pt/o a tr called Hap Hazzard, which bond appeared to be subscribed by RACHEL BEVINS and EBENEZAR CALLAWAY as witnesses, that the same time he informed the said ISAAC JONES it would be necessary for him to procure one of the witnesses to appear in a Court of Common Pleas and prove the execution of the said bond ... [same as

above]. Sworn before JOHN WILTBANK esqr and his associates justices. (B:pg 234)

24 Nov 1783. Petition and Deed. The petition of WM BEVINS (BIVINS) of Suss Co acting executor of the will of WILLIAM BEVINS Senr late of Worcester Co MD planter decd ... praying the court to cause an order to be made thereby impowering him to execute and ackn in open court a good and sufficient deed to the said ISAAC JONES for the 90 1/2 a. [see above] ... it was considered and ordered by the court that the said WILLIAM BEVINS executor afsd do execute and ackn a conveyance to the said ISAAC JONES ... WILLIAM BEVINS conveys the afsd tr of land unto ISAAC JONES for 30 pounds paid to WILLIAM BEVINS Senr in his lifetime and 5 shillings paid to the said WILLIAM BEVINS party to these presents ... . Wit: JNO RUSSEL, JOHN WOOLF. Ackn 24 Nov 1783. (B:pg 235)

25 Nov 1783. Deed. WOODMAN STOCKLEY of Indian River and Angola Hund Suss Co yeoman and ELIZABETH his wife for 160 pounds sold to WILLIAM MATTHEWS of Broadkill Hund same co yeoman ... a tr of land se side of Mill Cr Br in Broadkill Hund 85 a. pt/o a larger tr whereof RICHARD DOBSON late of same co died seized intestate & is part which was laid off agreable to the directions of the Orphans Court unto SARAH ANDERSON late SARAH DOBSON dau of the said RICHARD DOBSON late of said co widow decd who by her will did devise the same unto the afsd WOODMAN STOCKLEY and ELIZABETH his wife. Wit: SAMUEL ROWLAND, DAVID TRAIN. ELIZABETH STOCKLEY did declare that she became a party to the within deed of her own free will. Attest: JNO WILTBANK justice. Ackn 25 Nov 1783. (B:pg 239)

25 Nov 1783. Deed. SAMUEL ROWLAND and ALICE his wife of Suss Co for 30 pounds sold to WILLIAM JEFFERESS carpenter of same co ... a tr of land in White Oak Neck pt/o a larger tr originally granted by pattent to a certain HENRY HARMON and became the property of WILLIAM ALLEN esqr of Phila and he conveyed it to the executors of SAMUEL ROWLAND decd and after division made among his several heirs became the property of the present SAMUEL ROWLAND, adj the friends meeting house land ... 2 a. 10 perches. Wit: JAMES MARTIN, STEPHEN WARRINGTON. Ackn 26 Nov 1783. (B:pg 241)

5 Mar 1783. Quit Claim. JACOB WALKER of Lewes and Rehoboth Hund Suss Co yeoman for 5 pounds quit claim unto JOHN RUSSEL of Lewes same co scrivenor ... a parcel of woodland pt/o a larger tr called Coopers Hall bounded by Indian River Road and JOHN WILTBANK esqr ... 10 a. Wit: ADAM HALL, ELIZABETH HALL. Ackn 8 Aug 1783. (B:pg 242)

5 Mar 1783. Quit Claim. JOHN RUSSEL of Lewes Suss Co scrivenor for 5 pounds quit claim unto JACOB WALKER of Lewes and Rehoboth Hund same co yeoman ... a parcel of land pt/o a larger tr in hund afsd called Coopers Hall bounded by Kollocks Mill Pond, WILLIAM FISHER, JOHN WILTBANK esqr, Indian River Road, ROBERT

WHITE and TROTTER's pattent ... 56 1/2 a. Wit: ADAM HALL,
ELIZABETH HALL. Ackn 8 Aug 1783. (B:pg 243)

8 May 1777. Petition of SARAH LEWIS widow and relict of WRIXAM
LEWIS esqr late of Suss Co decd and SUSANAH and HESTER by
their guardian JACOB MOORE esqr and LYDIA LEWIS by her
guardian the said SARAH ... whereas the trustees of the Loan Office at
a Court of Common Pleas held in Aug Term 1774 recovered judgment
against WILLIAM ARNALL late of same co pilott for a debt of 30
pounds and 40 shillings 2 pence damages, and by a writ bearing date 24
Sep 1774 PETER ROBINSON esqr then high sheriff of Suss Co seized
in execution a messuage and lott of ground in town of Lewes bounded
by WRIXAM LEWIS esqr, Front Street, JOHN ADAMS and Second
Street and sold same to WRIXAM LEWIS esqr for 88 pounds he being
the highest bidder ... and the said PETER ROBINSON was removed
from his office of sheriff before any conveyance was made, and
WRIXAM LEWIS afterwards died intestate leaving the afsd SARAH
his widow and relict and issue the afsd SUSANNAH, HESTER and
LYDIA LEWIS whereby it desended to them ... your petitioner prays
the court to make an order for the present sheriff to execute a deed to
the said SARAH, SUSANNAH, HESTER and LYDIA LEWIS for the
said premises. Granted May Term 1777. (B:pg 245)

10 Apr 1782. Deed. ROBERT DAVIS of Kent Co yeoman and
SUSANNAH his wife for 10 pounds sold to ROBERT DAVIS Junr of
same co yeoman, and JACOB MOORE of Suss Co in a common
recovery ... a tr of land in Cedar Cr Hund pt/o a larger tr called Harts
Choice by Woolf Br ... 100 a. Wit: RICHARD BASSETT, RHOADS
SHANKLAND. SUSANNAH ackn that she became a party to the
within deed of her own free will. Attest: JNO WILTBANK. Ackn 10
May 1782. (B:pg 246)

27 Jan 1784. Deed. JAMES MURRAY the younger of Suss Co yeoman
for 123 pounds 10 shillings sold to LEVAN MILBY of same place
yeoman ... a parcel of land pt/o a 170 a. tr in Indian River Hund called
Dyers Choice ... 152 a. surveyed by RHOADS SHANKLAND deputy
surveyor on 22 Jan 1783 being the same land which a certain ALLEN
REED by deed bearing date 3 Feb last afsd conveyed to JAMES
MURRAY the elder who also by deed bearing date 5 Feb of said year
conveyed to JAMES MURRAY the younger. Wit: PETER ROBINSON,
GEORGE GREEN. Ackn 4 Feb 1784. (B:pg 248)

3 Sep 1783. Deed of Gift. ELIZABETH WHORTON Senr of Suss Co
widow woman for natural love and good will and 5 shillings give to my
grandson WRIXAM WHORTON of same place farmer ... all my
personal estate, 1 black horse that was bought of JOHN FULLER, 1
sorrill horse, 5 head of grown cattle, 2 calves, 1 feather bed and
furniture that I have made since my husband WILLIAM WHORTON's
decease, 6 head of sheep, 13 head of hogs ... ELIZABETH WHORTON
doth ordain JONATHAN NOTTINGHAM my atty to ackn this deed in
open court. Wit: ROBERT HOUSTON, JOS PRETTYMAN. Proved
and Ackn 4 Feb 1784. (B:pg 249)

2 Feb 1784. Deed. WILLIAM PERRY and JAMES MARTIN esqr of
Suss Co as attys to DAVID RANKIN of Westmoreland Co PA for 454
pounds sold to JOHN WALKER of Suss Co yeoman ... a tr of land,
whereas the afsd DAVID RANKIN by sundry purchs became possessed
with 436 a. in Broadkill Hund pt/o a large tr called Millfield Pattent in
manner following viz, JOSHUA FISHER as atty to EDWARD EVANS,
REBECCA EVANS his wife and ELIZABETH the only surviving issue
of WILLIAM CLARK decd, did on 10 Dec 1745 convey to MARY
LIGHT, BETTY LIGHT and BENIDICK TOWNSEND 200 a. of the
afsd patten binding on Gills Br, and the said BENIDICK TOWNSEND
and his wife on 2 May conveyed to a certain ADONIJAH LITTLE all
their right in the afsd 200 a. being 1/2 thereof, and the said
ADONIJAH LITTLE on 5 Feb 1765 conveys to the afsd DAVID
RANKIN the 100 a., and THOMAS NEWCOMB with BETTY his wife,
she being the afsd BETTY LIGHT, on 5 Feb 1765 convey to the afsd
DAVID RANKIN 50 a. of the 200 a. being all their right, and the afsd
MARY LIGHT on 3 Sep 1765 conveys all her right to the 200 a. unto
the afsd DAVID RANKIN, and also 150 a. more of the Millfield Pattent
by sundry conveyances became the right of HUGH THOMSON and
ELINOR his wife and they on 7 Feb 1738 convey the 150 a. unto a
certain JOHN STEPHENSON who mortgaged the same to the
trustees of the General Loan Office and the trustees caused the same
to be sold at publick vendue to discharge the monies due on said
mortgage and JOSEPH SHANKLAND then high sheriff on 2 Sep 1760
conveys the 150 a. unto WILLIAM MASON he being the highest
bidder, and he on 3 Sep 1765 conveys it to the afsd DAVID RANKIN,
and also a CATTY STUART executrix of the will of her husband
WILLIAM STUART decd sells on 10 Aug 1776 unto the afsd DAVID
RANKIN 86 a. being also a pt/o the afsd Millfield Pattent and adj unto
the other lands of the said DAVID RANKIN .... Wit: JOSEPH
DARBY, MARNIX VIRDEN. Ackn 4 Feb 1784. (B:pg 250)

-- -- 1784. Deed. WILLIAM SALMON Junr and SARAH his wife of
Suss Co for 100 pounds sold to CHARLES VEASEY of same co ... a
parcel of land called Narrow Chance in Dagsbury Hund s side of Indian
River granted unto a certain ISAAC COVINTON on 13 Oct 1748
bounded by Island Cr, land called Pointers Ignorance and land called
Aydelotts Meadow now in possession of WILLIAM WAPLES ... 183 a.
... WILLIAM SALMON and SARAH his wife hereby appoint their
trusty friends RHOADS SHANKLAND, PETER WHITE and JAMES
THOMPSON gent of afsd co or either of them our atty to ackn this
instrument in open court. Wit: JOHN WALKER, GEORGE
WHORTON. Proved and Ackn 4 Feb 1784. (B:pg 253)

4 Feb 1784. Deed. ELIZABETH OAKEY widow of THOMAS OAKEY
late of Suss Co for 65 pounds 15 shillings sold to WILLIAM WELCH of
same co yeoman ... a parcell of land in the forrest of Broadkill Hund
being the n 1/2 of a 106 a. parcell conveyed by HUGH and WILLIAM
STEVENSON to the said ELIZABETH OAKEY on 3 May 1780
bounded by JOHN HALL's fence, the County Road and Hairfields Br
... 53 1/2 a. Wit: RHOADS SHANKLAND, WM DELLANEY. Ackn 4
Feb 1784. (B:pg 254)

40

1 Feb 1784. Deed. REECE (REES) PAYNTER of Lewes and Rehoboth Hund Suss Co yeoman for the docking and baring of all estates tail and for setling the messuage and 5 shillings sold to JONATHAN BOYAN of hund & co afsd yeoman, and JOHN PAYNTER of hund & co afsd carpenter in a common recovery ... a tr of land in Lewes and Rehoboth Hund 209 a. pt/o 3 trs of land, Batchelors Folly, Grays Inn and Waltons Purch and is the same tr whereof REECE WOOLF formerly of Suss Co was seized who by his will bearing date 1 Mar 1772 divised the same to the said REECE PAYNTER ... . Wit: ELIJAH COLLINGS, J MOORE. Ackn 5 Feb 1784. (B:pg 255)

5 Feb 1784. Deed. ROBERT WHITE of Suss Co yeoman for 5 pounds sold to REECE (RICE) PAYNTER of same co house carpenter ... the n corner of a parcel of land adj land of ROBERT WHITE which he bought of JOHN WHITE being pt/o a small tr laid out by virtue of a warrant granted to ELISHA DICKSON and assigned to the said ROBERT WHITE ... 10 1/2 a. Wit: JOHN PAYNTER, RHOADS SHANKLAND. Ackn 5 Feb 1784. (B:pg 257)

4 Feb 1784. Deed. ISRAEL HOLLAND of Suss Co for 162 pounds 6 shillings 3 pence sold to THOMAS GODWIN of same co ... a messuage percell of land called Woodmans Folly in Little Neck ... 153 1/2 a. which tr was purch by Capt WILLIAM HOLLAND decd of a certain WILLIAM HAZARD of Suss Co, and WILLIAM HOLLAND did by his will bequeath the tr of land unto his son JOHN HOLLAND, and JOHN HOLLAND died intestate and without issue and the land descended to his brothers and sisters wherefore the afsd ISRAEL HOLLAND being eldest son to WILLIAM HOLLAND decd eldest brother to JOHN HOLLAND the right of acceptance was vested in him, together with 1 water mill. Wit: STEPHEN HILL, JOS HALL. Ackn 4 Feb 1784. (B:pg 258)

22 Aug 1783. Deed. JOHN MORGAN (son of SOLOMON) of Caroline Co MD and SARAH his wife for 15 pounds 10 shillings sold to JAMES HARRIS of same co ... a tr of land near the stone line that divides between DEL and MD called Morgans Timber Land that pt/o it formerly called Dorchester on s side of a path that leads from where DAVID WRIGHT lived to CHARLES KEMMEY's ... 15 1/2 a. ... JOHN MORGAN and SARAH his wife appoint JOHN CLOWES or WILLIAM POLK (son of ROBERT) justices of the peace for Suss Co to be their atty or either of them to ackn this deed in open court. Wit: JOHN DAWSON, HENRY SWIGGETT. Ackn 5 Feb 1784. (B:pg 260)

4 Feb 1784. Deed. JOHN SMITH of Suss Co yeoman for 40 pounds sold to JOSHUA COSTON of same co yeoman ... his right into an undivided tr of land, whereas JOHN SMITH in his lifetime having purch a 88 a. tr of land in the forrest of Broadkill Hund of a certain WILLIAM BUTCHER and being seized thereof dyed intestate leaving several children amonst whom the afsd first mentioned JOHN SMITH is one ... 88 1/2 a. Wit: JACOB KOLLOCK, DAN TRAIN. Ackn 5 Feb 1784. (B:pg 262)

20 Nov 1783. Deed. JOHN WILTBANK of Suss Co esqr and MARY his wife for natural and parental love and affection and 5 shillings give to ADAM HALL of the town of Lewis same co taylor and ELIZABETH his wife (their dau) ... a tr of land, whereas there is a parcel of land pt/o a larger parcel in the town of Lewis surveyed by RHOADS SHANKLAND deputy surveyor 22 Sep year afsd bounded by the said ADAM HALL's dwelling house, Shipcarpenters Street, Front Street and land late of ABRAHAM WILTBANK ... 150 sq perches during the term of their natural lives and then to the issue of the said ELIZABETH HALL, if the said ELIZABETH HALL should die before the said ADAM HALL and leave no issue, and the said ADAM HALL should afterwards intermarry with another woman and have issue by her then in such case the issue of the said ADAM HALL shall hold and enjoy the land during the term of their natural lives and no longer and immediately after, the estate shall descend to JAMES WILTBANK son of the said JOHN WILTBANK and MARY his wife. Wit: WM POLK, SIMON MARRINER. Ackn 5 Feb 1784. (B:pg 263)

3 Feb 1784. Deed. JACOB MESSICK of Suss Co yeoman for 65 pounds sold to JOHN COLLINGS of same co esqr ... pt/o a tr of land and forrest of Broadkill Hund which said tr was granted by vertue of a warrant unto a certain MARY WEST who became the w/o a certain JOSEPH LUFTON and the said JOSEPH LUFTON and MARY his wife did convey the afsd tr, excepting 100 a., unto a certain OBADIAH MESSICK and the said OBADIAH MESSICK did by his will give the tr unto the afsd JACOB MESSICK bounded by OBADIAH MESSICK's MD patent land, ISAIAH JOHNSON and land of JOHN COLLINGS ... 207 3/4 a. Wit: STEPHEN REDDEN, JOHN S. DORMAN. Ackn 9 Mar 1784. (B:pg 265)

24 Feb 1784. Deed. WILLIAM SHORT of Suss Co for 130 pounds sold to WILLIAM NEWBOLD of same co ... 2 trs of land on Shealos Br in Dagsburry Hund, one called Content granted by pattent from CHARLES proprietary of MD unto WILLIAM KILLUM dated 28 Jan 1748 ... 50 a., the other tr called Addition was granted by pattent to the afsd WILLIAM KILLUM bearing date 15 Jun 1750 by CHARLES proprietary of MD e side of land called Chance ... 25 a. the 2 trs was by the said WILLIAM KILLUM on 12 Mar 1762 conveyed to JOSEPH BROTHERER and by JOSEPH BROTHERER by deed of gift bearing date 7 Jun 1768 did give the 2 trs to his grandson WILLIAM SHORT ... 75 a. Wit: SIMON KOLLOCK, THOMAS DARTER. Ackn 9 Mar 1784. (B:pg 266)

9 Mar 1784. Petition of JOSEPH MARVEL of Suss Co humbly sheweth that whereas WILLIAM DELANNY at a Court of Common Pleas in 1782 recovered judgment against WILLIAM BEVINS & JOHN BEVANS late of Suss Co yeoman for 54 pounds 5 shillings and 42 shillings 6 pence damages, by a writ dated -- -- 1783 RHOADS SHANKLAND then high sheriff seized in execution a tr of land in Broadkiln forest 50 a. and a small improvement whereon JOHN BEVINS lately dwelt and sold same at publick vendue unto JOSEPH MARVEL, your petitioner, for 86 pounds he being the highest bidder ...

whereas the said RHOADS hath been since removed from his office of high sheriff without having executed a deed to your petitioner, your petitioner humbly prays your worships to make an order for CORD HAZZARD esqr present high sheriff to execute a deed unto your petitioner. Granted. (B:pg 268)

9 Mar 1784. Deed. CORD HAZZARD esqr high sheriff of Suss Co for 86 pounds paid to RHOADS SHANKLAND late sheriff and a further sum of 5 shillings conveyed to JOSEPH MARVEL ... a tr of land called Beavens (Bevens) Peace adj JOHN HALL ... 50 a. by virtue of a pattent granted by the proprietary of MD 2 Jul 1754 unto a certain JOHN BEVINS who devised the same unto his son JOHN BEVINS and one other 10 a. tr of land whereon the last mentioned JOHN BEVINS lately dwelt adj ... [see petition above]. Wit: CALEB CIRWITHIN, DAV TRAIN. Ackn 9 Mar 1784. (B:pg 269)

22 Dec 1729. Deed. HENRY BISHOP of Cedar Cr Hund Suss Co PA planter sold to THOMAS HILL of New London Chester Co PA ... 205 a. nw side of Herring Br which runs into Mispilion Cr bounded by JOSEPH LAINE, ROBERT SHANKLAND, JOSHAWA PORTOR and WM GREEN ... my Lord BALTIMORE and his heirs are excepted. Wit: GEORGE BISHOP, FRANCI FUTHY. (B:pg 272)

20 Mar 1784. Articles of Agreement between CURTIS SMITH, GEORGE SMITH and ALLEN SMITH, all brothers, that they should live in brotherly love together, hath by the will of their father GEORGE SMITH fell heirs to a tr of land called Luck by Chance in NW Fork Hund and we taking with us JOHN TENNENT and EZEKIEL BROWN with a skillfull surveyor and did proceed to divide the said land, to wit CURTIS SMITH to have land on the s side of a line drawn, GEORGE SMITH to have land adj JOHN TENNENT & ALLEN SMITH on n side. Wit: DANIEL POLK, WM POLK, HUGHITT LAYTON. (B:pg 273)

3 May 1784. Return on Division. JOHN TENNENT and EZEKIEL BROWN, appointed by GEORGE SMITH late of this co decd in his will to divide & lay off the lands he has left his 3 sons, viz CURTIS SMITH, GEORGE SMITH & ALLEN SMITH yeoman all of Suss Co wishing to establish peace & amity among the 3 brothers heirs to the land afsd we have entered upon the premises taking with us an able surveyor & proceeded to lay off & divide the said lands [see above]. (B:pg 274)

24 Feb 1776. Deed. ROBERT WATSON MCCOLLEY (MCCOLLY) of Suss Co yeoman for 100 pounds sold to MITCHELL SCOTT of same co yeoman ... pt/o a tr of land surveyed and laid off for JOHN MORRIS in Broadkill Hund on Green Br ... 128 a. Wit: MATHIAS JONES, RHOADS SHANKLAND. Ackn 24 Feb 1776. Attest: DAVID TRAIN dep prothonotary. (B:pg 275)

3 Mar 1690. Deed. CHARLES HAYNES (HAINS) of Lewis Suss Co PA chirurgeon for a certain sum of money sold to LANCELOTT BECK of

Kent Co PA cordwaynr ... a 4 a. tr of land in the town of Lewes adj
PHILIP RUSSELL and RICHARD PAYNTER. Wit: ALBERTUS
JACOBS, ROGER CORBETT. Ackn 3&4 Mar 1690/91. Attest: THO
PEMBERTON clerk. (B:pg 276)

1 Sep 1691. Assignment. THOMAS PEMBERTON of Suss Co PA doe
by virtue of power to me given under the hand of LANSLOTT BECK
bearing date 20 Aug 1691 convey all the right & claim of LANSLOTT
BECK unto the [above] premisses unto RICHARD WILLIAMS. Wit:
WM CLARK, LUKE WATTSON, JOHN HILL. Ackn day next afsd.
(B:pg 276)

4 Feb 1692/3. Deed. RICHARD WILLIAMS of Kent Co PA planter for
10 pounds sold to MARY HASELUM of Suss Co widow ... a 4 a. parcell
of land in the town of Lewis, formerly granted by Suss Co court unto
CHARLES HINDS & by him improved and sould unto one LANSLOTT
BECK & by him unto me RICHARD WILLIAMS. Wit: JAMES
BROWN, THO PEMBERTON. Ackn 5 Feb 1692/3. (B:pg 277)

30 Mar 1776. Deed. WILLIAM ELLEGOOD Senr of Suss Co PA
planter for 200 pounds sold to ROBERT ELLEGOOD of same place
planter ... a tr of land, whereas the said WILLIAM ELLEGOOD had by
the lordships of MD pattent dated 22 Apr 1760 1104 a. of land being
resurvey made of a tr of land bought of a certain WILLIAM
BENSTON and sold to the said WILLIAM ELLEGOOD ... 200 a. ne
end of Isables Choice. Wit: JOHN LAWS, J RODNEY. Ackn 30 Mar
1776. Attest: DAVID TRAIN dep prothonotary. (B:pg 278)

23 Jan 1733. Deed. DANIEL COE of Suss Co sadler son & legatee of
TIMOTHY COE decd for 160 pounds sold to RICHARD HINMAN of
same co yeoman ... 2 parcels of land near Kings Cr of Rehoboth Bay
300 a. pt/o a 800 a. tr called Averys Rest formerly granted unto Capt
JOHN AVERY decd by patent under the hand of Sir EDMOND
ANDROSS governor of NY bearing date 15 Jan 1675, one parcel 200 a.
being purch by the said TIMOTHY COE from EDWARD MORRIS &
SARAH his wife granddau & one of the heirs of the afsd JOHN
AVERY on 24 Aug 1715, and the other parcell 100 a. formerly sold out
of the tr by JOHN MORGAN & JEMIMA his wife, she being dau of
the said JOHN AVERY, unto one SAMUEL DICKASON who after
being legally possessed of the same did under his wife ANN's hand on
1 Nov last afsd convey the same unto the afsd TIMOTHY COE, the
said TIMOTHY COE being possessed of the 300 a. did by his will
bearing date 13 Jan 1720 bequeath unto his son the afsd DANIEL
COE all his plantation & lands. Wit: JAMES CULBERTON, PHIL
RUSSEL. Ackn 5 Feb 1733/4. (B:pg 279)

3 Aug 1736. Deed. MARY TOWNSEND adminr of the estate of JOHN
TOWNSEND late of Suss Co marriner decd for 35 pounds 10 shillings
sold at publick vendue to JOHN BOYD of same co blacksmith he being
the highest bidder ... a lott of land, whereas the said JOHN
TOWNSEND dyed possessed of 1 lott of land with a dwelling house in
Mulberry Street in the town of Lewis adj JOHN SIMONTON and lott

which was WILLIAM GODWIN's, in breadth 60 ft & in length 200 ft, and soon after the decease of the said JOHN TOWNSEND administration was granted by JACOB KOLLOCK deputy reg of Suss Co unto the afsd MARY TOWNSEND, at Orphans Court held May 1735 it was ordered the land & premisses to be sold to discharge the remainder of the debts. Wit: PHIL RUSSEL, JOHN WELBORE. Ackn Aug 1736. (B:pg 280)

14 May 1785. Deed of Gift. RACHEL MACKLIN of Suss Co now the w/o THOMAS MACKLIN for valuable considerations give unto JOBE MACKLIN of Suss Co 50 a. of woodlen land and plantation in Broadkill Hund nw side of Dobsons Beaver Dam Br pt/o a tr called Dobsons Folly. Wit: GEORGE MESSICK, AVIS MESSICK. (B:pg 282)

7 Feb 1775. Bond of Conveyance. DAVID JOHNSON of Worcester Co MD yeoman am firmly bound unto THOMAS ROBINSON esqr of Suss Co in the sum of 250 pounds ... the condition of this obligation is such that if DAVID JOHNSON and JOSEPH JOHNSON sons of the afsd and bounded DAVID JOHNSON and HANNAH his wife and half brother to ROBERT CRAIG decd who was the son of ALEXANDER CRAIG decd and the present HANNAH JOHNSON his then wife shall when they arive to full age or in case of their death before they come to full age then their legal representatives shall well & truly convey by a good and sufficient deed unto THOMAS ROBINSON a tr of land in Rehoboth Hund adj PETER PARKER's mill pond it being the same that ALEXANDER CRAIG bought of WILLIAM DAVIS gaoler 70 a., then this obligation to be void. Wit: LEATHERBERY BARKER, JOHN HAYWARD. Proved 9 May 1787. (B:pg 282)

9 May 1785. Assignment. THOMAS ROBINSON formerly of Suss Co and late of Nova Scotia do for a valuable consideration assign over all my right of the [above] bond unto PETER ROBINSON late of Suss Co merchant. Wit: JOHN BRADY, GEORGE ROBINSON. (B:pg 283)

2 Dec 1785. Assignment. PETER ROBINSON of Suss Co do for a valuable consideration assign over all my right of the [above] bond unto ANDERSON PARKER of same co. Wit: PETER F. WRIGHT, GEORGE ROBINSON. (B:pg 283)

27 Jan 1783 at Phila. Certificate of Discharge. JOHN CLIFTON soldier of DEL having been examined by me is found to be unfit for any further duty, either in the field or in garrison, having entirely lost his health in the service of the US, he is at his own request, recommended for a discharge. (signed) WALTER STEWART col insp northn army. Discharged 29 Jan 1783. (signed) W JACKSON assistant secr at war. Attest JOS CARLETON secy. (B:pg 283)

21 Jan 1786. NATHL YOUNG and WILLIAM PERRY justices of peace for Suss Co doe certify that we have examined the [above] discharge and adjudge the same to be genuine. Please to pay JOHN CLIFTON a wounded soldier being a citizen of DEL the sum of 1 pound 17 shillings 6 pence per month. (B:pg 284)

3 May 1786. Deposition. JOSHUA POTTER aged 18 years an inhabitant of Carteret Co NC appeared in open court at Lewes Town Suss Co and being sworn sayeth that he is the reputed son of JOSHUA POTTER that his mother was as he has been informed widow of ALEXANDER MCCULLAH by whom she had 2 children JOHN and MARY, that he had very little knowledge of JOHN, but that MARY who is now the w/o JOSEPH HARDISTON of Carteret Co is well known to him and that the said JOSEPH who is now present before the court is the said MARY's lawful husband. Proved in Court JNO WILTBANK. (B:pg 284)

14 Nov 1774. Deed in Trust. JOHN EDWARDS of Burden Town Burlington Co NJ and MARTHA his wife for 140 pounds sold to GEORGE KOLLOCK of Lewes and Rehoboth Hund Suss Co yeoman in trust for ALICE FISHER w/o a certain THOMAS FISHER during the term of her natural life and after her decease for the use of MARY FISHER dau of the said THOMAS and ALICE ... a messuage & 2 trs of land, whereas a certain MARTHA WOOD decd in her lifetime was seized of 1 messuage & 2 pieces of land in Lewes and Rehoboth Hund, one on the Great County Road between the tanyard & the house built by the afsd MARTHA WOOD ... 1 a., the other binding upon land of JACOB KOLLOCK, widow HART's and land called the Flatt Grounds ... 20 a. and so seized made her will bearing date 28 Jan 1769 and devised to wit, I bequeath unto my sister MARY's dau MARTHA MOORE all the residue of my estate and soon after died, and MARTHA MOORE afterwards intermarried with the afsd JOHN EDWARDS. Wit: ISRAEL BUTLER, SAMUEL BUTLER. (B:pg 285)

11 May 1775 at City of Burlington. Personally appeared before JOHN LAWRENCE esqr one of his majestys council for NJ & mayor of the City of Burlington, ISRAEL BUTLER one of the witnesses of the [above] deed who being one of the people called Quakers & duly afirmed saith that he was present & saw JOHN EDWARDS & MARTHA EDWARDS sign, seal & deliver the [above] instrument as their volintary act and that he signed his name with SAMUEL BUTLER the other subscribing wit, and MARTHA ackn that she executed the same of her own free will. (B:pg 286)

26 Jan 1783 at Phila. Certificate of Discharge. LEVIN POINTER soldier of DEL having been examined by me is found to be unfit for any further duty, either in the field or in garrison, from a wound he received in the service of the US, he is, at his own request, recommended for a discharge. (signed) WALTER STEWART col inspr northn army. Discharged 26 Jan 1783. (signed) W JACKSON assistant secry at war. Attest: JOS CARLETON secy. (B:pg 287)

11 Aug 1786. To the treasurer of DEL. Pay unto LEVIN POINTER a wounded soldier being a citizen of DEL the sum of $5 per month for and during his natural life. (signed) WILLIAM PERRY, N WAPLES. (B:pg 287)

23 Oct 1781. Receipt. ARCHABALD MCCALL received of JOS BAILY

46

40 pounds 2 shillings 6 pence being in part payment for his & my bond to REESE MERIDITH which I paid said MERIDITH, but no otherwise concerned than being his security. (B:pg 287)

13 May --. ARCHD MCCALL received of JOS BAILY 9 pounds on acct of his bond. Recorded 15 Sep 1786 per JNO RUSSEL recorder. (B:pg 287)

20 Jan 1778. Return on Division. RHOAD SHANKLAND, JOHN HARMONSON and WILLIAM THOMPSON being appointed and impowered in the will of STEPHEN GREEN late of Suss Co now decd to make division of his land ... did make the following division, laid off 100 a. on se pt/o the land near BALEY's patten, ED BOODLE's patten and Munckey Br agreeable to the will ... pt/o the land adj NATHAN BALEY and all the land on the ne side of the line we allott to RICHD GREEN 265 a., the remainder on sw side of the line 250 a. now belong to the other heirs of STEPHEN GREEN decd. (B:pg 288)

15 Jan 1675 at NY. Confirmation of Patent. Whereas there is a parcell or tr of land near unto the Whore Kill called Averyes Rest upon Rehoboth Bay which by vertue of a warrant hath been laid out for JOHN AVERY adj JOHN KING, Kings Cr and JOHN ROADS ... 800 a. EDMUND ANDROS esqr lieut and governr gen under his royall highness JAMES confirm and grant unto the said JOHN AVERY the afsd tr of land. Examined by MATTHIAS NICOLLS secr. Recorded 17 Apr 1787 per JNO RUSSEL recorder. (B:pg 288)

24 Aug 1715. Deed. EDWARD MORRIS of Phila tanner and SARAH his wife one of the daus and coheirs of ELIZABETH dau and coheir of JOHN AVERY late of Suss Co yeomam decd for 27 pounds sold to TIMOTHY COE of same co yeoman ... pt/o a tr of land, whereas the said EDWARD MORRIS in right of his wife SARAH now stands seized in 1/4 pt/o 800 a. near Kings Cr of Rehoboa Bay called Averys Rest [see above] ... 200 a. to be taken out of the 1/4 pt/o the 800 a. ... EDWARD MORRIS and SARAH his wife appoint PRESERVED COGGSHALL their atty to ackn these presents in open court. Wit: JOHN HINMAN, ROBERT JENKINS, JOHN CADWALADER. Proved 3 Sep 1715. Ackn Nov 1715. Attest: ROGER CORBETT clerk. Recorded 18 Apr 1787 per JNO RUSSEL recorder. (B:pg 289)

12 Apr 1786 at New Castle. Commission of the Peace. NICHOLAS VANDYKE esqr president captain generall and commander in chief of DEL to JOHN SIMPSON CAMPBELL and WILLIAM JORDON HALL of Suss Co esqrs, know ye that reposing special trust and confidence in your integrity and ability we have assigned you jointly and severally, justices the peace in Suss Co. Attest: JA BOOTH secy. (B:pg 291)

7 Aug 1787. Deposition. JOHN NEILL of NW Fork Hund Suss Co planter appeared in my office and requested me to record for him an accident which happened to his son CHARLES NEILL on 8 Feb 1783, the child being then aged about 7 years and 6 months which was as follows to wit, the said child was holding by the bridle a horse called

Prince who was eating when the child attempted to lead the said horse
from his food whereupon the said horse made a snap at the child and
bit off a piece of his left ear, this accident happened in presence of
JOSEPH NEILL and CHARLES LITTLETON, the said JOHN NEILL
brought with him and (showed) me the peace of the ear. JNO RUSSEL
recorder. (B:pg 291)

3 Jan 1788. Affidavit. Personally appeared before SIMON KOLLOCK
justice of the peace for Suss Co, THOMAS HOLSTON and made oath
that he was examined by Doctor JOSEPH HALL, and obtained a
certificate setting forth that he had served in the DEL regiment, in the
service of the US, that he was disabled at the Battle of Cow Pens in
SC by a wound he received in his arm and that he now lives in Suss
Co. (B:pg 292)

3 Jan 1788. Certificate of Disability. Doctr JOSEPH HALL do hereby
certify that having examined THOMAS HOLSTON late a common
soldier in the DEL regiment I find him much disabled by a wound
which he received in the service of the US and am of opinion that he is
intitled to $5 per month. (B:pg 292)

3 Jan 1788. Deed of Gift. ANN CALLAWAY of Suss Co for natural love
and affection give unto MATHEW CALLAWAY of same co a negro
man named HOPE, to have and to hold at my decease ... . Wit: JOHN
DASHIELL, WILLIAM LOW. (B:pg 292)

28 Nov 1787. Deed of Gift. ROBERT JONES of Suss Co yeoman for
natural love and affection give unto BRIDGET DASHIEL dau of
WINDER DASHIEL late of Somerset Co MD decd a negro girl named
RACHEL aged about 13 years together with all her future increase ... .
Wit: ISAAC HORSEY, CALEB BALDING. (B:pg 293)

12 Aug 1774 at Wor MD. Bond. JOHN COLLINS of co afsd planter am
firmly bound unto ROBERT HOUSTON of same place planter in the
sum of 200 pounds ... whereas JOHN COLLINS hath entered into an
agreement with the said ROBERT HOUSTON for errecting a saw mill
just above the mill JOSEPH COLLINS decd bequeathed to his son
GEORGE COLLINS, the said ROBERT to have 1/2 thereof, the
condition of this obligation is such that if the afsd JOHN COLLINS
shall and do at all times save harmless the said ROBERT HOUSTON
from all cost and charge and suites that may be brought in the name of
said GEORGE COLLINS for building the mill and allso defend 1/2
thereof to him against all manner of claims, then this obligation to be
void. Wit: BETTY VAUGHAN, DOLLY EDGAR, LEVIN VAUGHAN.
Proved 10 Aug 1786. (B:pg 293)

22 Nov 1782. Deed. THOMAS HAND heir to SAMUEL HAND decd,
WILLIAM HAND, JOHN HAND and THOMAS SKIDMORE all of
Suss Co for 24 pounds 11 shillings 2 pence sold to JOHN PONDER ...
a tr of land in Broadkill Hund w side of Round Pole Br on the road
leading to the town of Lewes ... 17 1/4 a. surveyed 10 Oct 1782 by
WILLIAM PERRY ... THOMAS HAND, WILLIAM HAND, JOHN

HAND and THOMAS SKIDMORE appoint RHOADS SHANKLAND, DAVID TRAIN and PHILLIP KOLLOCK for their attys to ackn this deed in open court. Wit: JOHN WILSON DEAN, DAVID MASEN, BAPTIS LAY. Proved and Ackn 8 Jan 1788. (B:pg 294)

6 Dec 1787 at Dover. Commission of the Peace. THOMAS COLLINS esqr president captain general and commander in chief of DEL to RHOADS SHANKLAND of Suss Co esqr, know you that reposing special trust and confidence in your integrity and ability we have assigned you justice the peace in co afsd .... Attest: JA BOOTH secy. (B:pg 295)

11 Feb 1788. Deposition. Personally appeared before JOHN S. CAMPBELL justice of the peace for Suss Co, JACOB COVINGTON of same co yeoman aged about 43 years or thereabouts and ESTHER COVINGTON aged about 42 years or thereabouts and both being solemnly sworn severally deposeth and saith that they saw MARY SMITH w/o JOB SMITH sign, seal and deliver as her act and deed a bond by the name of MARY YOUNG unto her grandchildren with a penalty of 500 pounds conditioned for the payment of 250 pounds unto her grandchildren with interest on or before 22 May next ensuing date of the bond, which bond these deponants thinks and believes was dated 22 Sep 1786, but these deponants further saith that they think and believe the said bond was dated back in order to make it bear date before the said MARY YOUNG intermarried with the said JOB SMITH, and these deponants further saith that the said MARY at the time of signing the said bond was the lawful w/o the said JOB SMITH to the best of their knowledge and belief. (B:pg 296)

8 Mar 1788. Certificate of Disability. Doctr JOSEPH HALL do hereby certify that having reexamined HAMILTON O'NEILL late a sergeant in the DEL regiment still find him incapable of gitting a livelyhood from a wound he received in the service of the US and am of the opinion that he is intitled to 1 pound 15 shillings per month. (B:pg 296)

8 Mar 1788. Affidavit. HAMILTON O'NEILL came before RHOADS SHANKLAND justice of the peace for Suss Co and made oath that he was examined by Doctr JOSEPH HALL, had his certificate examined seting fourth that he had served in the DEL regment and that he was disabled by a wound and that he now lives in Suss Co. (B:pg 296)

25 Feb 1788 at Dover. Commission of the Peace. THOMAS COLLINS esqr president captain general and commander in chief of DEL to CHARLES POLK of Suss Co esqr, know you that reposing special trust and confidence in your integrity and ability, we have assigned you one of the justices the peace in Suss Co .... Attest: JA BOOTH secy. (B:pg 297)

4 Apr 1788. Deed of Mortgage. GEORGE WALKER of Suss Co for 51 pounds 10 shillings 2 pence sold to GEORGE MITCHELL & JOSEPH DIRICKSON of same co ... 2 trs of land, whereas there is a certain tr of land in Baltimore Hund 50 a. pt/o a 100 a. tr granted to a certain

SOLOMON ROGERS by pattent bearing date 3 Apr 1750 e side of
Sound Road leading from JOSEPH DIRICKSON's mill or Vineses Cr to
Finwixes Island called Woodcrafts Venture on Indian Town Cr, adj
THOMAS WILDGOOS, which land was conveyed unto the afsd
GEORGE WALKER from GAMMAGE EVANS HODGE, also one other
tr 46 a. with 6 percent allowance for roads being said GEORGE
WALKER's devidend of a resurvey made by WILLIAM ROBINSON on
a tr called Sandy Ridge by virtue of a warrant from JOHN PENN, but
now called Addition to Sandy Ridge between GEORGE WALKER's
plantation on Woodcrafts Venture and JANE WILLIAMS which land is
to be conveyed unto the afsd GEORGE WALKER by bond for said
conveyance from WILLIAM ROBINSON of Suss Co bearing date 2
May 1771 ... 96 a. ... provided that if the said GEORGE WALKER do
well and truly pay unto the said GEORGE MITCHELL & JOSEPH
DIRICKSON the sum of 51 pounds 10 shillings 2 pence on or before 1
Mar next ensuing with lawfull interest then this present indenture
shall cease ... . Wit: SAMUEL DIRICKSON, ISAAC TUNNELL. (B:pg
297)

5 Apr 1788. Deed of Gift. JOHN AYDELOTT Senr of Suss Co for
natural love & effection and for better maintainance & livelihood give
to his son MATTHIAS AYDELOTT of same co ... all the messauges or
parcels of land in Baltimore Hund now in the hands of the said JOHN
AYDELOTT ... . Wit: THOMAS HAZZARD, JAMES AYDELOTT.
(B:pg 299)

5 Apr 1788. Deed of Gift. JOHN AYDELOTT Senr of Suss Co for
natural love and affection give unto my well beloved son MATTHIAS
AYDELOTT ... 2 negro boys named JAMES & SAML aged 12 & 18
years or thereabouts, 3 cows & calves, 1 yoke of oxen, 4 yews & lambs,
1 desk, 1 chest, 1 good bed & furniture to have and to hold after my
decease ... . Wit: THOS HAZZARD, JAMES AYDELOTT. (B:pg 300)

3 Apr 1787. Deed of Mortgage. ELIJAH CANNON of Suss Co for
securing the payment of a bond to GEORGE MITCHELL and 1 shilling
sold to GEORGE MITCHELL of same co merchant ... a tr of land
called Hanleys Luck which land was granted to MARMADUKE
HANLEY by pattent bearing date 21 Jul 1748, whereas WINGATE
CANNON of same co and the said ELIJAH CANNON by their
judgment bond bearing date 3 Apr 1787 stands bound to the said
GEORGE MITCHELL in the penal sum of 44 pounds in spanish milled
dollars at 7 shillings 6 pence each or half joes at 3 pounds each
conditioned for the payment of 21 pounds 15 shillings -- pence in like
money ... upon the condition that if the said WINGATE CANNON or
ELIJAH CANNON shall pay to the said GEORGE MITCHELL the
principal sum of money in the said bond mentioned with legal interest
to be paid yearly and every year as it arises due, together with the
charge of drawing and recording this conveyance, then this present
indenture shall cease. Wit: THOMAS INGRAM, THOMAS WEST.
(B:pg 300)

3 Apr 1787. Deed of Mortgage. ELIJAH CANNON of Suss Co for the

50

securing the payment of a bond to GEORGE MITCHELL and 1 shilling sold to GEORGE MITCHELL of same co merchant ... a tr of land called Folly which was granted to ELIJAH CANNON by pattent bearing date 10 May 1774, whereas ELIJAH CANNON and his son WINGATE CANNON of same co by their judgment bond bearing even date with this present indenture stand bound unto the said GEORGE MITCHELL in the penal sum of 100 pounds in spanish milled dollars at 7 shillings 6 pence each or half joes at 3 pounds each conditioned for the payment of 61 pounds 18 shillings 9 pence in like money ... upon the condition that if the said ELIJAH CANNON or WINGATE CANNON shall pay to the said GEORGE MITCHELL the principal sum of money in the said bond to be paid yearly and every year as it arises due, together with the charge of drawing and recording this conveyance, then this present indenture shall cease. Wit: THOMAS INGRAM, THOMAS WEST. (B:pg 301)

26 Mar 1788. Deed of Gift. MARY PORTER widow of Suss Co for natural love and affection give unto my beloved son CURTIS WILLIAMS ... a negro boy named JACOB aged 5 years ... . Wit: ISRAEL BROWN Junr, NELLEY S. WILLIAMS, REBECKAH CARLILE. (B:pg 302)

31 Mar 1788. Giving notice on 21 Mar 1788 to each member of the Methodist Episcopal Church in Lewis & Rehoboth Hund to meet at the new house belonging to RHOADS SHANKLAND esqr (being the usual place of meeting for publick worship) in order to choose trustees not exceeding 7 nor less than 3 ... we do certify JOHN WILTBANK esqr, WM WEST, WM COULTER, ABRAHAM HARGUS (HARGIS), SHEPARD PRETTYMAN, THOMAS COULTER & WILLIAM PRETTYMAN elected as trustees. Wit: CALEB RODNEY, RICHARD PAYNTER, JAMES COULTER. (B:pg 303)

7 May 1787. Deed. WILLIAM ROBINS of Suss Co shipright for 5 shillings sold to DANIEL HEAVERLO of same co yeoman ... pt/o a 160 a. tr of land in Broadkiln forrest on Gravely Br which was pattened to a certain ELENDER DOBSON by the propriator of MD on 20 Dec 1741 bounded by land taken up by ABRAHAM INGRIM now belonging to the afsd DANIEL HEAVELO called Bair Garden ... this tr called the Finishing Stroak which the said ELENDER DOBSON did by her will devise to her dau MARY, mother to a certain ALEXANDER PAIRMORE, who did on 21 Jan 1780 convey all his right of the land unto WILLIAM ROBINS party to these presents. Wit: WILLIAM CORD, LYDIA MILLARD. (B:pg 303)

3 Jul 1787. Deed of Mortgage. THOS BATSON of Suss Co for securing the payment of a bond to GEORGE MITCHEL and 1 shilling sold to GEORGE MITCHEL of same place ... 1 gray horse and 4 cowes, whereas the said THOS BATSON by his bond bearing date with this indenture stands bound unto the said GEORGE MITCHEL in the penal sum of 30 pounds spanish milled dollars at 7 & 6 each conditioned for the payment of 20 pounds 4 shillings 11 pence in like money ... upon the condition that if THOS BATSON shall pay to the

said GEORGE MITCHEL the afsd principal sum of money in the bond
mentioned with legal interest then this present indenture shall cease.
Wit: JOHN W. BATSON, KINDAL BATSON. (B:pg 304)

6 Mar 1788. Deed of Mortgage. JOHN EVANS of Suss Co taylor to
secure the payment of a bond to GEORGE MITCHEL and 1 shilling
sold to GEORGE MITCHEL of same co merchant ... 2 beads &
bedsteds, 1 coverled, 1 rug, 1 bed quilt 2 pair of sheets, 1 of them toe,
2 bed cords, 2 chests, 3 pine tables, 1 round tea table, 1 spining wheel,
1 pair of hand irons, 1 pair of tongs and 1 shovel, 2 iron potts, 1 tea
kittle, 1 coffee pott, 1 dozen cups & sausers, 1 dozen knives & forks, 2
small jugs, 10 chairs, 2 tea pots, 5 pewter plates, 1 pewter dish, 1
frying pan, 2 buckets, 1 meal tub, 2 earthen bowles, 1 bridle & saddle,
1 axe, 1 milk house, 1 taylors goose, 1 pair of taylors shears, 1 pair of
wool cards, 1 sow & pig, whereas the said JOHN EVANS by his bond
bearing even date with this present indenture stands bound to the said
GEORGE MITCHEL in the penal sum of 79 pounds 1 shilling 8 pence
in spanish milled dollars at 7 shillings 6 pence each or 1/2 joes at 3
pounds each conditioned for the payment of 39 pounds 10 shillings 10
pence in like money ... upon the condition that if the said JOHN
EVANS shall pay unto the said GEORGE MITCHEL the afsd principal
sum of money in the bond mentioned with legal interest to be paid
yearly and every year as it arises due, then this present indenture shall
cease. Wit: ISAAC TUNNELL, WILLIAM TINGLE Junr. (B:pg 305)

7 Apr 1788 at Kent Co. Commission for Trial of Negroes. To SIMON
KOLLOCK and RHOADES SHANKLAND esqrs justices our peace of
Suss Co, know ye that for the hearing, trying and determining the
crimes and offences that have been committed by any negro or negroes
or mullatto slaves, we have assigned you our justices to hold such
special court with the assistance of 6 substantial inhabitants
freeholders by you to be chosen and legally sworn to hear, try, convict
or acquit according to law, all and every such negro and negroes or
mullatto slaves as shall be guilty of committing any murder,
manslaughter, buggery, rapes, attempts of rapes, felonies, or any other
high or heinous offence ... . (signed) THOMAS COLLINS esqr
president captain general and commander in chief. Attest: JA BOOTH
secy. (B:pg 306)

7 May 1788. Deed. RHOADS SHANKLAND of Suss Co esqr for 7
shillings sold to JOHN WILTBANK esqr, WILLIAM WEST, WILLIAM
COULTER, ABRAHAM HARGIS, SHEPARD PRETTYMAN,
THOMAS COULTER & WILLIAM PRETTYMAN gent trustees of the
Methodist Episcopal Church in Lewis & Rehoboth Hund ... a parcel of
land nw side of South Street of the town of Lewis on Canary Cr ... 70
sq perches laid off 14 Apr 1788 for the use of the Methodist Episcopal
Church. Wit: THO GRAY, CALEB RODNEY. Ackn 9 May 1788. (B:pg
307)

19 Feb 1788. Power of Atty. JEHU CONWELL of Fayette Co PA
appoint JOHN STOCKLY of the town and co of Washington my atty to
recover all such sums of money that is due to me from any person in

DEL, and I am possessed of a right and claim in a tr of land in Suss Co I appoint the said JOHN STOCKLY my atty to sell the afsd lands ... . Ackn 21 Feb 1788 before JNO NOGE justice of the peace for Washington Co PA. (B:pg 308)

21 Feb 1788 at Washington Co PA. I certify that JOHN NOGE esqr before whom the [above] acknowledgement was taken was at the time of the taking thereof and still is one of ye justices of the peace in said co. (signed) for THOMAS SCOTT esqr prothonotary REAKIN BEALL. (B:pg 308)

28 Mar 1788. Deed. WILLIAM COULTER of Lewis and Rehoboth Hund Suss Co yeoman and SARAH his wife (late SARAH BAILY one of the daus of NATHANIEL BAILY late of same co decd) for 30 pounds sold to JONATHAN BAILY of same hund & co yeoman ... a parcel of land 19 a. pt/o a larger tr in hund afsd whereof the said NATHANIEL BAILY died seized which said 19 a. (together with 2 a. not hereby sold) were laid off to the said WILLIAM COULTER and SARAH his wife in right of the said SARAH as their pt/o the larger tr pursuant to the directions of the said NATHANIEL BAILY's will, adj JONATHAN BAILY's dividend. Wit: JNO WILTBANK, MARY EMORY. Ackn 4 Jun 1788. (B:pg 309)

7 Feb 1788. Deed of Mortgage. JOHN MARSHALL of the town of Lewis Suss Co pilot for 85 pounds 9 shillings 6 pence sold to WILLIAM ROBINS of same co ship carpenter and AARON MARSHALL of same co cordwainer as tenants in common and not as joint tenants ... a messuage and lott of land in the town of Lewis whereon the said JOHN MARSHALL now dwells in length 200 ft and in breadth 60 ft bounded by Lewis Cr, lott formerly belonging to a certain JACOB PHILLIPS now in the possession of HANNAH NUNEZ, Second Street and lot formerly belonging to JOHN and ALBERTUS JACOBS now in possession of JOHN BURTON, being the lott which the said JOHN MARSHALL purch of PETER WHITE and ELIZABETH his wife on 4 Jan 1782 (Book M fol 438) ... upon the condition that if the said JOHN MARSHALL shall well and truly pay unto the said WILLIAM ROBINS and AARON MARSHALL the full and just sum of 85 pounds 9 shillings 6 pence on or before 7 Feb next ensuing with lawful interest, then this present indenture shall cease ... untill default JOHN MARSHALL may peaceably and quietly occupy and enjoy the lands, receive and take the rents and profits thereof. Wit: WM WEST, WRIXAM WEST. Proved 5 Jun 1788 (B:pg 310)

7 Aug 1716. Deed of Gift. SAMUEL ROWLAND of Suss Co esqr give for pious & religious use, 1 a. of land near the town of Lewis fronting on Lewis River adj land which formerly belonged to WILLIAM CLARK decd now in ye possession of THOMAS BEDWELL ... to build thereon a church for a religous place of worship for the Church of England and to pay unto me and my heirs 1 grain of indian corn yearly forever if demanded. Wit: ANDERSON PARKER, PHIL RUSSEL Junr. Ackn Aug 1716. Attest: PRESERVD COGGSHALL clerk. (B:pg 312)

28 Jun 1788. Incorporation of Trustees. Agreeable to an advertisement dated 16 Jun 1788 giving notice to the congregation of St. Matthews Episcopal Church in Cedar Cr Hund to meet at the church to elect trustees ... we certify that NEHEMIAH DAVIS, THOMAS EVANS, ISAAC BEAUCHAMP, GEORGE WALTON, JACOB TOWNSEND, BETHUEL WATTSON & MARK DAVIS were elected trustees. Wit: JOHN LOFLAND, JOHN METCALF, WM DAVIS. (B:pg 312)

1 Jul 1788 at Kent Co. Commission. To JOHN CLOWES of Suss Co esqr, whereas our president and general assembly on 10 Jun 1788 did by joint ballot, elect and appoint you third justice of the Court of Common Pleas and Orphans Court of Suss Co, we do by these presents commissionate you third justice ... . (signed) THOMAS COLLINS esqr. Attest: JA BOOTH secy. (B:pg 313)

1 Jul 1788 at Kent Co. Commission. To ALEXANDER LAWS of Suss Co esqr, whereas our president and general assembly on 10 Jun 1788 did by joint ballot, elect and appoint you, fourth justice of the Court of Common Pleas and Orphans Court of Suss Co, we do by these presents commissionate you fourth justice ... . (signed) THOMAS COLLINS esqr. Attest: JA BOOTH secy. (B:pg 313)

4 Sep 1788. Deed. PETER FRETWELL WRIGHT esqr high sheriff of Suss Co sold to the honourable GEORGE MITCHELL esqr of same co ... a tr of land on Indian River and in Baltimore Hund called Irones First Adventure surveyed 3 May 1783 which was assigned by JOHN WINGATE and JACOB BURTON in Mar following, warrant was granted to the afsd WINGATE and BURTON 14 Oct 1776 106 a. which became the right of [blank] bounded by Woolf Point Ridge, land called Holly Grove, JOB DERICKSON and DAGWORTH's land called Timber Land Inlarged, and whereas SANDERS ROBERTS lately in a Court of Common Pleas recovered a debt against JACOB IRONS, and by virtue of a writ PETER FRETWELL WRIGHT sheriff seized in execution the afsd tr of land of RACHEL IRONS executrix of JACOB IRONS and sold same at public vendue to GEORGE MITCHELL esqr for 26 pounds 11 shillings on 12 Jul last past he being the highest bidder. Wit: RHOADS SHANKLAND, JOHN W. BATSON. Ackn 4 Sep 1788. (B:pg 314)

12 May 1786. Deed. WILLIAM CAHOON of Suss Co yeoman and MARY his wife for 100 pounds sold to JOHN SHARP of same co yeoman ... a tr of land, which a certain JOHN FOWLER late of same co by a deed bearing date 6 May 1779 did sell unto the afsd WILLIAM CAHOON in Broadkiln forest pt/o a tr granted to said JOHN FOWLER by a warrant dated at Phila 15 Mar 1754 bounded by CLOWE's 3 notched survey, JOHN SHARP, land formerly of WILLIAM DAUGHTEN now in possession of JOHN SHARP & line between JOHN FOWLER and his son WILLIAM FOWLER ... 95 a. Wit: PHILLIP KOLLOCK, W HARRISON. Ackn 6 Aug 1788. (B:pg 316)

8 Apr 1774. Bond of Conveyance. TIMOTHY MAY of Suss Co am

firmly bound unto JOHN CHANCE of same place in the sum of 60
pounds ... the condition of this obligation is such that THOMAS MAY
shall convey all his rite unto 12 a. of land being the land which
THOMAS DAVIS & JOHN DAVIS convaid unto SPENCER CHANCE
in 1761 unto JOHN CHANCE, then this obligation shall be void. Wit:
MESHACH COUCH, DRAPER MAY. 6 Aug 1788 Handwriting of
THOMAS MAY proved by oath of RHOADS SHANKLAND esqr. (B:pg
318)

16 Apr 1788. Assignment. WILLIAM BRADLEY for 60 pounds assign
over all my right of the [above] bond unto MARK DAVIS. (B:pg 318)

16 Jan 1777. Articles of Agreement. WILLIAM BAGWELL of Suss Co
am firmly bound unto JOHN CHANCE of same place in the sum of 37
pounds 10 shillings ... the condition of this obligation is such that
WILLIAM BAGWELL shall convey his rite to a tr of land s side of
Goits Br bounded by land of JOSHUA SPENCER formerly sold to him
by WILLIAM BAGWELL and JOHN CHANCE's other land ... 10 a.
which land the said JOHN CHANCE binds himself to pay unto
WILLIAM BAGWELL the sum of 37 shillings 6 pence, when bond is
completed then this obligation to be void. Wit: THOMAS CADE,
SARAH OWENS. Proved 6 Aug 1788. (B:pg 318)

Deed. WILLIAM BRADLEY of Kent Co and MARY his wife for 427
pounds 10 shillings sold to MARK DAVIS of Suss Co yeoman ... two trs
of land, whereas EDMOND ANDROSS esqr by pattent bearing date 29
Sep 1677 did grant unto a certain RICHARD HILL a 1000 a. tr of land
on Mispillion Cr which the said RICHARD HILL on 7 Jul 1678 did
convey unto a certain BENJAMIN COWDRY who granted 500 a. unto
HENRY SPENCER and SAMUEL SPENCER, and afterwards did on
26 Apr 1683 grant unto his dau FRANCES SPENCER w/o WILLIAM
SPENCER the remaining 500 a., which on 1 Oct 1690 confirmed unto
the said FRANCES SPENCER, HENRY SPENCER & SAMUEL
SPENCER by the honouerable WILLIAM PENN absolute proprietor of
PA, and whereas the afsd HENRY SPENCER by his will bearing date
28 Feb 1715/16 did devise unto his son JEHU SPENCER 85 a. pt/o the
afsd lands, which JEHU SPENCER on 14 Apr 1730 did sell unto a
certain WILLIAM CHANCE late of Suss Co decd, whereas the said
WILLIAM CHANCE being seized of the afsd land died intestate
leaving 2 sons SPENCER CHANCE and WILLIAM CHANCE to whom
the land descended, which said WILLIAM CHANCE by deed of release
bearing date 6 Feb 1758 did release unto the said SPENCER CHANCE
his right to the 85 a., whereas a certain JOHN DAVIS and THOMAS
DAVIS by deed of release bearing date 4 Feb 1750 did release unto the
said SPENCER CHANCE all their right to pt/o a tr of land called
Cullins Purch in Cedar Cr Hund e of the division line between them
and SPENCER CHANCE adj SAMUEL SPENCER, and SPENCER
CHANCE being seized of the lands released it unto the said WILLIAM
CHANCE and JOHN DAVIS, & THOMAS DAVIS died intestate
leaving 3 children JOHN CHANCE, MARY w/o WILLIAM BRADLEY
and SARAH CHANCE, to whom the said lands descended, which
JOHN CHANCE preferred a petition to the Orphans Court 26 Feb

1774 praying the court to appoint 5 freeholders to make partition
among the heirs of SPENCER CHANCE decd, the court did appoint
WILLIAM BELL, JOHN DRAPER, BETHUEL WATTSON, WILLIAM
HAZZARD and DAVID WILLIAMS, who laid off and allotted unto the
said JOHN CHANCE 183 a. 94 perches, and whereas JOHN CHANCE
purch of a certain THOMAS MAY 14 a. 106 perches adj to the said
allotment for conveyance of which the said THOMAS MAY did execute
a bond, which 2 trs contain 198 a. 40 perches ... by virtue of a writ
dated 12 Feb 1786 PETER FRETWELL WRIGHT esqr high sheriff of
Suss Co seized in execution the lands of JOHN CHANCE to satisfy
JAMES THARP a debt and damages which he had recovered against
MATTHIAS JONES and JOHN CHANCE, and sold same at publick
vendue to WILLIAM BRADLEY party hereto he being the highest
bidder ... 198 a. 40 perches and 80 a. 37 perches. Wit: JOHN
CLOWES, MARY CLOWES. Ackn 6 Aug 1788. (B:pg 319)

28 Jul 1788. Deed. HENRY SAFFORD of Suss Co planter for 200
pounds sold to OBEDIAH SMITH of same place planter ... pt/o a tr of
land called Yoark in the N.W.F. Hund ... 16 1/2 a. and also pt/o a tr of
land called Cow Gardain or any other tr for the quantity of 3 1/2 a.,
also pt/o a tr of land called Brothers Adventure surveyed for the afsd
HENRY SAFFORD ... 105 1/2 a. ... HENRY SAFFORD do appoint
JOHN WILTBANK and PHILLIP KOLLOCK of the town of Lewis
Suss Co esqrs or either of them atty to ackn this deed in open court.
Wit: FRANS JOHNSTON, DANIEL POLK. Proved and Ackn 6 Aug
1788. (B:pg 322)

28 Jul 1788. Deed. HENRY SAFFORD of Suss Co planter for 30
pounds sold to LEVI SAFFORD of same place planter ... pt/o a tr of
land called Brothers Adventure in N.W.F. Hund ... 15 1/2 a. ... HENRY
SAFFORD do appoint JOHN WILTBANK and PHILLIP KOLLOCK of
the town of Lewis Suss Co esqrs or either of them his atty to ackn this
deed in open court. Wit: FRANS JOHNSTON, DANIEL POLK. Ackn 6
Aug 1788. (B:pg 324)

7 Aug 1788. Deed. WILLIAM JONES of Suss Co yeoman for 75 pounds
sold to JAMES JONES of same co gent ... a messuage called Good Will
in Nanticot Hund adj land of THOMAS MARVEL and WM JONES
afsd both being pt/o the same tr taken up by MATTHIAS JONES of
same co and by him conveyed to the afsd WM JONES bounded by
ABRAM ADAMS ... 48 a. and also another messuage adj taken up by
ABRAM ADAMS and by him conveyed to MATTHIAS JONES afsd and
by said JONES conveyed to the afsd WM JONES called Support to
Double Purch bounded by ELIAS JOHNSTON ... 58 a. Wit: ISAAC
HARDY JONES, BENJAMIN JONES. Ackn 6 Aug 1788. (B:pg 325)

7 Aug 1788. Deed. JAMES JONES of Suss Co yeoman for 75 pounds
sold to JOHN MARTIN of same place farmer ... 2 trs of land [same as
above]. Wit: ISAAC HRD JONES, BENJAMIN JOHNSON. Ackn 6
Aug 1788. (B:pg 327)

28 Jul 1788. Deed. Col JOSHUA MITCHELL of Worcester Co MD for

22 pounds 10 shillings sold to JONATHAN BETTS of Suss Co yeoman
... a tr of land, whereas the proprietor of MD by his pattent did grant
unto THOMAS RALPH a tr of land called Ephrams Purch ... 15 a. and
THOMAS RALPH did convey the tr unto a certain ROBERT NELSON
who with a certain ESME BAYLY conveyed the land unto Col
JOSHUA MITCHELL ... JOSHUA MITCHELL hereby appoint
THOMAS BATTSON esqr, JOHN WINGATE, ELISHA DICKINSON,
ISAAC ATKINS and ROBERT LACEY of Suss Co his attys to ackn
this deed in open court. Wit: CHARLES COLLINGS, ELIZABETH
MUMFORD. Proved and Ackn 6 Aug 1788. (B:pg 329)

7 Aug 1788. Deed of Mortgage. JAMES BROWN Junr of Suss Co
yeoman in order to secure the payment of a sum of 540 pounds and
also for 5 shillings sold to NICHOLAS OWINGS and BEAL OWINGS
of Baltimore Town MD merchants ... several trs of land, whereas the
afsd JAMES BROWN together with WHITE BROWN of Suss Co
yeoman by their bill bearing date 5 this instant Aug became indebted
unto the afsd NICHOLAS OWINGS and BEAL OWINGS in the sum of
540 pounds ... Forrest Land 50 a., Clarks Forest 66 a., Addition to Four
Trs 80 a., Mohorom Hill 81 a., Browns Support 23 a. which 5 trs are
the dwelling plantation of the said JAMES BROWN bounded by JOHN
HANDY, WHITE BROWN, JOHN NEILL, RICHARD CANNON, also
a tr called Canaan Improved 122 a. adj HUMPHRIES BROWN,
JAMES BROWN Senr and JACOB KINDER and now in the tenure of
BARTHOLOMEW TAYLOR, all lands in NW Fork Hund, if the afsd
JAMES BROWN shall well and truly pay unto NICHOLAS OWINGS
and BEAL OWINGS the afsd sum of 544 pounds with lawful interest
on or before 7 Nov next ensuing, then this present indenture shall be
void ... . Wit: JOSEPH DAWSON, EDWD BROWN. Ackn 7 Aug 1788.
(B:pg 330)

3 Oct 1772. Bond of Conveyance. JOHN HAMMOND and SABRA his
wife of Dorchester Co MD am firmly bound unto JAMES SPENCER of
Kent Co in the sum of 200 pounds ... the condition of this obligation is
such that if JOHN HAMMOND and SABRA his wife and JOHN
HAMMOND Junr son of afsd JOHN HAMMOND when the said JOHN
HAMMOND Junr arives to the age of 21, make over unto the said
JAMES SPENCER by way of a general warrentee a tr of land called
Batcheldors Folly 100 a. in Marshehope e side of the NE Fork Br of
Nanticoke River and Doublefork Br then this present obligation to be
void. Wit: HENRY SAFFORD Junr, NEHEMIAH NICOLLS. Ackn 7
Aug 1788. (B:pg 332)

18 Jun 1788. Deed. LEVI HILL of Suss Co for 70 pounds sold to
ANDERSON HUDSON of same co ... a tr of land in Broadkiln Hund
pt/o 2 larger trs, one called Cool Spring and the other was granted to a
certain HUGH VIRDEN which said 200 a. by sundry mesne
conveyances became the right of GEORGE HILL and he by his will
bearing date 28 Nov 1786 divised the tr to his 2 sons LEVI HILL party
to these presents and GEORGE HILL, on County Road leading to the
Ironworks adj WILLIAM PERRY, Mill Cr, JOSEPH DODD and
SAMUEL HUDSON ... 200 a. Wit: ROBERT HOOD, WILLIAM

VIRDEN. Ackn 8 Aug 1788. (B:pg 332)

7 Aug 1788. Deed. JONATHAN WOOLF of Lewis Suss Co inkeeper and RUTH his wife for 200 pounds sold to JAMES GORDON of Lewis and Rehoboth Hund same co house carpenter ... a messuage and parcel of land pt/o a larger tr called St. Martins in Lewis and Rehoboth Hund 2 mi from the town of Lewis in the fork of the Indian River Road and the road leading from Lewis to Dover adj PERRY PRETTYMAN's child and JAMES HEPBURN ... 12 a. 26 perches. Wit: JOSEPH DARBY, WILLIAM DELLANEY. RUTH doth say that she signed this conveyance of her own free will. Attest: JOHN CLOWES judge. Ackn 8 Aug 1788. (B:pg 334)

1 Sep 1788. Petition of SYDENHAM THOM (who intermarried with BETTY CRAPPER the surviving executrix of the will of LEVIN CRAPPER esqr late of Suss Co merchant decd) and BETTY his wife humbly sheweth that whereas the said LEVIN CRAPPER in his lifetime was seized of 3 percels of land in Cedar Cr Hund one called Portors Folly e side of Bowmans Br which was granted by warrant unto GABRIEL WEST and assigned unto LEVIN CRAPPER, one other tr w side of Bowmans Br being the same which a certain RICHARD HAYS Senr of same co sold unto JOHN TRUITT who afterwards (and before any conveyance to him made) conveyed the same to the afsd LEVIN CRAPPER 100 a., and one other tr adj the first whereon NICHOLAS VEIGHT Junr lately dwelt 509 a., and LEVIN CRAPPER being so seized by his bond bearing date 25 Jan 1768 did ackn himself bound unto DAVID WILLIAMS of Dorset Co farmer for 1000 pounds with condition that if the said LEVIN CRAPPER did convey by special warrantee the lands after the full purch money paid, then that obligation should be void, LEVIN CRAPPER after first making his will appointing BETTY CRAPPER executrix and MOLTON CRAPPER executor, after which the said SYDENHAM THOM intermarried with the said BETTY CRAPPER and the said MOLTON CRAPPER died without having executed any deed to DAVIS WILLIAMS, he having paid the consideration money, and whereas DAVID WILLIAMS also died having first made his will by which he did bequeath unto his son JOHN WILLIAMS the afsd 100 a., after which the said JOHN WILLIAMS died intestate leaving no issue whereby the 100 a. descended to his several brothers and sisters, whereof WILLIAM WILLIAMS the eldest surviving brother had 75 a. 69 perches of the recited land (leaving 29 a. 91 perches for his mothers thirds) which he sold with his right to his mothers thirds to SAMUEL BASNETT, after which MARY PORTOR the mother of the said WILLIAM WILLIAMS also died whereupon the said SAMUEL BASNETT had the remaining 29 a. 91 perches, SAMUEL BASNETT sold the 100 a. to WILLIAM JOHNSON Junr (son of SAMUEL JOHNSON) ... . Bond wit: DAVID WILLIAMS. Your petitioner pray your worships to make an order for them to convey the 100 a. unto the said WILLIAM JOHNSON in discharge of the bond. (B:pg 336)

1 Sep 1788. Deed. PETER FRETWELL WRIGHT esqr high sheriff of Suss Co for 400 pounds sold to LEVIN HILL of Baltimore Hund same

co ... a tr of land, whereas JOHN DICKSON of same co on 27 Nov 1755 did sell unto AARON IRONS of Worcester Co MD now Suss Co a tr of land pt/o a 500 a. tr called Friendship originally granted by patent by CHARLES Lord Baron of Baltimore unto a certain MARTIN CURTIS of Somerset Co MD who sold the same to a certain WILLIAM DICKSON of co afsd, who by his will devised the same to his 2 sons STURGISS DICKSON and JOHN DICKSON, which said JOHN DICKSON afterwards died leaving issue JOHN DICKSON party to recited indenture, whereby JOHN became seized of 1/2 of the 500 a. on Baltimore River ... 250 a. whereas AARON IRONS by his will bearing date 4 Oct 1774 did devise unto his son JACOB IRONS the 250 a. who being seized died intestate within the co afsd, and administration of the estate was committed unto RACHEL IRONS widow and relict of the said JACOB IRONS decd, and HENRY NEILL in a Court of Common Pleas May Term 1785 had recovered against the said RACHEL IRONS adminr a debt of 160 pounds and damages of 3 pounds 4 shillings, by virtue of a writ dated 8 Nov 1786 PETER FRETWELL WRIGHT high sheriff seized in execution the tr of land of JACOB IRONS in the hands of RACHEL IRONS and on 23 Dec 1786 sold same at public vendue to LEVIN HILL he being the highest bidder. Wit: ALEXR LAWS, JNO WILTBANK. Ackn 1 Sep 1788. (B:pg 338)

8 Mar 1788. Deed. KEZIAH WRIGHT of Suss Co widow and JEREMIAH CANNON of same co sold at publick vendue to WILLIAM SLUBY and JOHN SMITH, as tenants in common and not as joint tenants, for 978 pounds they being the highest bidders ... several trs of land in NW Fork Hund, whereas PETER HUBBERT late of Suss Co merchant died intestate on 10 Mar 1777 and administration of the said decd was granted unto the afsd KEZIAH WRIGHT (then KEZIAH HUBBERT) and JEREMIAH CANNON by PHILLIP KOLLOCK esqr register appointed for the probate of wills and granting letters of administration, whereas in an Orphans Court on 6 Sep 1785 the said KEZIAH WRIGHT and JEREMIAH CANNON were granted an order to sell the real estate of the said decd to discharge his just debts ... pt/o a tr called Cannons Regulation 50 a., also pt/o a tr called Spring Hill 40 a., also pt/o a tr called Luck, also a tr called Clarksons Meadow 68 a., also a tr called Hubberts Regulation 507 a., and a tr called Clarksons Lott 100 a. ... KEZIAH WRIGHT and JEREMIAH CANNON appoint JOHN RODNEY and PHILLIP KOLLOCK of the town of Lewis gent our attys to ackn this deed in open court. Wit: WM BRADLEY, PHILLIP KOLLOCK. Proved and Ackn 1 Sep 1788. (B:pg 340)

1 Sep 1788. Deed. PETER FRETWELL WRIGHT esqr high sheriff of Suss Co for 2 pounds 5 shillings sold at public vendue to PHILLIP KOLLOCK he being the highest bidder ... 19 a. pt/o 41 a. allotted to HERCULAS KOLLOCK, whereas a certain SHEPARD KOLLOCK late of same co gent decd in his lifetime was seized of a tr of land 397 a. pt/o a larger tr near Lewes Town called Middleborough originally granted by patent to a certain ALEXANDER MOLISTON decd, and being so seized made his will bearing date 24 Jun 1756 wherein he did devise the following ... to his well beloved wife MARY KOLLOCK for

and during the time of her widowhood, but in case she again marries she shall enjoy no more than an equal portion with her children ELIZABETH KOLLOCK, COMFORT PRETTYMAN, GEORGE KOLLOCK, SIMON KOLLOCK, ALICE KOLLOCK, HERCULAS KOLLOCK and SHEPARD KOLLOCK, and I hereby appoint the said MARY my executrix of my will, and MARY being so seized on 1 Sep 1761 for 39 pounds 10 shillings sold unto JACOB KOLLOCK and RYVES HOLT esqrs, trustees of the General Loan Office, a tr of land and plantation in the hund of Lewis and Rehoboth 100 a. pt/o a larger tr called Middleborough, from FENWICK STRETCHER and HESTER his wife to SHEPARD KOLLOCK late decd, 29 Mar 1749 (Book H fol 218) which indenture provides that if the said MARY should well and truly pay unto the said JACOB KOLLOCK and RYVES HOLT or their successors, 59 pounds 10 shillings with interest then the said indenture should be void, and whereas the said MARY KOLLOCK afterwards, before she had paid the principal monies and interest, died intestate by means whereof administration of the estates of MARY KOLLOCK and of the said SHEPARD KOLLOCK committed unto GEORGE KOLLOCK eldest son of the said SHEPARD KOLLOCK ... in an Orphans Court GEORGE KOLLOCK obtained an order of court and sold unto a certain WILLIAM GILL 70 a. pt/o the first afsd lands and in pursuance of the second order of court did sell the mansion house and 40 a. of land adj and became the purchasor thereof himself, and GEORGE KOLLOCK on 4 Mar 1767 petitioned the court to appoint 5 freeholders to divide the residue among the several heirs, DAVID HALL, GILBELSHER PARKER, STEPHEN GREEN, JOHN WILTBANK and PETER PARKER were appointed to make petition, and taking with them RHOADS SHANKLAND a skilful surveyor, having viewed the said lands division was made ... allotted to HERCULES KOLLOCK 41 a. which on 7 Mar 1769 for 100 pounds he sold to JACOB KOLLOCK late of Suss Co esqr decd (Book L fol 15) and whereas MARGARET KOLLOCK executrix of the will of the afsd JACOB KOLLOCK did on 17 Jul 1787 convey unto PHILLIP KOLLOCK the 41 a., and whereas JOSEPH HALL esqr trustee of the General Loan Office at Aug Term 1787 obtained a judgment against JOHN RUSSEL, PHILLIP KOLLOCK and ELIZABETH DRAIN, late ELIZABETH KOLLOCK, tenants of the land in the indenture of mortgage, by virtue of a writ the sheriff seized in execution and sold the 100 a. on 12 Jan 1788. Wit: JOHN CLOWES, WILLIAM DAVIS. Ackn 2 Sep 1788. (B:pg 342)

2 Sep 1788. Deed. PETER FRETWELL WRIGHT esqr high sheriff of Suss Co for 15 pounds sold at public vendue to HANNAH EVANS she being the highest bidder ... a tr of land in Baltimore Hund called Rickards Chance, whereas HANNAH EVANS of same co widow in Aug Term 1785 recovered a judgment against a certain LUKE TOWNSEND for 70 pounds with legal interest, by virtue of a writ dated 7 Feb 1787 the sheriff attached pt/o 2 trs of land in possession of CHARLES WHALEY who together with JONES RICKARD he had summoned as garnishees, and sold same unto HANNAH EVANS the plantiff. Wit: JNO RUSSEL, ELIZABETH RUSSEL. Ackn 2 Sep 1788. (B:pg 346)

3 Sep 1788. Deed. ELIZABETH DRAIN of Lewis and Rehoboth Hund
Suss Co widow for 105 pounds sold to WILLIAM COLEMAN of Lewis
same co silversmith ... a tr of land near the town of Lewis originally
granted by pattent to a certain ALEXANDER MOLISTON 600 a.
called Middleborough who sold 476 a. to a certain PETER LEWIS, who
together with GRACE his wife sold 440 a. unto JACOB KOLLOCK late
of Lewes Town cooper decd, who by his will devised the land among his
children, in which division the lands were assigned to his son SIMON
KOLLOCK who afterwards died seized thereof intestate leaving 4
children, SHEPARD, MARY, HESTER and COMFORT who being all of
full age, divided the land, and the said HESTER intermarried with a
certain FENWICK STRETCHER, and the said COMFORD
intermarried with a certain JAMES TYBOUT, which said FENWICK
STRETCHER and HESTER his wife, and the said JAMES TYBOUT
and COMFORT his wife, conveyed their respective parts unto
SHEPARD KOLLOCK who became seized of 397 a. and being so
seized made his will wherein he did devise his whole estate unto his
wife MARY KOLLOCK [see B:pg 342] ... 40 a. Wit: JNO RUSSEL,
PETER F. WRIGHT. Ackn 3 Sep 1788. (B:pg 347)

3 Sep 1788. Bond of Warranty. PETER FRETWELL WRIGHT of Suss
Co esqr am firmly bound to WILLIAM COLEMAN of Lewis same co
silversmith in the sum of 260 pounds ... whereas a certain SHEPARD
KOLLOCK in his lifetime was seized of a tr of land [see B:pg 342] ...
whereas SHEPARD KOLLOCK (the son) sold the land allotted to him
to his brother SIMON KOLLOCK by his bond conditioned to make a
good & sufficient title to SIMON KOLLOCK, but whereas SIMON
KOLLOCK did assign all his right to the bond to GEORGE KOLLOCK,
and GEORGE by his bond bearing date 6 Feb 1776 did become bound
to the said PETER FRETWELL WRIGHT condition for conveyance of
the parcel of land with general warranty, and GEORGE KOLLOCK
afterwards died without having made any deed and having first made
his will appointed his wife ELIZABETH executrix, and PETER
FRETWELL WRIGHT did secure 130 pounds to the said GEORGE
KOLLOCK in his lifetime, and did pay unto ELIZABETH on 24 Jun
1777 65 pounds pt/o the purch money, whereas the said ELIZABETH
by her bond in the penal sum of 260 pounds unto the said PETER
FRETWELL WRIGHT with condition if ELIZABETH shall make over
a sufficient deed to the said PETER FRETWELL WRIGHT, then the
obligation to be void, and whereas JOSEPH HALL esqr trustee of the
General Loan Office caused the mortgage to be sued out and the lands
sold and the 40 a. were purch by ELIZABETH DRAIN late
ELIZABETH KOLLOCK, and afterwards PETER FRETWELL
WRIGHT sold the 40 a. unto the afsd WILLIAM COLEMAN [see
above] ... in the further and better securing to the said WILLIAM
COLEMAN a good and sufficient title to the land, if ELIZABETH
DRAIN should prove insufficent to support her warrantee, then the
condition of this obligation is such that if the afsd PETER FRETWELL
WRIGHT shall save keep harmless and indemnifyed the said WILLIAM
COLEMAN in the full peaceable and quiet possession of the said 40 a.
from the claim and property of the said SHEPARD KOLLOCK (the
son) and SIMON KOLLOCK from the future claim of all and every

other persons, then this obligation to be void. Wit: JOSEPH MILLER, JNO RUSSEL. Proved 3 Sep 1788. (B:pg 351)

2 Sep 1788. Petition of SARAH HARMONSON late SARAH LEWIS late widow and relict of WRIXAM LEWIS esqr late of Suss Co decd in behalf of herself and other heirs of the said WRIXAM LEWIS humbly sheweth, that whereas the trustees of the General Loan Office at a Court of Common Pleas held in Aug Term 1774 recovered a judgment against WILLIAM ARNALL late of same co pilot for a debt of 30 pounds and damages of 40 shillings 2 pence, by virtue of a writ PETER ROBINSON esqr then high sheriff seized in execution a messuage and lott of land in the town of Lewis bounded by WRIXAM LEWIS esqr, Front Street, JOHN ADAMS and Second Street, and sold same at public vendue unto WRIXAM LEWIS esqr for 88 pounds he being the highest bidder, and whereas the said PETER ROBINSON was removed from his office before a deed was made and whereas WRIXAM LEWIS died intestate leaving your petitioner his widow and relict and 3 children SUSANNAH, HESTER and LYDIA LEWIS, and whereas the consideration money is paid, and whereas SUSANNAH afterwards intermarried with a certain JOHN MARSH of Suss Co physician and the said HESTER hath intermarried with a certain ALEXANDER MCCALLEM of Talbut Co MD gent, your petitioner prays your worships to make an order for the present sheriff to execute a deed to the said SARAH, JOHN MARSH & SUSANNAH his wife, ALEXANDER MCCALLEM and HESTER his wife and LYDIA LEWIS for the lott of land and premises. Granted 2 Sep 1788. (B:pg 353)

2 Sep 1788. Deed. PETER FRETWELL WRIGHT esqr high sheriff of Suss Co for 88 pounds paid to PETER ROBINSON then sheriff and a further sum of 5 shillings conveys unto SARAH HARMONSON, JOHN MARSH & SUSANNAH his wife, ALEXANDER MCCALLEM and HESTER his wife and LYDIA LEWIS ... a tr of land [see above petition]. Wit: JNO RUSSEL, JOS DARBY. Ackn 2 Sep 1788. (B:pg 354)

3 Feb 1787. Deed. ELIZABETH DRAIN late ELIZABETH KOLLOCK of Suss Co executrix of the will of GEORGE KOLLOCK late of same co decd for 260 pounds sold to JAMES THOMPSON of same co ... a parcel of land in Lewis Hund near the town of Lewis pt/o a tr which SHEPARD KOLLOCK of same co in his lifetime was seized and dying intestate the tr was divided among his several heirs, pt/o the tr was laid off to the afsd GEORGE KOLLOCK and one other part was laid off to ALICE KOLLOCK son and dau of the said SHEPARD KOLLOCK, and ALICE by the name of ALICE HENDERSON on 4 May 1769 conveyed her share except 1 a. to the afsd GEORGE KOLLOCK who sold 20 a. pt/o the share laid off to him unto PETER WHITE and afterwards by his will bearing date 27 Apr 1776 devised the remaining pt/o the 2 shares to be sold for paying his just debts adj land belonging to the heirs of DAVID HALL esqr decd ... 84 a. Wit: D HALL, JOSEPH MILLER. Ackn 3 Sep 1788. (B:pg 357)

3 Sep 1788. Deed. PETER FRETWELL WRIGHT esqr high sheriff of

Suss Co for 60 pounds sold at public vendue unto BENJAMIN
HUDSON he being the highest bidder ... a tr of land, whereas
BRIDGET CONNOLLY adminr of the estate of FRANCES
CONNOLLY late of same co decd in Nov Term 1786 recovered a
judgment against WILLIAM TURNER, RICHARD COVERDALE and
MARGARET TRUITT executrix of JOHN TRUITT late of same co
decd for 1000 pounds together with 15 pounds 1 shilling damages, by
virtue of a writ 8 Aug 1787 the sheriff seized in execution a tr of land
in Cedar Cr Hund 100 a. said to be late the property of the said JOHN
TRUITT in the hands of MARGARET TRUITT his executrix and sold
same unto BENJAMIN HUDSON ... beginning at BENJAMIN
TRUITT's land, to ELIZABETH TRUITT's line, to COVERDALE
COLE's new ground, to WALTON's Mill Road, by the old school house,
to Herring Run Br, to ROBERT HOUSTON's land, to DITT's land ...
160 1/2 a. surveyed 16 Apr 1776 by CALEB CIRWITHIN called Spittle
Field. Wit: HAP HAZZARD, DANIEL ROGERS. Ackn 3 Sep 1788.
(B:pg 358)

3 Sep 1788. Deed. PETER FRETWELL WRIGHT esqr high sheriff of
Suss Co for 605 pounds sold at publick vendue to DANIEL ROGERS of
same co merchant he being the highest bidder ... a tr of land and
marsh in Cedar Cr Hund n side of Cedar Cr on Spring Br and
Beaverdam Br, adj THOMAS PURNALL, JOHN CLINDANIELS, land
late belonging to JOHN PLOWMAN decd, w side of THOMAS
OZBURN and GEORGE BLACK's land and WILLIAM BELL ... 300 a.
conveyed by WILLIAM BELL Senr on 14 Jun 1783 unto his son JOHN
BELL being pt/o a larger tr conveyed by BENJAMIN WYNKOOP and
SARAH WOODDROP his wife by deed bearing date 9 Oct 1767 unto
the said WILLIAM BELL, whereas WILLIAM BELL Junr in Aug Term
1787 at Court of Common Pleas recovered against the afsd JOHN
BELL 2626 pounds 14 shillings 8 pence debt and 4 pounds 4 shillings 6
pence damages, by virtue of a writ 6 Feb 1788 the sheriff seized in
execution the afsd tr of land and sold same unto DANIEL ROGERS.
Wit: PHILLIP KOLLOCK, HAP HAZZARD. Ackn 3 Sep 1788. (B:pg
360)

30 Aug 1788. Deed. WILLIAM LUCKER and CATHARINE his wife of
Suss Co for 50 pounds sold to JOHN KING of same co yeoman ... a tr
of land, whereas there was a 400 a. tr of land called Newcombs
Barrons in Broadkill Hund bounded by Broad Cr and Mill Cr which
said tr was resurveyed by JOSEPH BARKSTEAD 13 Jul 1685 for a
certain BAPTIST NEWCOMB and he did on 8 Dec 1686 convey the tr
to a certain PHILLIP THSELEMNAM then late of Phila in the books
when NEHEMIAH FIELD was clerk, and on 23 Apr 1723 a certain
JOHN SMITH, having possession of the said tr of land by his will doth
bequeath the same to his 4 children, HESTER SMITH, ANN SMITH,
PATIENCE SMITH & FEBY SMITH, and the afsd PATIENCE dying
without issue, the 3 surviving sisters, HESTER the widow of THOMAS
NEWCOMB, ANN then w/o JAMES RICORDS and PHEBY then w/o
ROBERT WARE did by their deed of partition 14 Dec 1744 divide the
tr equally amonst them (Book H fol 58), and JAMES RICORDS and
ANN his wife did convey their dividend unto JOHN CLOWES esqr of

co afsd, and JOHN CLOWES by his will bairing date 8 Apr 1761 did
devise unto his 4 sons and 3 daus, WILLIAM, JOHN, DAVID,
GERHARDUS, CATHARINE, MARY and LYDIA all the lands, and the
said WILLIAM dyed intestate, leaving issue 4 children CATHARINE,
party to this deed, MARY, LYDIA and JOHN to whom his pt/o the said
lands descended, and the survivors of the afsd 7 children did on 17 Dec
1772 divide all the testators lands, when Lot No 5 became the property
of the afsd WILLIAM's 4 children (Lib L fol 270), and CATHARINE
dau of the afsd WILLIAM intermarried with a certain PETER
DICKERSON who petitioned the Orphans Court for a division of Lot
No 5 amongst the heirs of the said WILLIAM, being granted 3
freeholders were ordered to set a true valuation thereon which order
being complyed with the said PETER DICKERSON accepted the same
in right of his wife CATHARINE ... 17 1/2 a. adj HAZARD's old field ...
WILLIAM LUCKER and CATHARINE his wife appoint HAPP
HAZZARD to ackn this deed in open court. Wit: ANDW WILLY, ROBT
JONES. CATHARINE did say that she executed this deed of her own
free will. Attest: JOHN COWES. Proved and Ackn 3 Sep 1788. (B:pg
363)

3 Sep 1788. Deed. JOHN TIMMONS of Suss Co yeoman for 60 pounds
sold at publick vendue to NEWBOLD VINSON he being the highest
bidder ... a tr of land, whereas JESSE THOMPSON late of same co
yeoman died intestate within the said co on or about 6 Mar 1773 and
administration of his estate was granted unto the afsd JOHN
TIMMONS by PHILLIP KOLLOCK register appointed for the probate
of wills and granting letters of administration, and whereas at an
Orphans Court on 4 Jun 1788 the said JOHN TIMMONS preferred a
petition setting forth that the said JESSE THOMPSON in his life
obtained letters of administration on the estate of GEORGE
THOMPSON upon settlement of which estate the said JESSE fell in
debt to the heirs of the said GEORGE THOMPSON the sum of 29
pounds 4 shillings 9 pence 1/2 penny, and prayed the court to grant an
order impowering him to make sale of so much of the real estate of the
said decd to enable him to pay & discharge the debts afsd, the court
ordered that the said JOHN TIMMONS do sell by public vendue as
much of a tr of land in Little Cr Hund to amount of 60 pounds ... tr
called Cox's Craft adj Bald Cypruss Swamp Br of Broad Cr and
CALDWELL's shingle cabbin ... and pt/o a tr called Cox's Folly 27 1/2
a. Wit: D HALL, JOS MILLER. Ackn 3 Sep 1788. (B:pg 365)

4 Apr 1788. Deed of Lease. BARKLEY (BARKELY) (BERCKLEY)
TOWNSEND of Suss Co in consideration of the yearly rents and
covenants aftermentioned lease to MANAEN BULL of same co ... a lott
of ground s side of Broad Cr ... 1 a. MANAEN BULL is to give full use
to the public of 50 ft sq of the land at the water side for a road during
the term of 7 years paying yearly rent of 5 pounds in and upon 4 Apr
next ensuing paying every year ... . Wit: CHAS MOORE, WILLIAM
POLK. (B:pg 367)

21 Aug 1787. Deed. JAMES HOWARD for 8 pounds 17 shillings 3
pence sold to Capt ROBERT EWART mariner ... a tr of land s side of

Broad Cr called Howards Lot 3 1/4 a. Wit: JAMES BRATTON, JONA
BOYCE. Ackn 5 Nov 1788. (B:pg 369)

21 Aug 1787. Power of Atty. JAMES HOWARD do appoint JAMES
BRATTON & PETER WHITE my attys to make over the [above] deed
in open court. Wit: CHAS MOORE, JAMES BRATTAN, JONA
BOYCE. Proved 5 Nov 1788. (B:pg 370)

5 Nov 1788. Sureties Bond. THOMAS EVANS esqr high sheriff of Suss
Co and RICHARD HAYS Junr, EDWARD STAPLEFORD, JOHN
WOOLF & JOHN METCALF of same co gent are firmly bound unto
the DEL State in the sum of 2000 pounds ... the condition of this
obligation is such that if THOMAS EVANS do well and truly execute
the office of sheriff then this obligation to be void. Wit: JOHN
CLOWES, W HARRISON. Proved 5 Nov 1788. (B:pg 370)

4 Nov 1778 at Fort George, City of NY. Certificate of Probate. His
Excellency WILLIAM TRYON esqr captain, general and governor in
chief in NY chancellor and vice admaral of the same, know ye that at
Richmond Co on 27 Jul 1778 before BENJAMIN SEAMAN esqr
thereunto appointed to the last will of PETER WINANT decd and his
codicil thereto were proved and the said decd having whilst he lived
and at the time of his death goods and chattles and credits within the
province by means whereof the registering the said will and codicil and
the granting of administration and the auditting and final discharging
the account thereof doth belong unto me, the administration of the will
is granted unto JOHN MICHEAN and HENRY PERINE the executors
in the said will named. (B:pg 371)

10 Nov 1788. Personally appeared before PAUL MICHEAN judge of
the Court of Common Pleas for Richmond Co NY JOHN MICHEAN
who declared on his oath that he and HENRY PERINE are appointed
executors to the will of PETER WINANT late of same place decd [see
above] and that he is duly qualified and that he is the only surviving
executor of said will and finding debts due to the said PETER
WINANT decd in Worcester Co MD for the recovering thereof has
appointed CORNELIUS COLE of Richmond Co NY his atty. (B:pg 371)

15 Oct 1788. Power of Atty. JOHN MICHEAN of Richmond Co NY
surviving executor of the will of PETER WINANT late of said co have
appointed my trusty friend CORNELIUS COLE of same co my atty to
recover and receive all sums of money which are or shall be due to me
as executor of said estate of PETER WINANT decd ... . Wit: PAUL
MICHEAN, PAUL MICHEAN Junr. The seal hereunto annexed is the
seal of Richmond Co. Attest: JNO MERSERIE clerk. (B:pg 372)

15 Oct 1788. Deed of Mortgage. JAMES AYDELOTT & SAML
AYDELOTT of Suss Co for securing the payment of a bond to
GEORGE MITCHELL and 1 shilling sold to GEORGE MITCHELL of
same place merchant ... 3 cows & 1 yearlin, 1 yoke of oxen, 1 young
horse, 1 young mare, 2 young heifer & 2 young stear yearlins, whereas
the said JAMES AYDELOTT & SAML AYDELOTT by their bond

bearing this date stand bound unto the said GEORGE MITCHELL in the penal sum of 40 pounds 6 pence conditioned for the payment of 20 pounds with lawfull interest ... upon the condition that if the said JAMES & SAML shall pay unto the said GEORGE MITCHELL the principal sum of money recited with legal interest, this present indenture shall cease. Wit: TAMER AYDELOTT, HODAY ONIONS. (B:pg 372)

20 Nov 1788. Deed. THOMAS BELL of Cedar Cr Hund Suss Co yeoman for 700 pounds sold to DANIEL ROGERS of same place merchant ... a tr of land and marsh which a certain WILLIAM BELL purch of BENJAMIN WYNKOOP and WOODROP his wife in the hund afsd called Harts Tr beginning at part conveyed to JOHN BELL n side of Cedar Cr, to property of DANIEL ROGERS, to Beaverdam Br, to ROBERT HART's 100 a., to THOMAS PURNALL's line ... 400 a. being the same land conveyed by WILLIAM BELL Senr on 1 Aug 1783 unto his son THOMAS BELL party hereto, pt/o a larger tr conveyed by BENJAMIN WYNKOOP and SARAH WOODDROP his wife on 9 Oct 1767 unto the said WILLIAM BELL. Wit: WILLIAM JOHNSON Junr, NOAH SPENCER. Ackn 4 Dec 1788. (B:pg 373)

2 Mar 1764. Bond of Conveyance. SAMUEL SPENCER & JOHN SPENCER am firmly bound unto LEVIN COLLINGS of Suss Co yeoman in the sum of 350 pounds ...the condition of this obligation is such that if SAMUEL SPENCER & JOHN SPENCER make over a good & lawfull deed of sail of the tr of land whereon CHARLES RAWLINS now lives adj Herren Br & Piney Br of Musmilion Cr 200 a. in Seder Cr Hund unto LEVIN COLLINGS, then this obligation to be void. Wit: HENCOCK COLLINS, GEORGE CARPENTER. (B:pg 375)

6 Sep 1771. Assignment. LEVIN (LEVEN) COLLINGS of Suss Co for 200 pounds assigned unto ROBERT HOUSTON yeoman all my right unto the [above] bond. Wit: WM HAZZARD, THOMAS COLLINGS. (B:pg 375)

6 Nov 1788. Assignment. Whereas ROBERT HOUSTON Senr decd by his will devised the lands in the [above] bond unto one of his sons ROBERT HOUSTON Junr, I the said ROBERT HOUSTON Junr for 260 pounds assign unto NEHEMIAH CAREY of Suss Co yeoman all my right unto the [above] bond. Wit: D HALL, JOSEPH HOUSTON. (B:pg 375)

24 Nov 1788. I do hereby certify that the handwriting of SAMUEL SPENCER one of the [above] obligors was proved in open court 6 Nov 1788 by LUKE SPENCER, and the hand writing of JOHN SPENCER the other obligor was proved at the same time by WILLIAM PERRY esqr and the handwriting of WM HAZZARD, a wit to ye assignment, by THOMAS EVANS. (signed) NATH MITCHELL prothonotary. (B:pg 376)

The petition of LUKE SPENCER and WILLIAM DRAPER surviving executors of the will of SAMUEL SPENCER late of Suss Co yeoman decd and SARAH MIFFLIN late SARAH SPENCER adminr of the estate of JOHN SPENCER late of same co esqr decd, humbly sheweth that whereas the said SAMUEL SPENCER & JOHN SPENCER in their lifetimes by their bond [see B:pg 375] ... and whereas the said SAMUEL SPENCER and JOHN SPENCER are both since decd without executing any deed and having received full consideration money, and whereas LEVIN COLLINS assigned his right to the bond unto a certain ROBERT HOUSTON, and ROBERT HOUSTON by his will bearing date 23 Jan 1788 devised the tr unto his son ROBERT HOUSTON, and whereas the said ROBERT HOUSTON hath sold the tr unto NEHEMIAH CAREY of Cedar Cr Hund same co, your petitioners therefore pray your honors to grant them an order impowering them to execute a deed of conveyance unto the said NEHEMIAH CAREY. Granted & order made 6 Nov 1788. NATHL MITCHELL prothonotary. (B:pg 376)

6 Nov 1788. Deed. LUKE SPENCER, WILLIAM DRAPER both of Suss Co yeoman and SARAH MIFFLIN of same co widow for 150 pounds paid unto SAMUEL SPENCER and JOHN SPENCER in their lifetime and 5 shillings to them sold to NEHEMIAH CAREY ... a tr of land called Rich Land s side of Herring Br and w side of Piney Br ... 200 a. [see above petition and bond] ... . Wit: D HALL, JOSEPH HOUSTON. Ackn 6 Nov 1788. (B:pg 377)

17 Feb 1775. Bond of Conveyance. DAVID JOHNSON of Worcester Co MD am firmly bound unto THOMAS ROBINSON esqr of Suss Co in the sum of 300 pounds ... the condition of this obligation is such that if DAVID JOHNSON and JOSEPH JOHNSON sons of the afsd DAVID JOHNSON and HANNAH his wife and half brothers to ROBERT CRAIG decd who was the son of ALEXANDER CRAIG decd and the present HANNAH JOHNSON his then wife, shall when they arrive to full age, or in case of their death before they come to full age, then their legal representatives, shall convey by a good and sufficient deed unto THOMAS ROBINSON, all right in a tr of land in Rehoboth Hund s of Kings Road that leads from Coldspring to Lewis Town and the same land that ROBERT CRAIG the elder by his will devised to his grandson ROBERT CRAIGE 120 a. that DAVID JOHNSON and JOSEPH JOHNSON fell heirs to by the death of the said ROBERT CRAIG the younger, then in that case this obligation to be void. Wit: LEATHERBERY BARKER, JOHN HAYWARD. Proved 5 Nov 1788. (B:pg 379)

3 Jun 1788. Deed. JACOB HAZZARD for 5 shillings sold to JOSHUA FISHER ... a tr of land 2 mi from the town of Lewis in Quaker Town on Pagan Br adj JOSEPH SHANKLAND, JOSEPH ELDRIDGE, WALTON's land and ALEXANDER MOLESTON ... 112 a. whereas JACOB HAZZARD by a writ of entry against JOSHUA HALL ... and JOSHUA HALL as his right and inheritance and into which the said JOSHUA HALL had not entry but after the descision which HUGH HUNT unjustly and without judgment made to the said JACOB HAZZARD within 30 years then last past ... JOSHUA HALL a good and perfect common recovery was had ... . Wit: DANL RODNEY,

JOHN MASSEY Junr. Ackn 5 Jun 1788. (B:pg 380)

1 Nov 1788. Deed of Mortgage. JOHN ADAMS of Suss Co pilot for 500
pounds sold to JOHN BURTON Senr of same co ... a tr of land in Long
Neck in Indian River Hund adj Rehoboth Bay 330 a., provided that if
the said JOHN ADAMS shall pay unto the said JOHN BURTON Senr
the sum of 500 pounds on or before 1 Nov 1793 in one entire payment
together with lawful interest, then this present indenture shall cease.
Wit: PETER RICORDS, JAMES F. BAYLES. Ackn 5 Nov 1788. (B:pg
381)

23 Aug 1791. Receipt. JOHN BURTON the mortgagee in the [above]
recorded deed received of JOHN ADAMS the mortgagor full
satisfaction and therefore release and quit claim to the lands and
premises [above] mentioned. JNO RUSSEL recorder. (B:pg 382)

6 Nov 1788. Petition of HINMAN (HENMAN) WHARTON of Suss Co
yeoman humbly sheweth that by virtue of a writ issued out of the
Court of Common Pleas 6 Aug last past PETER FRETWELL WRIGHT
esqr late high sheriff seized in execution the lands and premises of
JOSHUA ROBINSON late of same co in the hands of MARTHA
ROBINSON and JOSEPH ROBINSON executors to satisfy PETER
ROBINSON of same co a debt of 250 pounds and 5 pounds 4 shillings
11 pence damages which the said PETER ROBINSON lately in a Court
of Common Pleas recovered against the said MARTHA and JOSEPH,
and sold same at public vendue to your petitioner on 19 Oct last past
for 205 pounds 10 shillings, the said PETER FRETWELL WRIGHT
before the said day of sale was removed from his office of sheriff and
thereby disabled from making a deed to your petitioner, your petitioner
prays your worships to make an order authorizing THOS EVANS the
present sheriff to execute a legal deed of conveyance. Granted 6 Nov
1788. (B:pg 383)

6 Nov 1788. Deed. THOMAS EVANS esqr high sheriff of Suss Co for
200 pounds 10 shillings paid to PETER FRETWELL WRIGHT sold to
HINMAN WHARTON ... a tr of land [see petition above] ... . Wit:
JOSEPH DAWSON, MITCHELL KIRSHAW. Ackn 6 Nov 1788. (B:pg
383)

The petition of FRANCIS WRIGHT humbly sheweth that a tr of land
in NW Fork Hund lately the property of JOHN JESSOP late decd
hath been taken in execution for the payment of his debts and sold at
public vendue by the late sheriff, and your petitioner was the highest
bidder for the same, your petitioner humbly prays the court to make
an order for the present sheriff to execute to your petitioner a deed.
Granted and order made 7 Nov 1788. (B:pg 385)

7 Nov 1788. Deed. THOMAS EVANS present high sheriff of Suss Co
for 19 pounds conveys to FRANCIS WRIGHT ... a tr of land in NW
Fork Hund s side of Bridge Br called Ridge Point 100 a. which after
sundry mesne conveyances became the right of a certain JOHN
JESSOP late of Suss Co decd by a deed of sale from CURTIS BROWN

& others, and whereas ISAAC BRADLEY in Nov Term 1787 in a Court of Common Pleas recovered judgment against the estate of the said JOHN JESSOP in the hands of EUNCE JESSOP adminr for 37 pounds 17 shillings 8 pence and 4 pounds 15 shillings damages, by virtue of a writ PETER FRETWELL WRIGHT then high sheriff seized in execution the tr of land and sold same at public vendue unto the said FRANCIS WRIGHT he being the highest bidder [see petition above]. Wit: JOS MILLER, D HALL. Ackn 7 Nov 1788. (B:pg 385)

5 Nov 1788. Petition of JESSE TULL of Suss Co yeoman humbly sheweth that by virtue of a writ dated -- May 1788 PETER FRETWELL WRIGHT esqr then high sheriff seized in execution the lands of JEREMIAH WARWICK at the suit of JOHN MITCHELL and sold same to your petition for 64 pounds on 24 Jun 1788 he being the highest bidder, and the sherifalty of the said PETER FRETWELL WRIGHT expired before he had executed any deed, your petitioner prays your honors to grant an order authorizing THOMAS EVANS esqr the present high sheriff to execute a deed of conveyance. Order made 5 Nov 1788. (B:pg 387)

5 Nov 1788. Deed. THOMAS EVANS high sheriff of Suss Co for 64 pounds sold to JESSE TULL of same co yeoman ... a tr of land pt/o a larger tr called Courtesey ... 150 a. [see petition above] .... Wit: JOHN WINGATE, D HALL. Ackn 5 Nov 1788. (B:pg 388)

28 Oct 1788. Deed of Gift. DAVID THORNTON of Broadkiln Hund Suss Co gent and ELESHE his wife for the great and pious love they have and do bear towards the rights and ceremonies of the Episcopal Church (usually called the Church of England) and also 5 shillings give to NEHEMIAH DAVIS, THOMAS EVANS, ISAAC BEAUCHAMP, GEORGE WALTON, JACOB TOWNSEND, BETHUEL WATTSON and MARK DAVIS all of Cedar Cr Hund same co gent trustees of St. Matthews Episcopal Church in Cedar Cr Hund duly elected (Lib B fol 312) ... a parcel of land 2 a. 5 1/2 sq perches in the hund afsd purch by the said DAVID THORNTON of NEHEMIAH DRAPER esqr decd and conveyed to him from SARAH and ALEXANDER DRAPER executors of the said NEHEMIAH DRAPER by deed bearing date 31 May 1772 adj DRAPER's old mill pond, surveyed and divided off 10 Apr 1770 by CALEB CIRWITHIN together with the church house. Wit: JOHN CLOWES, BURTON ROBINSON, RACHEL ATKINSON DAVIS. Ackn 5 Nov 1788.
5 Nov 1788. Deed. RACKLIFF CONNER of Suss Co taylor and AMY his wife for 250 pounds sold to ARTHUR WILLIAMS of same co planter ... a tr of land called Johnsons Lott in Baltimore Hund on Herring Cr ... 150 a. Wit: JOHN EVANS, LITTLETON TOWNSEND, LEAH WILDRAGE. AMY did allow that she became a party to the within deed of her own free will. Attest: ALEXR LAWS justice. Ackn 5 Nov 1788. (B:pg 390)

5 Jun 1788. Deed. JOHN ROBINSON and JENNEY his wife of Baltimore Hund Suss Co planter for 41 pounds 10 shillings sold to EZEKIEL WILLIAMS of same co planter ... a tr of land pt/o a tr

granted by the proprietor of MD unto a certain WILLIAM
WHITTINGTON by pattent bearing date 9 Jun 1694 in Baltimore
Hund called Sumerfield adj Shrimp Gut of Indian Assawamon Cr,
JAMES MURRAY, JOHN ROBINSON's old plantation and land called
Scottish Plott ... 41 1/2 a. ... EZEKIEL WILLIAMS do appoint
LITTLETON TOWNSEND, MATTHIAS AYDELOTT, ISRAEL
HOLLAND and NEHEMIAH HOWARD or either of them to ackn this
deed in open court. Wit: THOS BATSON, WILLIAM LOCKWOOD,
JOSEPH WILDGOOSE. Ackn 5 Nov 1788. (B:pg 393)

5 Nov 1788. Deed. ARTHUR WILLIAMS and TABATHA his wife both
of Suss Co planter and seamster and LEAH WILDRAGE of same co
widow for 80 pounds sold to EZEKIEL WILLIAMS of same co ... a tr of
land pt/o a tr granted by the proprietor of MD unto a certain AMBROS
WHITE in Baltimore Hund on the seaboard side called Cow Quarter
adj WILLIAM WOODCRAFT decd ... 39 a. Wit: JOHN EVANS, ISAAC
HARDY JONES, RACKLIFF CONNER. TABITHA became a party to
the deed of her own free will. Attest: ALEX LAWS justice. Ackn 5 Nov
1788. (B:pg 394)

19 Sep 1788. Deed. JOSEPH HALL of Suss Co for 75 pounds sold to
GEORGE WALKER of same co ... a tr of land in Indian River Hund
granted by warrant bearing date 13 -- 1761 to a certain JOSEPH
WARRINGTON called Welches Folly and the said JOSEPH
WARRINGTON on 13 Dec 1775 did oblidge himself to convey the tr
unto a certain JAMES STAFFORD, and JAMES STAFFORD did
assign the same unto the afsd JOSEPH HALL, and JOSEPH
WARRINGTON dying before any conveyance was made, RHOADS
SHANKLAND and ALEXANDER WARRINGTON executors of his will
by deed bearing date 2 May 1780 did convey the afsd tr unto the afsd
JOSEPH HALL adj ROBERT HOLMES ... 190 a. Wit: WILLIAM
PERRY, MARGARETTA PERRY. Ackn 5 Nov 1788. (B:pg 396)

27 Oct 1788. Deed. SOLOMON PARIMORE (PARMORE) of Suss Co
yeoman for 122 pounds 5 shillings sold to NEHEMIAH REED of same
co yeoman ... pt/o a tr of land, whereas THOMAS TILTON,
ELIZABETH HILL and THOMAS DAVOCK had granted to them by
sundry pattents a 500 a. tr of land and did by sundry conveyances
become the property of the afsd THOMAS DAVOCK, and THOMAS
DAVOCK did by his will bearing date 27 Jan 1718 bequeath to his son
THOMAS DAVOCK the afsd land, and THOMAS DAVOCK the
younger dyed intestate without issue whereupon the tr became the
right of his 2 sisters MARY and NEOMEY which they by mutual
compact did divide, and NEOMEY intermarried with a certain
MICHAEL GODWIN of Worcester Co by whom she had several
children, and by her will did bequeath her divident of the tr to her
eldest son WILLIAM GODWIN, and MICHAEL GODWIN in order to
confirm the title to him did by his will -- Dec 1765 bequeath unto him
the dividend of land, and the said WILLIAM GODWIN on 29 Aug 1772
did convey 250 a. unto the afsd SOLOMON PARIMORE (Lib L fol
265) ... on Long Bridge Br w side of the County Road adj land
belonging to the heirs of WILLIAM CLARK decd and land of JOSEPH

COULTER ... 81 1/2 a. Wit: JOHN CLOWES, JOSEPH MORRIS.
Ackn 6 Nov 1788. (B:pg 397)

4 Nov 1788. Deed. WILLIAM WALTON and SARAH his wife of Suss
Co for 375 pounds sold to CLEMENT ROSS of Dorchester Co MD
yeoman ... a tr of land, whereas a certain WILLIAM WALKER
obtained a warrant 17 Jun 1681 for 1000 a. of land in Broadkill called
Walkers Choice (copy of survey in secretary's office at NY), and
WILLIAM WALKER being possessed of the land did by virtue of his
will dated 20 Feb 1687/8 give the land to a certain Major WILLIAM
DYER, and WILLIAM DYER did bequeath unto his son WILLIAM
DYER all his plantation or land in Broadkill now called Rumbless Place
2000 a. and did bequeath to his youngest son JAMES DYER 300 a. in
the fork of Broadkill on Beverdam and Primehook Cr with 100 a. of
marsh adj, and whereas a certain THOMAS GROVE (great
grandfather to the afsd WILLIAM WALTON) obtained a warrant 13
May 1696 for all the lands and marsh between the lines of WILLIAM
DYER and the Primehook and Little Cr laid off 3 May 1697 by
THOMAS PEMBERTON deputy surveyor and found to contain 215 a.
of marsh and 356 a. of land, and the said WILLIAM DYER on 6 Mar
1698/9 did convey the afsd THOMAS GROVE gun smith 418 a. s side
of Primehook Cr, which the said THOMAS GROVE dyed and all his
lands became the property of his son THOMAS GROVE, and the said
JAMES DYER to whom the afsd 300 a. and 100 a. was by Major
WILLIAM DYER's will bequeathed, did on 18 Aug 1725 convey to the
last mentioned THOMAS GROVE of Suss Co yeoman 300 a. and 100 a.
of marsh adj thereto, and THOMAS GROVE after selling some pt/o the
400 a. to a certain WILLIAM STUART died intestate possessed of the
residue together with the land from the warrant to his father granted
(leaving issue THOMAS, SAMUEL, SUSANNAH and SARAH) to
whom the lands descended, and they divided the land and by their
deeds of leas and releas the whole became property of THOMAS and
SAMUEL, SAMUEL's part now in possession of WILLIAM HAZZARD
and the said THOMAS GROVE purch of a certain JOHN POTTER 75
a. adj his part 4 May 1785 and also 5 a. of a certain JACOB ADDISON
for the conveyance of which the said ADDISON gave a bond 8 Nov
1785, and THOMAS GROVE being seized of the land died having first
made his will bearing date 4 Apr 1787 in which he bequeath to my
nephew WILLIAM WALTON all my land down the neck ... adj
BEVINS MORRIS, JOHN HAZZARD & WILLIAM HAZZARD, 5 a.
purch of JACOB ADDISON and JONATHAN ADDISON ... now
surveyed for 372 a. Wit: HUGH PATTERSON, JAMES W. NAIGHT.
SARAH did sign this deed of her own free will. Attest: JOHN
CLOWES. Ackn 6 Nov 1788. (B:pg 399)

24 Oct 1788. Deed. SOLOMON PARAMORE (PARRAMOR)
(PARRAMER) of Suss Co yeoman for 52 pounds sold to EBENEZER
PETTYJOHN of same place ... a parcel of land pt/o the tr SOLOMON
now dwells on near Long Bridge Br ... 47 a. Wit: STEPHEN
PARROMORE, WILLIAM PARROMORE. Ackn 6 Nov 1788. (B:pg 402)

8 Oct 1788. Deed. SARAH MASON of Broadkiln Hund Suss Co widow

and adminr of the estate of ELIAS MASON late of same place cloather
decd for 178 pounds 15 shillings sold at public vendue to BURTON
JOHNSON of same place shop joyner he being the highest bidder,
pursuance to an order of the Orphans Court to discharge the debts of
the said ELIAS MASON ... a tr of land, in Broadkiln Hund binding on
Pembertons Br being the greater pt/o the same tr of land conveyed to
the said SARAH as widow of the said ELIAS MASON and their
children in 1775 from JOSEPH BAILY late of same co pilot decd ... 143
a. per late survey by RHOADS SHANKLAND esqr bounded by JOHN
CLOWES esqr's fulling mill land, SARA MASON doth appoint JOHN
CLOWES and THOMAS EVANS her attys to ackn this deed in open
court. Wit: JOHN W. DEAN, RHOADS SHANKLAND. Proved and
Ackn 6 Nov 1788. (B:pg 403)

14 May 1788. Deed. JOSEPH BURTON of Suss Co yeoman and
MARTHA his wife (late MARTHA WALKER) executrix of the will of
JACOB WALKER late of same co yeoman for 42 pounds 7 shillings 6
pence sold at public vendue to WILLIAM BAILEY of same co yeoman
he being the highest bidder, in pursuance of a order of the Orphans
Court to pay the said JACOB WALKER's debts ... a tr of land, whereas
the said JACOB WALKER at the time of his death was seized of a
parcel of land pt/o a larger tr in Lewis and Rehoboth Hund called
Coopers Hall ... bounded by KOLLOCK's mill pond, land late of
WILLIAM FISHER decd, JOHN WILTBANK esqr, Indian River Road
and ROBERT WHITE ... 56 1/2 a. Wit: JNO RUSSEL, ESTHER
CALE. Ackn 6 Nov 1788. (B:pg 405)

15 May 1788. Deed. WILLIAM BAILEY of Lewis and Rehoboth Hund
Suss Co yeoman and ANN his wife for 48 pounds 17 shillings 6 pence
sold to JOHN WILTBANK of same place esqr ... a tr of land [same as
above]. Wit: JNO RUSSEL, ESTHER CALE. Ackn 6 Nov 1788. (B:pg
407)

3 Nov 1788. Deed. JOSEPH HALL son of PH[?] of Suss Co &
ELIZABETH his wife for 25 pounds sold to ISAAC ATKINS
cordwinder of same co ... a tr of land in Indian River Hund called
Welches Folly which tr was granted by warrant in 1762 unto JOSEPH
WARRINGTON and the said JOSEPH WARRINGTON (now decd) on
24 Feb 1776 did convey 251 a. of the land unto the afsd JOSEPH
HALL (Lib M fol 245), and the said JOSEPH HALL did convey 100 a.
unto JOHN FLEMMING and 56 a. more unto WILLIAM BLIZARD ...
97 a. 44 sq perches. Wit: N WAPLES, JAMES VENT, JAS WILEY,
ADAM HALL. Ackn 6 Nov 1788. [plat shown] (B:pg 408)

12 Jul 1787. Deed of Gift. JOHN BROWN of Suss Co for natural love
and affection and for their advancement and for 7 shillings paid by
THOS LAWS give to his sons WILLIAM BROWN and JOHN BROWN,
and his daus BETSEY BROWN and MARY BROWN ... the following
articles, to my sons WILLIAM and JOHN 200 a. with my dwelling
plantation and woodland adj, and if either of them should die without
heirs or before they should arive to the years of 21 then the whole 200
a. should belong to the longest liver and also to my dau BETSEY

72

BROWN 1 negro girl named DINAH and her increase and to my dau
MARY BROWN 1 negro girl named LEAH and her increase provided
the afsd negroes should not be taken out of my possession during my
natural life or out of the possession of my wife during her natural life
should she out live me ... JOHN BROWN doth appoint the afsd
THOMAS LAWS and DAVID TRAIN esqr my attys to ackn this deed
in open court. Wit: THOMAS LAWS, AMELIA LAWS, MARY LAWS.
Proved and Ackn 6 Nov 1788. (B:pg 410)

6 Nov 1788. Deed. WILLIAM WHITE of Suss Co gent for baring
docking and cutting all estates tale and remainders and 5 shillings, and
RHOADS SHANKLAND esqr of same place in a good and perfect
common recovery, sold to JOSHUA HALL of same place gent ... 50 a.
(15 a. of arable land & 31 a. of woods land) 5 mi from the town of
Lewis on the road to Dagsbury and near to Indian River Chappel,
bounded by JOHN LITTLE, patten called Watsons Purch, pt/o a tr
surveyed 27 Jun MDCCLXXII by RHOADS SHANKLAND esqr, the
warrant granted unto SARAH WHITE widow for 150 a. Wit:
TRUSTIN LAWS POLK, FRANS JOHNSON. Ackn 6 Nov 1788. (B:pg
411)

9 Aug 1788. Deed. JOSHUA BURTON and MARY his wife,
NATHANIEL HICKMAN and PHEBE his wife and ESTHER
CARPENTER all of Suss Co for 14 pounds 10 shillings sold to
WILLIAM SHOCKLEY and ELI SHOCKLEY both of same co yeoman
... the undivided right in a 69 1/4 a. tr of land, whereas a certain
JAMES CARPENTER late of same co decd was in his lifetime seized of
a tr of land in Cedar Cr Hund and being so seized died intestate
leaving SARAH his widow and 7 children JOHN CARPENTER, LUKE
CARPENTER, SARAH CARPENTER, MARY w/o JOSHUA BURTON,
ELIZABETH w/o ELIJAH NORMAN, PHEBE w/o NATHANIEL
HICKMAN and ESTHER CARPENTER to whom the lands descended,
and whereas in an Orphans Court held 10 Dec 1776 five freeholders
were appointed to make partition, to the widow her right of dower 69
1/4 a. adj TILL's land originally WILLIAM BELLAMY's and JACOB
JONES, during her natural life, the remaining 2/3's would not admit
division without marring and spoiling the whole, whereupon 3
freeholders valued the said remaining 2/3's at 69 pounds 12 shillings 6
pence, adjudged by the court to LUKE CARPENTER, the second son,
and whereas SARAH CARPENTER widow of the intestate, lately died
by whose death the lands allotted to her descended to the afsd children
... the grantors appoint PHILLIP KOLLOCK and PETER FRETWELL
WRIGHT esqrs or either of them to ackn this deed in open court. Wit:
JOHN CLOWES, JOHN HAND, JOHN W. DEAN. Proved and Ackn 9
Aug 1788. (B:pg 412)

20 Nov 1780. Bond of Conveyance. THOMAS WHARTON (WARTON)
(WORTON) of Suss Co am firmly bound unto WILLIAM LOFLAND of
same co in the sum of 100 pounds ... the condition of this obligation is
such that if THOMAS WHARTON conveys a tr of land that REAVEL
WORTON decd from a division fence that was made between is farter
and him 50 a., also that the said THOMAS WHARTON shall quitt

possession at the request of the said WILLIAM LOFLAND, then this obligation to be void. Wit: JOHN LOFLAND, JOB TOWNSEND. Proved 5 Feb 1789. (B:pg 414)

3 Dec 1788. Petition of JOHN ROBINSON of Suss Co humbly sheweth that by virtue of a writ dated 6 Aug 1788 PETER FRETWELL WRIGHT esqr high sheriff seized in execution a parcel of land 90 a. late the estate of JOHN CIRWITHIN decd in Cedar Cr Hund, at the suit of JOSEPH HALL esqr trustee of the General Loan Office, and sold same at public vendue to your petitioner for 22 pounds 13 shillings he being the highest bidder, and PETER FRETWELL WRIGHT was removed from his office of sheriff before he had executed any deed, your petitioner therefore prays your worships to grant an order authorizing THOMAS EVANS esqr the present sherriff to execute a legal deed. Granted and ordered 3 Dec 1788. (B:pg 415)

3 Dec 1788. Deed. THOMAS EVANS esqr high sheriff of Suss Co for 22 pounds 13 shillings paid to PETER FRETWELL WRIGHT conveys to JOHN ROBINSON ... a tr of land, whereas JOHN CIRWITHIN on 14 May 1776 by deed of mortgage to JOHN RODNEY esqr trustee of the General Loan Office for 60 pounds did sell a tr of land in Cedar Cr Hund 90 a. pt/o a 300 a. tr which CALEB CIRWITHIN grandfather of the said JOHN CIRWITHIN purch of a certain WILLIAM PILES, and CALEB CIRWITHIN being so seized did by his will devise the same to his son CALEB CIRWITHIN father of the afsd JOHN CIRWITHIN, by means whereof the said JOHN CIRWITHIN upon the death of his father became heir in tail to the said 300 a., JOHN CIRWITHIN in a common recovery conveyed 236 a. to his brother CALEB CIRWITHIN ... nevertheless that if the said JOHN CIRWITHIN should pay to the said JOHN RODNEY or his successor trustee 60 pounds with interest, then the said indenture should be void, and whereas JOHN CIRWITHIN afterwards (before he had paid the principal monies and interest) died intestate, whereupon administration was committed unto NANNY CIRWITHIN widow of the intestate, who afterwards intermarried with a certain JOHN MOORE now of Phila, and JOSEPH HALL esqr trustee of the General Loan Office obtained a judgment against JOHN MOORE and NANNY his wife [see petition above] ... on Beverdam Br adj THOMAS COLLINS, LUKE PRIDE and JOSEPH COLLINS ... 190 a. by a late survey. Wit: GEORGE HAZZARD, PHILLIP KOLLOCK. Ackn 3 Dec 1788. (B:pg 415)

20 Dec 1788. Bill of Sale. GEORGE MITCHELL of Suss Co for 100 pounds sold to WILLIAM BELL of NJ ... 1 negro man called ISAAC & 1 negro woman named LIDD with his child. Wit: BERNARD HANLON, JAMES LITTLE. (B:pg 418)

1 Jan 1789. Bill of Sale. WILLIAM TENNENT BELL of Suss Co for 75 pounds sold to NATHANIEL MITCHELL of same co ... 1 negro man called ISAAC. Wit: JOHN W. BATSON, GEO MITCHELL. (B:pg 418)

12 Jan 1789. Deed of Gift. ABIGAIL (MARY) JOHNSON of Suss Co for natural love and affection give to my son GEORGE JOHNSON ... 1

negro woman called HAGER, 1 negro boy called SAUL, 2 beds and furniture. Wit: LITTLETON TOWNSAND, JAMES WHARTON, BETSEY TOWNSAND. (B:pg 418)

29 Jun 1788. Bill of Sale. ELIJAH CANNON of Suss Co for 400 pounds sold to SAMUEL HALL and JEREMIAH CANNON of same co ... 6 beads, 3 tables, 2 desks, 1 1/2 dozen of chiars, all my pewter and earthen ware and glass and fur iron pots and 20 head of cattle, 20 head of sheep, 30 head of hogs, 5 head of horses, 12 negros MESS BESM MINGS ROSS MANUEL STEPHEN SAM NELL TAMER ROSS SILBE GIN and the crop now growing on the ground, plour and harrows. Wit: DANIEL MILSON, WINGATE HALL. (B:pg 419)

1 Dec 1788. Deed of Gift. JOHN FLATT of Woodbridge Middlesex Co NJ son and heir of the late WILLIAM FLATT of same place decd who was the son of JAMES FLATT who was husband of ELIZABETH DEPRAY the dau of JOHN DEPRAY for love good will and affection give to my cozen JOHN FLATT of Hartford Co MD ... a parsel of land formerly belonging to JOHN DEPRAY formerly called Horkills but now Lewes Town below Phila. Wit: DAVID EVENS, JACOB CAMPTON, JOHN MCCLUIR. Ackn 1 Dec 1788 before JEREMIAH MANING judge of the Inferior Court of Common Pleas of Middlesex Co. (B:pg 419)

1 Dec 1788 at Midlesex Co NJ. Appeared before AJARIAH DUNHAM judge of the Inferior Court of Common Pleas, JOHN MCCLUIR wit to the [above] deed who being sworn deposeth and saith that he saw JOHN FLATT sign and seal and deliver the [above] deed. (B:pg 420)

1 Dec 1788. JONATHAN DEARE CLARK of the Court of Common Pleas for Midlesex Co NJ do hereby certify that the foregoing is a true coppy from the record of the original deed ackn and proff recorded in the clarks office (Book D pg 338-339) and that JAREMIAH MANING and AJARIAH DUNHAM are judges of the said court and duly authorized to take the same. (B:pg 420)

22 Jan 1789. Deed. JOHN HOPKINS Junr of Suss Co and his wife ALICE (ALSE) for 143 pounds sold to NEHIMIAH REED of same co ... a tr of land in Indian River Hund pt/o a large tr granted by warrant unto ANDERSON PARKER dated at Phila 24 Aug 1750 and by sundry conveyances became the property of JOHN HOPKINS Senr, also one other tr of land surveyed at the request of one ANN LANDRESS on 13 Apr 1734 laid off for 55 a. and by sundry conveyances became the property of JOHN HOPKINS Senr which 2 parsells adj WILLIAM HOPKINS ... 143 1/2 a. and the said JOHN HOPKINS Senr and his wife SOPHIAH by their deed of release bearing date 8 May 1782 did convey the same land unto JOHN HOPKINS Junr. Wit: JOS MILLER, JOHN TAM. ALICE sayeth that she did become a party to the within deed of her own free will. Attest: JOHN CLOWES. Ackn 4 Feb 1789. (B:pg 421)

7 Jan 1789. Deed. JESSE GRIFFITH and MARY his wife, CLEMENT

ROSS and SARAH his wife for 210 pounds sold to ALEXN LAWS esqr
of Suss Co ... 212 1/2 a. in W Fork Hund their pt/o a 367 1/2 a. tr
called Davids Hope, pt/o a 85 1/2 a. tr called Adventure and pt/o a 78
3/4 a. tr called Puirntion?, all the 531 3/4 a. of land pattented to
DAVID POLK the elder decd or purch by said DAVID POLK, and
willed by him to his grandson WM POLK and his heirs and for the
want of such heirs then the lands to be the write and property of his 4
daus ELIZABETH ROBERTS, MARY JUITT, LOVEY COLLINS and
EMELAH LAWS, and WM POLK dyed and left no such heirs and the
discribed lands since fell to the heirs of said daus, and MARY
GRIFFITH w/o JESSE GRIFFITH one of the said daus and SARAH
ROSS the only heir of LOVEY COLLINGS ... JESSE GRIFFITH and
MARY his wife and CLEMENT ROSS & SARAH his wife appoint our
true and trusty friends JOHN WILTBANK, JOHN RODNEY and
PHILLIP KOLLOCK esqrs our attys to convey this land in open court.
Wit: JOB INGRAM, JNO RUSSEL. Ackn 4 Feb 1789. (B:pg 422)

7 Jan 1789. SARAH ROSS w/o CLEMENT ROSS not of full age and
MARY GRIFFITH w/o JESSE GRIFFITH being at full age did declare
that they become parties to the [above] deed of their own free will.
Attest: JOHN CLOWES. (B:pg 424)

4 Feb 1789. Deed. JONATHAN ADDISON of Suss Co yeoman for 200
pounds sold to JOHN HAZZARD and WILLIAM HAZZARD of same co
yeoman ... a tr of land, whereas JACOB ADDISON late of same co died
seized of a tr of land in Broadkiln Hund leaving 3 sons, JOHN, JACOB
and JONATHAN and whereas they did enter into a mutual obligation
bearing date 19 Feb 1783 to abide the award and determination of
CALEB CIRWITHIN, STRINGER TILORY, JOHN HAZZARD,
WILLIAM HAZZARD and JOHN H[?] by the parties appointed to
make division of the land, the said JONATHAN ADDISON did enter
into a writing obligation bearing date 12 Oct 1786 to convey to his
brother JACOB ADDISON pt/o the afsd land and JACOB ADDISON
assigned the same to JOHN and WILLIAM HAZZARD ... adj JOHN
HAZZARD and Beaverdam Br ... 99 a. of land and 10 a. of marsh adj
ZAIL HALL and BEAVINS MORRISS on Primehook Cr. Wit:
SAMUEL WILTBANK, CORNELIOUS WILTBANK, EMANUEL
RUSSEL. Ackn 4 Feb 1789. (B:pg 424)

11 Aug 1788. Deed. SOLOMON TRUITT and JANE (JEAN) his wife of
Kent Co for 80 pounds sold to WILLIAM RECORDS and MILLS
RECORDS of Suss Co farmers ... a messuage plantation and tr of land
in Ceder Cr Hund adj NANNEY BLACK ... 70 3/4 a. pt/o a tr called
[Page and Labanon?] which became the right of DAVID SMITH esqr
and by him devised to his grandson JOHN SMITH reserving the use
and proffits to his wife SARAH and his son WILLIAM father to the
said JOHN pursuance to his will dated 26 Apr 1753 during their
natural lives, and the said JOHN SMITH since the death of his father
WILLIAM SMITH and grandmother SARAH sold pt/o the said devise
above the County Road and part below leading from Ceder Cr to
CIRWITHIN's mill and 1 mi from Ceder Cr unto MITCHELL BLACK
father to the afsd JANE, the afsd MITCHELL BLACK died intested

leaving 4 children to whom the lands descended and by order of the
Orphans Court the lands became divided amongst 3 surviving heirs,
one of his children dying in the minority and without issue, the afsd
land allotted to JANE w/o SOLOMON TRUITT ... SOLOMON
TRUITT and JANE his wife appoint JOHN CLOWES to ackn this
deed in open court. Wit: JAMES MCNIGHT, PRISILLA SIMPLER.
Proved and Ackn 4 Feb 1789. (B:pg 426)

29 Oct 1788. Deed. BENJAMIN JOHNSON and MARY his wife of
Suss Co for 135 pounds sold to WILLIAM MORRIS of same co yeoman
... a 130 a. tr of land, whereas BEVINS MORRIS father of the afsd
WILLIAM MORRIS of same co had conveyed to him from a certain
RICHARD TEMPLIN of same co 106 a. of land in Broadkill Hund on
Pembertons Br adj THOMAS CARLILE and RICHARD TEMPLIN on
4 May 1750 by REBECAH BRICE adminr of JOHN BRICE, and the
said BEVINS MORRIS also purch of a certain FRANCIS CORNWELL
250 a. in same hund adj which he assigned a bond unto the said
BEVINS MORRIS on 14 Dec 1754 for the conveyance thereof baring
date 10 Dec 1753 signed by WILLIAM SHANKLAND then surveyor of
Suss Co, the said BEVINS MORRIS after his said purch seated the 2
trs of land and being so seized made his will in which he bequeathed
unto his 2 sons WILLIAM MORRIS and BEVINS MORRIS all his
lands, and WILLIAM and BEVINS did on 7 May 1776 by their deed of
partition divide the said testators lands between them, adj BENJAMIN
MIFLIN & DENNIS MORRIS, the se side of line became property of
BEVINS and all the lands on ne side of said line became the property
of WILLIAM, and BEVINS on 1 Jun 1782 did convey 130 a. to the said
BENJAMIN JOHNSON. Wit: JOHN CLOWES, JOB PARMORE. Ackn
4 Feb 1789. (B:pg 428)

30 Jan 1789. Deed. HAYWARD CANNON & REBECAH his wife and
MARY his mother of Suss Co yeoman for 40 pounds sold to WILLIAM
NOBLE (NEWBLE) of Dorchester Co MD ... a tr of land in NW Fork
Hund called Friendship w side of Chappel Road whereon the said
HAYWARD CANNON at present dwells 25 a. ... HAYWARD CANNON
& REBECAH his wife and MARY his mother appoint our well beloved
friends WILLIAM PERRY esqr or RHOADS SHANKLAND esqr to
ackn this deed in open court. Wit: ALEX LAWS, JOHN TENNANT.
Ackn 4 Feb 1789. (B:pg 430)

30 Mar 1774. Bond of Conveyance. JOHN LACY of Suss Co planter am
firmly bound unto BENJAMIN BENSTON of same co coop in the sum
of 130 pounds ... the condition of this obligation is such that if JOHN
LACY convey unto BENJAMIN BENSTON a tr of land called New
Port 150 a. w side of JOHN WILLIAMS's land, this obligation to be
void. Wit: ROBERT LACEY SENR, ROBERT LACEY Junr. Proved 12
Feb 1789. (B:pg 432)

20 Jan 1789. Assignment. BENJAMIN BENSTON the elder and ANN
his wife do assign over all my right to the [above] bond to BENJAMIN
BENSTON the younger. Wit: WILLIAM BUCHER Senr, WILLIAM
HARRIS. (B:pg 432)

24 Oct 1784. Deed. WILLIAM HUDSON of Suss Co yeoman for 100
pounds sold to his son JOHN HUDSON of same place farmer ... a tr of
land in the forrest of Ceader Cr Hund pt/o a larger tr which was
surveyed for JONAS WEBB by virtue of a warrant, and JONAS
WEBB by his will gave the same to his son JOHN WEBB, and JOHN
WEBB died intestate whareby the said land became the property of
the afsd BINGAMIN WEBB [sic] ... 110 a. Wit: JAMES HUDSON,
GABRIEL LOFLAND. Ackn 4 Feb 1789. (B:pg 433)

4 Feb 1789. Deed. WILLIAM SHOCKLEY Senr of Suss Co farmer for
6 pounds sold to ELI SHOCKLEY of same place yeoman ... pt/o a tr of
land granted by warrant from BENJAMIN EASTBURN surveyer
general baring date at Phila 8 Jun 1737 in Ceder Cr Hund at the head
of Slaughter Neck nw side Little Bridge Br of Primehook Cr which
land is called Grubby Plain pt/o a larger tr adj WILLIAM WINSLEY,
DILTO's line, land which formally belonged to JOSHUA TUNER and
land of ISAAC WATSON ... 171 a. Wit: NATHL MITCHELL, JNO
RUSSEL. Ackn 4 Feb 1789. (B:pg 434)

4 Feb 1789. Deed. WILLIAM SHOCKLEY Senr of Suss Co farmer for
6 pounds sold to his son WILLIAM SHOCKLEY Junr of same place
yeoman ... pt/o a tr of land granted by virtue of a warrant from
BENJAMIN EASTBURN surveyor general baring date at Phila 8 Jun
1737 in Ceder Cr Hund at the head of Slaughter Neck nw side of Little
Bridge Br of Primehook Cr which land is called Gruby Plain pt/o a
larger tr adj JOHN SMITH and JOHN POSTLE ... 60 a. Wit: NATHL
MITCHELL, JNO RUSSEL. Ackn 4 Feb 1789. (B:pg 435)

2 Nov 1788. Receipt. HENRY FISHER received of JOSEPH BAILY 63
pounds 5 shillings 4 pence it being in full of all accts to this day. (B:pg
436)

29 Jul 1779 at Phila. Receipt. WILLIAM SCHILLINGER received of
JOSEPH BAILY 52 pounds 10 shillings being the full consideration of a
bond which the said BAILY gave me bearing date 4 Apr 1773. Wit:
ANDREW HIGGONS, MARY PERRY. (B:pg 436)

30 Aug 1779. Receipt. JACOB CROWELL received of JOSEPH
BAILEY 52 pounds 10 shillings it being in full for the 1/2 of a pilot bote
called the Tite Match for which 1/2 of said boat I gave my bond but
Mr. CROWWELL not having my bond I payed the money on his giving
me this receipt. Wit: ELIZABETH TIBBS, CATHARINE PARKS. (B:pg
436)

13 Oct 1779. Receipt. DANIEL MURPHEY received of JOSEPH
BAILY 28 pounds 7 shillings in full of all accompts. (B:pg 436)

4 Feb 1780. Receipt. DANIEL MURPHEY received of JOSEPH
BAILEY (BALEAY) 16 pounds 3 shillings 6 pence in fool of all
accountes. (B:pg 436)

25 Apr 1789. Deed of Mortgage. ABRAM (ABRAHAM) BETTS Senr of

Suss Co for 1 judgment obtained against him & MATTHEW HILFORD
for 9 pounds 8 shillings 3 pence including cost dated 18 Apr 1789 and
one other judgment against the same for 6 pounds 17 shillings
including cost, and for a bond bearing equal date with this mortgage for
9 pounds 3 shillings 8 pence, sold to GEORGE MITCHELL of same
place ... 1 yoke of oxen, 1 mare, 2 cows & 3 young cattle 2 of which is 2
years old & 1 a year old, 1 sow & 6 pigs, 7 shoah and sundries of
household & kitchen furniture, the whole I now possess, upon the
condition that if ABRAM BETTS pay unto the afsd GEORGE
MITCHELL the above recited judgments & bond then the articles to
become the right of the said BETTS. Wit: WILLIAM EVANS,
WILLIAM FREEMAN. (B:pg 437)

18 Dec 1780. Manumition. Whereas MARIAH a negro woman aged 45
years formerly the property of JOHN SPENCER esqr afterwards of
LAWRENCE RILEY (REILEY) by marriage with his widow, and on
decease of the said RILEY purch by his widow SARAH now the w/o
BENJAMIN MIFFLIN being desirous of freedom & we being convinced
that it is inconsistant with christianity and derogatory of that just and
equitable command of the Savior of mankind to do unto others as we
would, were we in like circumstances, they should do to us, to hold our
fellow mortals in slavery, therefore we BENJA MIFFLIN & SARAH
his wife, grant unto the said MARIAH her natural right of freedom and
do hereby hence forth and forever quit claim to the servitude or
slavery of her and pronouce her a free woman. Wit: BAPTIS LAY,
PHEBE VIRDIN, PHILENA LAY. (B:pg 437)

29 Nov 1783. Deed. HENRY SWIGGIT of Suss Co farmer for 75
pounds sold to LEVI EATON (EAYTON) of Caroline Co MD farmer ...
the remaining part not sold by HENRY SWIGGIT to LEVI EATON of
a tr of land called Pritchells Adventure 42 a. and pt/o a tr adj called
Adams Fortune 18 a., and pt/o a tr adj afsd 2 trs called Loyds Care 10
a. ... HENRY SWIGGIT hereby appoint ISAAC BRADLEY or DANIEL
POLK or JOHN LAWS or JOSHUA POLK justices of the peace for
Suss Co to be his atty to ackn this deed in open court. Wit: LEVI
STAFFORD, WM NICOLLS. Ackn 7 Feb 1789. (B:pg 437)

22 May 1789. Manumition. JAMES NEWBOLD of Lewis and Rehoboth
Hund Suss Co adminr of the estate of SARAH JACOBS late of same
hund & co decd late widow and relict of ALBERTUS JACOBS late of
same hund & co yeoman decd ... in pursuance of a particular promise of
the said SARAH JACOBS in her lifetime that her negro man slave
called CATTO should be mannumitted and set free after her decease,
the said JAMES NEWBOLD in pursuance of the promise of SARAH
JACOBS sett free and at full liberty the said negro man CATTO aged
27 years or thereabouts ... known by the name of CATTO FREEMAN
.... Wit: JNO RUSSEL, RICHD GREEN. (B:pg 439)

25 May 1789. Manumition. MARGARET GILL of Suss Co in
consideration of the faithful services rendered unto me by my negro
man PARIS, release and discharge him from all manner of service due
to my heirs after my decease, and hereby declare the said negro PARIS

to be a free man immediatly after my decease. Wit: JOSHUA HALL, WILLIAM COLEMAN. (B:pg 439)

12 Sep 1760. Bond of Conveyance. JOHN BURK (BOURK) of Somerset Co MD planter am firmly bound unto JOHN GIBBINS of Worcester Co MD blacksmith in the sum of 60 pounds ... the condition of this obligation is such that if JOHN BURK convey unto JOHN GIBBINS his right to 100 a. of land in Worcester Co near the head of Indian River called Clare, then this obligation to be void. Wit: JOS COLLINS, CHAS MOORE. Proved 6 May 1789. (B:pg 440)

5 Apr 1785. Assignment. JOHN GIBBINS Senr of Suss Co for love and effection assign unto my son JOHN GIBBINS Junr all my right of the [above] bond. Wit: JOHN PHILLIPS, HANNAH PHILLIPS, ANN PHILLIPS. (B:pg 440)

1 Jun 1789. Power of Atty. MARY GIBBINS of Kent Co widow was by the will of JOHN GIBBINS late of Suss Co decd appointed executrix jointly with JOSHUA GIBBINS of same place ... MARY GIBBINS doth appoint JOSHUA GIBBINS afsd my atty to sell the lands and late dwelling plantation belonging to the said JOHN GIBBINS to a certain WILLIAM SHARP of same place 100 a. Wit: WAITMAN BOOTH, BENJAMIN COOMBE Junr, SARAH CARPENTER. Attest: JOHN DILL justice of the peace. Proved 3 Jun 1789. (B:pg 440)

3 Jun 1789. Deed. MARY GIBBINS and JOSHUA GIBBINS executors of the will of JOHN GIBBONS late of Suss Co decd for 120 pounds sold to WILLIAM SHARP of Dagsbury Hund Suss Co yeoman ... a tr of land in Dagsburry Hund originally granted by pattent from the proprietary of MD on 23 Jul 1756 unto a certain JOHN BURK s side of Sheals Br bounded by land called First Choice in posession of WILLIAM SHARP ... 100 a. called Clare originally surveyed on 6 Jan 1749 and the said JOHN BURK sold the same unto a certain JOHN GIBBINS the elder late of Somerset Co MD decd, as by his bond bearing date 12 Sep 1760, and the said JOHN ELDER on 5 Apr 1785 did transfer all his right of the said bond unto his son JOHN GIBBONS the younger, and JOHN GIBBONS the younger being so seized died having first made his will bearing date 3 Nov 1786 whereof he appointed the said MARY GIBBINS his then wife his executrix and JOSHUA GIBBINS his executor and did order them to sell the said lands, and whereas MARY GIBBINS is now resident in Kent Co and by her power of atty [see above] appointed the said JOSHUA GIBBINS her atty. Wit: W HARRISON, JNO RUSSEL. Ackn 3 Jun 1789. (B:pg 441)

19 May 1789. Deed of Mortgage. THOMAS BATSON esqr of Suss Co for the securing the payment of a bond to the said GEORGE MITCHELL and 1 shilling sold to GEORGE MITCHELL of same place ... turn working stears from 3 to 9 years of age, 5 cows & 5 calves, 3 cows and 3 yearlins, 2 heffers 3 years oald each, 1 bay hors about 8 years oald, whereas the said THOMAS BATSON by his bond bearing date with this indenture stands bound unto the said GEORGE

MITCHELL in the penal sum of 90 pounds 2 shillings 4 pence in
spanish milled dollars conditioned on the payment of 45 pounds 1
shilling 2 pence ... if the said THOMAS BATSON shall pay to the said
GEORGE MITCHELL the afsd principle sum of money with legal
interest with the charge of drawing and recording this conveyance then
this present indenture shall cease. Wit: SARAH ROGER, THOMAS
BATSON Junr. (B:pg 443)

8 May 1789. Deed of Mortgage. WILLIAM DIRICKSON of Suss Co for
the securing the payment of a bond to GEORGE MITCHELL and 1
shilling sold to GEORGE MITCHELL of same place ... 1 waggon, 1
black mare, 1 black hors, 1 yoke of oxen & all the gears belonging to
said waggon, a crop of rye & corn now in the ground, 2 ploughs and 2
harrows, 6 hors and 4 akes, 3 beads, beadstead & beding, 3 pots & 3
kettles, 1 trammel, 3 chests, 3 spining wheels, 14 head of hogs, 6
chains, 1 pare of fore waggon wheals, and all other personal property
now in the possession of the said WILLIAM DIRICKSON, whereas the
said WILLIAM DIRICKSON by his bond bearing date with this
indenture stands bound unto the said GEORGE MITCHELL in the
penal sum of 41 pounds 18 shillings 8 pence conditioned for the
payment of 20 pounds 7 shillings 6 pence ... if the said WILLIAM
DIRICKSON shall pay unto the said GEORGE MITCHELL the afsd
principle sum of money with legal interest, then this present indenture
shall cease. Wit: WM MOOR, WILLIAM FURMAN. (B:pg 444)

22 May 1789. Deed of Mortgage. JOHN LIGGATE for the securing the
payment of a bond to GEORGE MITCHELL and 1 shilling sold to
GEORGE MITCHELL both of Suss Co ... 1 waggon & gears fited up
for horses, 1 cow, 5 sheep & 1 lamb, 1 case of drawers, 1 table, 7 oald
hogs & their increas, 1 square cupboard and a certain debt due to me
from ELIJAH FAUSETT which a suit is now depending for the
recovery of the same, whereas the said JOHN LIGGATE by his bond
bearing date with this indenture stands bound unto the said GEORGE
MITCHELL in the penal sum of 33 pounds 3 shillings 4 pence for the
payment of 16 pounds 11 shillings 8 pence ... if the said JOHN
LIGGATE shall pay to the said GEORGE MITCHELL the afsd
principle sum of money with legal interest, then this present indenture
shall cease. Wit: WILLIAM FURMAN, ISAAC TUNNELL. (B:pg 445)

8 Sep 1788. Deed. SYDENHAM THOM and BETTY his wife,
WILLIAM WILLIAMS of Suss Co yeoman and NANCY his wife,
SAMUEL BASNETT of same co blacksmith and SARAH his wife in
discharge of the recorded bond and for 500 pounds paid to LEVIN
CRAPPER in his lifetime by DAVID WILLIAMS and also 5 shillings
paid to SYDENHAM THOM and BETTY his wife by WILLIAM
JOHNSON and for 160 pounds paid to WILLIAM WILLIAMS and
NANCY his wife by SAMUEL BASNETT and also 5 shillings paid to
WILLIAM WILLIAMS and NANCY his wife by WILLIAM JOHNSON
sold unto WILLIAM JOHNSON ... a 100 a. tr of land [see bond &
petition at B:pg 336] ... . Wit: NEHEMIAH CARY, BELITHA LAWS,
ROBERT HOUSTON. NANCY & SARAH became party to this deed of
their own free will. Attest: ALEXR LAWS judge. Ackn 2 Jun 1789.

(B:pg 445)

7 Dec 1789. Certificate. Docter JOSEPH HALL hereby certify that I have examined THOMAS HOLSTON late a common soldier in the DEL Regiment and find him much disabled by a wound in his right arm, which he received in the service of the US and am of opinion that he is intitled to 1 pound 10 shillings per month. (B:pg 450)

11 Jan 1790. Affidavit. Personally appeared before NATHANIEL YOUNG justice of peace for Suss Co, THOMAS HOLSTON & made oath that he was examined by Docter JOSEPH HALL & obtained the [above] certificate & that he now lives in Suss Co. (B:pg 450)

27 Jan 1790. Certificate. Docter JOSEPH HALL hereby certify that having reexamined JOHN CLIFTON late a common soldier in the DEL Regiment do find him still disabled from a wound he received in the service of the US and intitled to 1 pound 17 shillings 6 pence per month. (B:pg 451)

27 Jan 1790. Affidavit. Came before WILLIAM PERRY justice, JOHN CLIFTON a soldier of the DEL Regiment formerly in the service of the US and made oath that he hath been reexamined by Docter JOSEPH HALL and obtained the [above] certificate. (B:pg 451)

26 Mar 1684 at Phila. Confirmation of Patent. Whereas there is a tr of land called Abrahams Lott nw of Cold Spring Br bounded by CORNELIOUS JOHNSON, JOHN VINES and JOHN SMITH ... 300 a. granted by Suss Co Court 27 Jan 1681 and laid out by ye surveyor 20 Mar next following to ABRAHAM POTTER ... WILLIAM PENN proprietary govern of PA confirms a pattent unto the said ABRAHAM POTTER for the 300 a. (B:pg 451)

13 Oct 1775. Bond of Conveyance. JAMES REYNOLDS of Suss Co yoman am firmly bound unto THOMAS REYNOLDS Junr of same place yoman in the sum of 600 pounds ... the condition of this obligation is such that if JAMES REYNOLDS shall convey to THOMAS REYNOLDS Junr his right in a tr of land adj JOHN FOWLERS Senr, SOLOMON DODDS and BENJAMIN MIFFLIN, it being the place where the said JAMES REYNOLDS now lives on, then this obligation to be void. Wit: ROBT W. MCCALLEY, ELI MCCALLEY. Proved 5 Mar 1790. (B:pg 452)

Bond of Conveyance. THOMAS GODWIN and RHODA his wife both of Suss Co are firmly bound unto PEARSON ONIONS of same place taylor in the sum of 300 pounds ... the condition of this obligation is such that if THOMAS GODWIN and RHODA his wife shall make over unto PEARSON ONIONS all their right unto a parcell of land in Little Neck called Woodmans Folly 153 1/2 a. which land was purch by the afsd GODWIN of ISRAEL HOLLAND, and the said ONIONS paying for the same then this obligation to be void and of none effect else to remain in full force. Wit: NOAH COLLINS, ISAAC JOHNSON. Proved 2 Mar 1790. (B:pg 453)

9 Oct 1789. WILLIAM RICKARDS adminr of PEARSON ONIONS decd do assign all my right to the [above] bond unto ISRAEL HOLLAND. Wit: JOHN ONIONS, ELOSE WEST. (B:pg 453)

3 Mar 1786. ALBERTUS (ALBERT) JACOBS sets his negro TONEY free from all persons or otherwise shall pay 150 pounds ... . Wit: WILLIAM SHOCKLEY, ELIZABETH HOLLAND. Proved 1 May 1786 and WILLIAM HOLLAND & DAVID TRAIN esqr became security. Attest: D HALL clerk. (B:pg 453)

30 Mar 1776. Deed. WILLIAM ELLEGOOD Senr of Suss Co planter for 200 pounds sold to JOHN ELLEGOOD of same place planter ... 200 a. of land, whereas WILLIAM ELLEGOOD had by the proprietor of MD's pattent granted unto him 22 Apr 1760 1104 a. being a resurvey made on a tr of land that said WILLIAM ELLEGOOD bought of a certain WILLIAM BENSON that the said BENSON tuck up and had a pattent for the same and sold the land to WILLIAM ELLEGOOD for 100 a. called Isables Choice ... . Wit: JOHN LAWS, J RODNEY. Ackn 13 Mar 1776. (B:pg 454)

6 Nov 1790. Power of Atty. JOHN YOUNG of Phila merchant have appointed my trusty and worthy friend ADONIJAH STANDSBOROUGH gent now of same city to sell and convey my 1/2 of 1440 a. in the forrest of Broadkiln which BENJAMIN MIFFLIN decd resided (with GUNNING BEDFORD esqr) and also my 1/4 pt/o 980 a. contigious thereto, in comp with GUNG BEDFORD esqr and the heirs of REESE MEREDITH esqr decd also to settle with the several tenants for rent and arears rents, and also to settle with and prosecute any persons who have committed waste or cut timber without authority on the said lands ... . Wit: BARNETT DAWSON, RICHARD RENSHAW. Proved before CHARLES YOUNG notary and tabellion public of Phila 6 Nov 1790. (B:pg 455)

8 Sep 1790. Certificate. Doctr JOSEPH HALL hereby certify that having reexamined THOMAS HOLSTON late a common soldier in the DEL Regiment do find him still disabled from a wound which he received in the service of the US and intitled to $5 per month. GEORGE BUSH esqr. (B:pg 456)

11 Sep 1790. Affidavit. Personally appeared before NATHANIEL YOUNG justice of the peace for Suss Co, THOMAS HOLSTON & made oath that he was examined by Docter JOSEPH HALL & obtained the [above] certificate, and that he now lives in Suss Co. (B:pg 456)

8 Sep 1790. Certificate. Docter JOSEPH HALL hereby certify that having reexamined WILLIAM REDDEN late a serjeant in the DEL Regiment do find him still disabled from a wound he received in the service of the US and intitled to $5 per month. GEORGE BUSH esqr. (B:pg 456)

13 Nov 1790. Affidavit. WILLIAM REDDEN came before N WAPLES

justice of Suss Co and made oath that on 8 Sep last past he was
examined by Docter JOSEPH HALL and obtained the [above]
certificate. (B:pg 456)

15 Oct 1774. Receipt. ANDERSON PARKER received of GEORG
WALKER the sum of 24 pounds 5 shillings 10 pence in full against a
bond dated 1 Oct 1771 principle 18 pounds 44 shillings & interest &
cost amounting to 24 pounds 5 shillings 10 pence, received in full for
said bond interest & costs and in full of all demands whatsoever. (B:pg
456)

15 Dec 1778. Bond of Conveyance. JOHN BELL yeoman of Suss Co am
firmly bound unto JAMES REYNOLDS Senr (REYNDOLS) of same co
in the penal sum of 770 pounds ... the condition of this obligation is
such that if JOHN BELL shall on the receipt of 385 pounds paid by
JAMES REYNOLDS, convey a tr of land in Broadkill Hund 140 a. adj
lands of WILLIAM REYNDOLS, SOLOMON DODD and land now in
possession of JAMES WOODS that then this obligation to be void. Wit:
JOHN W. DEAN, JOHN WATSON. Proved 6 May 1791. Attest: NATH
MITCHELL prothonotary. (B:pg 457)

14 Oct 1784. Bond of Conveyance. JAMES REYNDOLS (REYNOLDS)
yeoman of Suss Co am firmly bound unto RICHARD BLOXOM
(BLOXSOM) of same place in the penal sum of 360 pounds ... the
condition of this obligation is such that if JAMES REYNDOLS shall on
the receipt of 180 pounds paid by RICHARD BLOXOM convey a tr of
land in Broadkill Hund 100 a. adj lands formerly of WILLIAM
REYNDOLS, SOLOMON DODD and lands now in possession of
RICHARD ABBOT that then this obligation to be void. Wit: JOHN W.
DEAN, BENEDICT PENNINGTON. Proved 6 May 1791. Attest:
NATH MITCHELL prothonotary. (B:pg 457)

7 May 1791. Receipt. Whereas a final settlement made between
CURTIS SHOCKLEY and ELZEY (ELSEY) HILL (heir of JONATHAN
HILL late of Suss Co) for 258 pounds, 1 mair and bedd, as I am now
21 years of age, do hereby receive for myself the full of all my pt/o my
fathers estate left to me in the hands of the afsd CURTIS SHOCKLEY
... and further I do hereby engage to defend the afsd SHOCKLEY in a
suit now commenced against WILLIAM CONWAY and HAIL SPICER
in behalf of my sister ELENOR HUTSON so far as to defend the said
SHOCKLEY from paying any costs accruing upon suit. Wit: WM
REDDEN, SOMMERSET DICKERSON COSTON, WOODMAN
PRETTYMAN. (B:pg 458)

8 Sep 1791. Certificate. Docter JOSEPH HALL hereby certify that
having examined TIMOTHY SAYFIELD late a common soldier in the
DEL Regiment do find him still disabled by a wound which he received
in the service of the US and other ways & incapacitated by disease so
as to render him less capable of doing any thing for his support,
therefore do think him entitled to 1 pound 10 shillings per month. JAS
TILTON esqr. (B:pg 458)

8 Sep 1791. Affidavit. TIMOTHY SAYFIELD came before JOSEPH HAZZARD esqr justice of the peace for Suss Co and made oath that he was in the Battle at Camdon in SC under General GREEN and commanded by [Col?] ROBERT KIRKWOOD in said battel he received a bad wound in the left leg and being examined by Dr JOSEPH HALL obtained the [above] certificate and that he was discharge after the ware seised and that he is the very man and not an impostor. (B:pg 458)

10 Sep 1791. Certificate. Doctr JOSEPH HALL do hereby certify that having examined WILLIAM REDDEN late a serjeant in the DEL Regiment do find him still disabled from a wound he received in the service of the US and entitled to 1 pound 17 shillings 6 pence per month. JAS TILTON esqr. (B:pg 459)

10 Sep 1791. Affidavit. Personally appeared before RHOADS SHANKLAND justice of the peace of Suss Co WILLIAM REDDEN and made oath that he was examined by Doctr JOS HALL & obtained the [above] certificate and that he now lives in Suss Co. (B:pg 459)

10 Sep 1791. Certificate. Doctr JOSEPH HALL do hereby certify that having examined THOMAS HOLSTON late a private soldier in the DEL Regiment do find him still disabled from a wound he received in the service of the US and intitled to 1 pound 17 shillings 6 pence per month. JAS TILTON esqr. (B:pg 459)

10 Sep 1791. Affidavit. Personally appeared before RHOADS SHANKLAND justice of the peace for Suss Co, THOMAS HOLSTON & made oath that he was examined by Doctr JOS HALL & obtained the [above] certificate and that he now lives in Suss Co. (B:pg 459)

17 Apr 1731 at Phila. Letter. To loving friend ROBERT SHANKLAND. The bearer hereof JACOB KOLLOCK hath requested that about 200 a. of land might be surveyed to him, he assures me that it is clear of all surveys, in the forrest, I have made an entry in his favour and request thee to survey such a quantity for him as requested, I hope in a very little time to see our proprietary here to confirm to the people those lands which have been surveyed to them who have made regular applications for the same, I am with good wishes thy real loving friend. (signed) JAMES STEEL. A true copy in my office at Lewes, examined & compared therewith 20 Mar 1770 WILLIAM SHANKLAND deputy surveyor. Coppied 20 Mar 1770 by RICHARD LITTLE at the Unity Foarge, JOS SHANKLAND had original letter to Phila from W.S.D.S. Recorded at the request of FRANCIS CORNWELL the present owner of the land surveyed in pursuance of the foregoing letter 5 Mar 1792. Attest: JNO RUSSEL recorder. (B:pg 459)

12 Feb 1776. Bond of Conveyance. WILLIAM BURTON of Broadkilln Hund Suss Co yeoman am firmly bound unto LUKE CARPENTER of same place planter in the penal sum of 240 pounds ... the condition of this obligation is such that if WILLIAM BURTON shall make over to LUKE CARPENTER a deed of sale for 62 a. of land pt/o the tr

whereon WILLIAM MATTHEWS now lives to be laid off from the Barrs along the line of SAML ROWLAND's land then this obligation to be void. Wit: WM MATTHEWS, ISAAC SMITH. (B:pg 460)

29 Apr 1777. Assignment. JOSHUA BURTON of Suss Co taylor executor of the will of LUKE CARPENTER for 77 pounds 10 shillings assign over to HAP HAZZARD of Broadkiln Hund same co yeoman all my right unto the [above] bond. Wit: SAMEL EDWARDS, WILLIAM MAULL. (B:pg 460)

1 Mar 1792. Bond. JAMES WILLEY of Broadkiln Hund Suss Co innkeeper am firmly bound unto ANDREW WILLEY of Lewes same co merchant in the sum of 80 pounds ... the condition of this obligation is such that if JAMES WILEY shall pay unto ANDREW WILLEY the sum of 40 pounds upon the arrival at age of ANN WILEY dau of the said JAMES without interest then this obligation to be void. Wit: D HALL, JOHN STEEL. (B:pg 461)

1 Mar 1792. Assignment. ANDREW WILLEY of Lewis Suss Co merchant for natural love and affection and 5 shillings assign to my niece ANN WILLEY dau of JAMES WILLEY all my right to the [above] bond to be paid to her upon her arrival at the age of 21 years, but in case she should die before her arrival to the age of 21 years then the bond to be considered as cancelled and of none effect. Wit: D HALL, JOHN STEEL. (B:pg 461)

1 Feb 1792. Receipt. SAMUEL CARPENTER received from RICHARD HOWARD 9 pounds 8 shillings 3 pence in full of my personall estate and of the rents and profits arising from my pt/o the house and lot. Wit: RICHARD LITTLE. (B:pg 462)

2 Apr 1792. Certificate. Doctr JOSEPH HALL do hereby certify that I have examined NEHEMIAH NICHOLS late a private soldier in the DEL Regiment and find him disabled from a wound which he received in his right arm in an engagement at Guilford Court House, as he himself says and certifyed by WILLIAM REDDEN, by which he is rendered incapable of gitting his living, therefore think him entitled to 1 pound 2 shillings 6 pence per month. (B:pg 462)

Receipt. A bill 22 Oct 1786: 1 negro wench caled DINAR 50 pounds; 1 mar, 1 bed and furniture, 30 pounds; cash paid 173 lbs of bacon 22 pounds 2 shillings 9 pence; 1 cow and calf, 3 head of sheep 3 pounds 12 shillings 6 pence; 1 pare of sadle bags, 1? bushels of petatoes 12 shillings 6 pence; LETHEBER BARKER's note 1 pound 17 shillings, 6 pence, received of PERCLAR HEARN and LOWDER HEARN the full of all accounts by JOSEPH HEARN. (B:pg 462)

31 Mar 1792 at MD. Bond. NATHAN WILLIAMS of Dorcester Co MD am firmly bound unto JOHN TWIFORD of same place in the sum of 100 pounds ... the condition of this obligation is such that if NATHAN WILLIAMS and MARGARET his wife do convey all their rights of a tr of land called Outtens Mistake unto JOHN TWIFORD except that part

that WILLIAM CROCKETT give to his brother RICHARD
CROCKETT by will than this obligation to void. Wit: JNO CRAPPER,
A PRITCHARD. (B:pg 462)

18 Apr 1992 at Dover. To EDWARD DINGLE, ISAAC DRAPER,
DANIEL POLK and LEVIN HILL of Suss Co esqrs, know ye that
reposing special trust and confidence in your integrity and ability, we
assign you justices of the peace ... . (signed) JOSHUA CLAYTON esqr
president and commander in chief. Attest: JAS BOOTH secy. (B:pg
463)

30 Apr 1792. Deed. PHILLIP KOLLOCK and HESTER MOORE
executors of the will of JACOB KOLLOCK late of Suss Co esqr decd
for 54 pounds 12 shillings 6 pence sold at public sale to HAP
HAZZARD he being the highest bidder ... a tr of land, whereas JACOB
KOLLOCK was in his lifetime seized of an island of marsh in Lewis Cr
... 40 a. 74 perches called Kollocks Island and whereas the said JACOB
KOLLOCK made his will bearing date 17 Feb 1767 and impowered his
executors to make sale of all his lands. Wit: MARGARET DUNN, W
HARRISON. Ackn 9 May 1792. (B:pg 463)

9 May 1792. Deed. HAP HAZZARD of Suss Co and MARY his wife for
54 pounds 12 shillings 6 pence sold to HESTER MOORE of same co
widow ... a tr of land [same as above]. Wit: MARGARET DUNN, W
HARRISON. Ackn 30 Apr 1792. (B:pg 464)

30 Apr 1792. Deed. PHILLIP KOLLOCK and HESTER MOORE
executors of the will of JACOB KOLLOCK late of Suss Co esqr decd
for 151 pounds sold at public sale to HAP HAZZARD he being the
highest bidder ... a messuage and sundry lots of ground, whereas the
said JACOB KOLLOCK decd was in his lifetime seized of a messuage
and sundry lots of ground in the town of Lewis adj Docter JOSEPH
HALL, SAMUEL PAYNTER, Lewis Cr and South Street, and JACOB
KOLLOCK made his will bearing date 17 Feb 1767 and did impower
his executors to make sale of all his lands. Wit: MARGARET DUNN,
W HARRISON. Ackn 9 May 1792. (B:pg 465)

30 Apr 1792. Deed. HAP HAZZARD of Suss Co and MARY his wife
sold to HESTER MOORE of same co ... a messuage and sundry lots of
ground [same as above]. Wit: MARGARET DUNN, W HARRISON.
Ackn 9 May 1792. (B:pg 466)

26 Apr 1792. Manumition. JAMES ELLIOTT and JOHN HILL of Suss
Co do hereby declare free the negros SALL and SARAH (that was left
by GEORGE HILL's will to his dau SARAH HILL now SARAH
ELLIOTT) aged about 9, to be free at 18 years of age the time that
she is to be free from the indenture that LEVIN STRADLEY now has
on her, hereby ackn the said negro discharged from all claim of service
and right of property whatever from us. Wit: WILLIAM CONWEL,
SALLY KING. (B:pg 467)

8 Nov 1791. Deed. GEORGE MITCHELL, ROBERT HOUSTON,

WILLIAM MOORE, JOHN COLLINS and RHOADS SHANKLAND as commissioners, in behalf of Suss Co for 17 pounds 10 shillings sold to GEORGE COOKE of same co ... 1 lott of land in George Town at the new Court House lately built being #12 bounded by Bedford Street and Coopers Ally ... the commissioners appoint KENDAL BATSON their atty to ackn this deed in open court. Wit: WM SHANKLAND, ROBERT SHANKLAND Junr. Ackn 9 May 1792. (B:pg 467)

4 Aug 1791. Deed. JOHN RICHARDS of Cedar Cr Hund Suss Co yeoman for 18 pounds 15 shillings sold to THOMAS STAPLEFORD of same place yeoman ... 2 trs of land ... 62 a. 86 sq perches divided off 26 Jul last past by WILLIAM JOHNSON pt/o a 500 a. tr called Richards Purch, and also 83 a. pt/o a larger tr afsd which a certain JOSEPH RICHARDS on 5 Aug 1761 conveyed to a certain EPHRAIM HOLEGAR (Lib I fol 334) which 83 a. was seized in execution and sold for the payment of the debts of the said EPHRAIM HOLEGER and purch by the said JOHN RICHARDS from THOMAS EVANS esqr high sheriff of Suss Co ... JOHN RICHARDS doth hereby appoint THOMAS EVANS and JOHN RUSSEL of Lewis gent his attys to ackn this deed in open court. Wit: ISAAC BEAUCHAMP, SYLVESTER WEBB. Proved and Ackn 9 May 1792. (B:pg 468)

9 Apr 1791. Deed. WILLISS CLARKSON and MARY his wife of Suss Co planter for 150 pounds sold to DANIEL POLK esqr of same place farmer ... pt/o a tr of land called Williams Lott and also pt/o a tr called Luck in NW Fork Hund including the dwelling plantation where BENNIAH CLARKSON did live 150 a. including all the land that WILLISS CLARKSON's father BENNIAH CLARKSON held under his father WILLIAM CLARKSON's will ... WILLISS CLARKSON and MARY his wife have ordained JOHN WILTBANK and PHILLIP KOLLOCK of Lewis Suss Co esqrs their attys to ackn this deed in open court. Wit: TRUSTIN L. POLK, ALEXANDER POLK, HENRY SMITH, CHARLES POLK. Proved and Ackn 9 May 1792. (B:pg 469)

31 Mar 1792. Deed. JOHN W. BATSON of Suss Co for 100 pounds sold to ABRAHAM HARRIS Senr of same co ... pt/o a tr of land called Low Ground Tr in Broadkill Hund 100 a. it being the part conveyed by CHARLES CLARK unto the said ABRAHAM HARRIS. Wit: ROSS THOMSON, ABRAM HARRIS Junr. Ackn 11 May 1792. (B:pg 470)

-- Mar 1792. Deed. ABRAHAM HARRIS Senr of Broadkiln Hund Suss Co house carpenter for 100 pounds sold to ABRAHAM (ABRAM) HARRIS Junr of same place ... a tr of land where ABRAHAM Junr now lives in Broadkiln Hund bounded by land called Low Ground Tr, ELIZABETH CONNER, JOSHUA PEPPER and Court House land ... 250 a. Wit: ROSS THOMSON, JOSHUA COSTON. Ackn 11 May 1792. (B:pg 471)

23 Apr 1792. Deed. THOMAS LOCKERMAN and FANNY his wife of Dorchester Co MD for 60 pounds sold to JULIAS AUGUSTUS JACKSON of Suss Co ... 2 trs of land called Gibrolter and Straights of Gibrolter on Nanticoke River adj the said JULIAS AUGUSTUS

JACKSON's dwelling plantation ... THOMAS LOCKERMAN and
FANNY his wife appoint their friend JOSHUA OBEIER of Suss Co
their atty to ackn this deed in open court. Wit: JOHN STEVENS,
PETER ROSS Junr, RUST JACKSON. Proved 10 May 1792 by
JEREMIAH R. JACKSON. (B:pg 472)

23 Apr 1792 at Dorchester Co MD. Appeared personally before JNO
STEVENS justice of the peace, FRANCES LOCKERMAN w/o
THOMAS who ackn the [above] deed to be her own free will. (B:pg
473)

30 Apr 1792 at Dorchester Co MD. I hereby certify that JOHN
STEVENS gent before whom the [above] acknowledgement appear to
have been made was one of the justices of the peace for Dorchester Co
MD. (signed) H DICKINSON clerk. (B:pg 473)

7 Apr 1792. Deed. JOSIAH GRIFFETH and ELIZABETH his wife of
KY for 22 pounds 10 shillings sold to JESSE GREEN of Suss Co
merchant ... a tr of land called Glassgow in NW Fork Hund adj Collo
JOHN RIDER, Mill Cr alias Clear Brook Br and Nanticoke River ... 11
a. to be holden of the Manner of Nanticoke by virtue of a warrant
granted SAMUEL GRIFFETH for 24 a. on 18 Apr 1753 & laid off for
him by HENRY ENNELLS dy surveyor of Dorchester Co on 11 Sep
1753 ... JOSIAH GRIFFETH and ELIZABETH his wife appoint our
well beloved friends THOMAS LAWS esqr & WILLIAM PERRY esqr
to ackn this deed in open court. Wit: JESSE GRIFFETH, JEREMIAH
R. JACKSON. Proved and Ackn 10 May 1792. (B:pg 473)

9 May 1792. Deed. GEORGE MITCHELL, ROBERT HOUSTON,
WILLIAM MOORE, JOHN COLLINS and RHOADS SHANKLAND
esqrs commissioners in behalf of Suss Co for 7 pounds 10 shillings sold
to JESSE GREEN of same co ... a lot of ground #11 in George Town
on Coopers Ally ... 25 perches ... the commissioners appoint JOHN W.
BATSON and THOMAS LAWS esqrs to ackn this deed in open court.
Wit: THOS FISHER, KENDLE BATSON. Proved and Ackn 10 May
1792. (B:pg 474)

9 May 1792. Deed. GEORGE MITCHELL, WILLIAM MOORE,
ROBERT HOUSTON, JOHN COLLINS and RHOADS SHANKLAND
esqrs commissioners in behalf of Suss Co for 2 pounds 5 shillings sold
to JACOB HAZZARD of same co ... a lot of ground #70 in George
Town bounded by Race Street, Coopers Ally ... 25 sq perches ... the
commissioners appoint JOHN W. BATSON and THOMAS LAWS esqr
our attys to ackn this deed in open court. Wit: JEHU EVANS,
STEPHEN STYER. Ackn 10 May 1792. (B:pg 475)

10 May 1792. Deed. GEORGE MITCHELL, ROBERT HOUSTON,
WILLIAM MOORE, JOHN COLLINS and RHOADS SHANKLAND
esqrs commissioners in behalf of Suss Co for 5 pounds 5 shillings sold
to JACOB HAZZARD of same co ... 2 lots of ground #71 & #72 in
George Town bounded by Race Street, Lawrel Street & Coopers Ally ...
56 sq perches ... the commissioners appoint JOHN W. BATSON and

THOMAS LAWS esqr to ackn this deed in open court. Wit: JEHU
EVANS, STEPHEN STYER. Ackn 10 May 1792. (B:pg 476)

9 May 1792. Deed. GEORGE MITCHELL, ROBERT HOUSTON,
WILLIAM MOORE, JOHN COLLINS and RHOADS SHANKLAND
esqrs commissioners in behalf of Suss Co for 5 pounds sold to JOSEPH
RICKITS (RICKETS) of same co ... 2 lotts of ground #51 & #52 in
George Town bounded by Cherry Ally, Lawral Street and Coopers Ally
... 56 sq perches ... the commissioners appoint JOHN W. BATSON and
RHOADS SHANKLAND esqrs to ackn this deed in open court. Wit:
THOMAS LAWS, JOHN HAZZARD. Proved and Ackn 10 May 1792.
(B:pg 477)

19 Mar 1792. Deed. PURNAL VEACH of Suss Co and MARY his wife
for 81 pounds 17 shillings 6 pence sold to RICHARD HUDSON of same
place yeoman ... a tr of land in Cedar Cr Hund bounded by SOLOMON
DEPUTY & SYLVESTER DEPUTY ... 150 a. which was conveyed on
27 Oct 1789 from a certain NUNCZ DEPUTY of same co unto the afsd
PURNAL VEACH (Lib O fol 114) which the said NUNCZ DEPUTY
became possessed of at the decease of his father. Wit: JOHN
GISLING, CHARLES POLK. Ackn 10 May 1792. (B:pg 477)

19 Mar 1792. Power of Atty. PURNAL VEACH and MARY his wife
hereby appoint JOHN W. BATSON and NATHANIEL MITCHELL
both of Suss Co or either of them to ackn the [above] deed in open
court. Wit: JOHN GISLING, CHARLES POLK. Proved 10 May 1792.
(B:pg 478)

11 May 1792. Deed. THOMAS LAWS esqr of Suss Co for 40 pounds
sold to JOSEPH RICHARDS (RICKETTS) of same co ... a tr of land
called Partnership in NW Fork Hund 33 a. bounded by the County
Road leading from St. Johns Town to Cool Brooke Br and land of
JONATHAN HATFIELD. Wit: BURTON ROBINSON, KENDLE
BATSON. Ackn 11 May 1792. (B:pg 479)

11 Apr 1792. Deed. ABRAHAM HARRIS Senr of Suss Co house
carpenter for 100 pounds sold to his son BENTON HARRIS of same
place ... a tr of land in Broadkiln Hund being composed of 3 trs of land
conveyed by divers persons to the said ABRAHAM HARRIS Senr
bounded by Hogs Quarter, heirs of WILLIAM BOGGS LACEY,
BURTON WAPLE, LUKE THOMAS's dividend of 24 a., Kenneys
Savannah, ABRAHAM HARRIS Junr and ELIZABETH MCCONNELL
... 150 a. Wit: KENDLE BATSON, WILLIAM HARRIS, ROSS
THOMSON. Ackn 11 May 1792. (B:pg 480)

30 Apr 1781. Bond of Conveyance. JOHN COWES of Suss Co mariner
am firmly bound to GEORGE CONWELL of same co yeoman in the
sum of 120 pounds ... whereas ELNATHAN INKLY late of same co
died intestate leaving 3 daus ANNA, SARAH and MARY being seized
at the time of his death with 217 a. of land which became the right of
the daus, ANNA and SARAH sold their parts, MARY died intestate
leaving 1 dau who also died intestate in her minority leaving no issue

and her mothers pt/o said land unsold, after which PARIZ CHIPMAN father to the afsd MARY's dau being the next nearest of kin conveyed MARY's part to JOHN CLOWES undivided, and whereas JOHN SPENCER esqr and MATTHEW PARIMORE assinees to the said ANNA and SARAH hath in virtue of their purch divided the 217 a. between them ... the condition of this obligation is such that if JOHN CLOWES conveys unto GEORGE CONWELL the undivided right of MARY dau afsd then this obligation to be void. Wit: STEPHEN REAVELL, ISAAC ALLEE. 10 May 1792 JOHN WILTBANK esqr proved the hand writing of JOHN CLOWES. (B:pg 481)

10 May 1792. Petition of MARY CLOWES and ISAAC CLOWES exors of JOHN CLOWES late of Suss Co esqr decd humbly sheweth that the said JOHN CLOWES in his lifetime became bound unto GEORGE CONWELL [see above] ... that JOHN CLOWES since decd and no deed of conveyance hath yet been made altho pt/o the consideration money was paid to the said JOHN CLOWES in his lifetime and the residue since his death to your petitioner, your petitioner prays your honors to give an order impowering them to convey the tr of land to the said GEORGE CONWELL. Granted 10 May 1792. Attest: NATHL MITCHELL prothonotary. (B:pg 481)

10 Jun 1791 [sic]. Deed. MARY CLOWES and ISAAC CLOWES executors of the will of JOHN CLOWES esqr late decd of Suss Co for 60 pounds sold to GEORGE CONWELL of same co yoman [see above bond and petition] ... on Long Bridge Br adj DAVOCK and CORD ... 58 a. ... MARY CLOWES and ISAAC CLOWES appoint ISAAC WILLSON of George Town their atty to ackn this indenture in open court. Wit: ISAAC DRAPER, JOHN CLARK. Proved and Ackn 10 May 1792. (B:pg 482)

9 May 1792. Deed. GEORGE MITCHELL, ROBERT HOUSTON, WILLIAM MOORE, JOHN COLLINS and RHOADS SHANKLAND esqrs commissioners in behalf of Suss Co for 12 pounds 13 shillings sold to ROBERT JONES of same co ... a lot of ground #41 in George Town bounded by Bedford Street and Strawberry Ally ... 25 perches ... the commissioners appoint JOHN W. BATSON and THOMAS LAWS esqrs to ackn this deed in open court. Wit: ABRAHAM HARRIS, KENDLE BATSON. Proved and Ackn 10 May 1792. (B:pg 483)

25 Mar 1783. Deed. ZADOCK SAFFORD of Suss Co for 2 pounds pur a. for the patent land and 1 pound 10 shillings pur a. for all the warant adj sold to THOMAS LEDNUM of same co yeoman ... a tr of land called Saffords Lot in NW Fork Hund n side of Mudy Br of Nanticoke River ... ZADOCK SAFFORD doth appoint JOHN RODNEY and JOHN RUSEL of Lewis gent or either of them my atty to ackn this deed in open court. Wit: ABRAHAM SAFFORD, DANIEL HURT. Proved and Ackn 9 May 1792. (B:pg 484)

28 Mar 1783. Bond. ZADOCK SAFFORD do hereby oblige myself in the sum of 100 pounds to be paid to THOMAS LEDENUM and I agree with the said THOMAS LEDENUM in the above if I cant purch the

above sums and debts I owe to THOMAS LEDENUM that he is to
have the [above] land and further bind myself not to morgage the said
land on this money nor sell to any other person for any sum or sums.
Wit: ABRAHAM SAFFORD, ZADOCK LEDENUM. Proved 9 May
1792. (B:pg 484)

10 May 1792. Deed. WILLIAM RICORDS (RICCORDS) (RICKARDS)
of Suss Co and ELIZABETH his wife for 115 pounds sold to NUTTER
LOFLAND of same co ... a tr of land in Slaughter Neck and Cedar Cr
Hund which by sundry conveyances became the estate of a certain
WILLIAM HICKMAN late of same co, which he being seized of the
land died intestate leaving RACHEL (RACHELL) his widow and 4
children, JOHN HICKMAN, MARY w/o afsd NUTTER LOFLAND,
BETSEY w/o afsd WILLIAM RICORDS, and JACOB HICKMAN to
whom the said lands did desend, in a Orphans Court held 8 Dec 1789
five freeholders were appointed to lay off the said RACHEL
HICKMAN her right of dower and make partition of the remaining 2/3,
laid off unto WILLIAM RICORDS and ELIZABETH his wife adj
BAKER JOHNSON and NUTTER LOFLAND and MARY's part ... and
also the right of them unto the 1/3 laid off to RACHEL HICKMAN.
Wit: PHILLIP KOLLOCK, W HARRISON. ELIZABETH did declare
that she became a party to the within deed of her own free will. Attest:
PETER ROBINSON judge. Ackn 10 May 1792. (B:pg 485)

2 Jun 1783. Bond of Conveyance. JONATHAN DOLBEE yeoman am
firmly bound unto JESSE WINDSOR (WINDZOR) of Suss Co in the
penal sum of 400 pounds ... the condition of this obligation is such that
if JONATHAN DOLBEE shall convey all his right unto JESSEE
WINDSOR an indefezable estate of inheritance in fee simple in 1/2 a
stream whereon is an old saw mill and grist mill being in partnership
with ISAAC DOLBEE on the head of Deep Cr which part is forming to
ISAAC DOLBEE that then this obligation to be void. Wit: ROBERT
ROBINSON, ISAAC DOLBEE. Proved 9 May 1792. (B:pg 486)

Manumition. These are to certify that JNO WILTBANK hath thought
proper to give his negro man JACOB a discharge from slavery whose
lawful property he was by purch from the estate of a certain JOHN
BRUEN and it is my desire that the afsd JACOB take upon himself
the additional name of BRUEN and that in all cases where it may
become necessary he be distinguished by the name of JACOB
BREWEN, I hereby give him the said JACOB BREWEN free liberty to
act and deal for himself he behaving well as other free men of this
state have, and I do further certify that any person who may incline to
employ said negro may depend on his being a faithful fellow for
business except reaping, he cuts well with a sythe nakd or with a
cradle, he is an extrodinary hand to schoar in and block off for a
carpenter in giting timber, sets post and rail fence and can saw well in
the pit with a whip saw, he has been raised on a farm from about 7
years old and been kept chiefly at that business with the subscriber
who further says that the said JACOB now JACOB BREWEN has
been the faithfullest slave amongst many the subscriber ever owned,
and for which reason the subscriber hath given him his liberty. Sir

92

please to record the within instrument of writing and you will (at the request of my father) oblidge your obt servt. (signed) JAS WILTBANK. Recorded 5 Jul 1792 W. JNO RUSSIL recorder. (B:pg 486)

21 Jul 1792. Deed of Mortgage. SAMUEL DIRRECKSON of Suss Co for securing the payment of a bond to GEORGE MITCHELL and 1 shilling sold to GEORGE MITCHELL of same place ... a tr of land called Babet Addition whereas SAMUEL DIRRECKSON and JAMES DIRRECKSON by their bond dated 18 May last past stands bound unto the said GEORGE MITCHELL in the penal sum of 320 pounds 13 shillings 2 pence conditioned for the payment of 164 pounds 16 shillings 7 pence with legal interest ... in Baltimore Hund 578 a. condition that if SAMUEL DIRRECKSON or JAMES DIRRECKSON shall pay unto GEORGE MITCHELL the afsd principal with legal interest then this present indenture shall cease. Wit: ISAIAH DIRRECKSON, ISAAC MURRAY. (B:pg 487)

26 Apr 1792. Deed. ISAAC CALLAWAY and ELENOR his wife of Suss Co for 75 pounds sold to DANIEL KILLEY of same place ... pt/o a tr of land called Addition adj the tr where the afsd DANIEL KILLEY now lives ... 75 a. pt/o a larger tr surveyed for THOMAS GORDAN 1685 and conveyd by the afsd GORDAN to a certain LIN who mortgaged the same to CHARLES PERRY and after his death his widow and JAMES BAILY and wife conveyd the tr to ISAAC CALLOWAY and at his death he devised the same to his son LOWDER CALLAWAY 100 a. next to Nanticoke River, and to his son EDWARD CALLAWAY 50 a., to his son ISAAC CALLAWAY 100 a. ... ISAAC CALLAWAY and ELENOR his wife appoint THOMAS LAWS esqr high sheriff & FRANCIS BROWN both of NW Fork Hund Suss Co our attys to ackn this deed in open court. Wit: SETH GRIFFETH, THOMAS ELLEGOOD. Proved and Ackn 5 Sep 1792. (B:pg 488)

18 Jun 1792. Manumition. HESTER MOORE, ALEXANDER MCCALLUM, HANNAH NUNCZ, PHILLIP KOLLOCK, NEHEMIAH FIELD, MARY FIELD and JNO MARSH heirs and legatees of JACOB KOLLOCK late of Suss Co esqr decd in consideration of the faithful services of a certain negro woman named SALRO, belonging to the estate of the said decd have freed the said negro SALRO from all manner of service and labour, and declare the said negro SALRO to be a free woman. (B:pg 489)

4 Feb 1793. Manumition. WILLIAM MORRIS of Broadkiln Hund Suss Co doth manumit and forever discharge from my service after 1 Jan 1794 my negro man named SIMON aged about 35 years and that after 1 Jan next I give and grant unto him his full and absolute freedom and will defend the same against my heirs and assigns forever. Wit: ISAAC DRAPER. (B:pg 490)

21 Dec 1791. Articles of Agreement between LEVI SPENCER & SAMUEL SPENCER on the one part and SYLVESTER WEBB on the other part, the said LEVI & SAMUEL covenant & agree with the said SYLVESTER to sell a piece of marsh adj Paynters Island Gut, the said

SYLVESTER doth covenant and agree to pay LEVI & SAMUEL at the rate of 20 shillings per a. for the afsd marsh, we bind ourselves in the penalty of 100 pounds to perform & execute the articles of agreement. Wit: JAMES P. WILSON, JOHN PURNELL. (B:pg 490)

8 Feb 1793. Manumition. SOLOMON VINSON of Suss Co do hereby declare free the negro PHILLIS aged 22 years to be free Jan 1793. Proved 8 Feb 1793. Wit: ISAAC COOPER. (B:pg 490)

23 Mar 1793. Manumition. WILLIAM JOHNSON Senr have given my negro woman named HANNAH aged 22 years her full freedom forever disclaiming all right either to her or her service, but by her consent, from the date hereof forever. Wit: NAOMI JOHNSON, WILLIAM JOHNSON Junr. (B:pg 490)

1 Mar 1793. Bill of Sale. JOSIAH COLLINGS planter of Suss Co am bound unto JONATHAN HEARN planter of same place to deliver up 2 horses, 5 head of cattle and 14 head of hogs, 3 feather beds and furniture ... the condition of this obligation is such that if JOSIAH COLLINGS shall pay the sum of 40 shillings on or before 1 Jan next or the afsd articles to be delivered unto JONATHAN HEARN to which payment on delivery I bind myself. Wit: ISAAC HEARN, ELIJAH HEARN. (B:pg 491)

6 Apr 1776. Bond of Conveyance. JOSHUA MOORE of Suss Co planter am firmly bound unto ISAAC MOORE Junr of same co planter in the sum of 600 pounds ... the condition of this obligation is such that if JOSHUA MOORE shall convey unto ISAAC MOORE a good estate of inheritance in fee simple unto 50 a. to be laid out on the upper side of a tr called Advantage and 1/2 of a saw mill on Husky Br and 1/2 of all mills and wrights ... then this obligation to be void. Wit: WM POLK, WILLIAM MOORE. (B:pg 491)

6 Mar 1778. Bond. JOHN MITCHELL of Suss Co at Broad Cr am firmly bound unto SAMUEL WILSON of New Castle Co in the sum of 5000 pounds ... the condition of this obligation is such that if JOHN MITCHELL shall convey unto SAMUEL WILSON a tr of land called Royelland whereon WILLIAM LOVIT now lives, and 120 a. whereon WILLIAM MCNEILL now lives, and also all the land that he has or shall include by resurvey of land formerly lying in Dorset Co but now in Suss Co adj to ROBERT OWENS and CONSTANT CANNON, then this obligation to be void. Wit: JOHN MITCHELL Junr, ALEX SMITH. Proved 9 May 1793. Attest: NATHL MITCHELL prothonotary. (B:pg 492)

6 Apr 1777. Bond of Conveyance. JOSHUA MOORE of Suss co planter am firmly bound unto ISAAC MOORE Junr of same co planter in the sum of 400 pounds ... the condition of this obligation is such that if JOSHUA MOORE conveys unto ISAAC MOORE a good estate of inheritance in fee simple unto 100 a. to be laid out of a tr called Moores Lott to be laid off to the best advantage to the plantation whereon the said ISAAC MOORE now lives, then this obligation to be

void. Wit: WILLIAM POLK, WILLIAM RELPH. (B:pg 492)

18 May 1786. Bond of Conveyance. GEORGE RALPH (RELPH) of
Suss Co am firmly bound unto THOMAS MOORE & JOHN MOORE
of same co in the sum of 500 pounds ... the condition of this obligation
is such that if GEORGE RALPH convey unto the said THOMAS
MOORE and JOHN MOORE pt/o a tr of land called Good Luck
whereon the said GEORGE RALPH now dwells, that pt/o the land that
was devised to the said GEORGE RALPH by his father WILLIAM
RALPH then this obligation to be void. Wit: MARY RALPH,
CHARLES MOORE. (B:pg 493)

20 Feb 1787. Assignment. THOMAS MOORE & JOHN MOORE of
Suss Co for 100 pounds assign unto ISAAC HORSEY the [above] bond.
Wit: DAVIS BACON, MATH HORSEY. (B:pg 493)

9 May 1793. Assignment. WILLIAM MOORE one of the executors of
ISAAC HORSEY esqr decd for 100 pounds assigned unto WILLIAM
MOORE, son of JOSHUA, the [above] bond. Wit: JNO RUSSEL, WM
COULTER. (B:pg 493)

27 Dec 1792. Deed of Mortgage. JOHN YOUNG of Phila merchant in
consideration of several debts and for the better and more effectual
securing the payment thereof and 5 shillings sold to JOHN
SPARHAWK of same city merchant ... 1/2 pt/o a 1445 a. tr of land,
whereas JOHN YOUNG together with GUNNING BEDFORD of same
city esqr by one bond bearing date 21 Mar 1789 did become jointly and
severally bound unto the said JOHN SPARHAWK in the penal sum of
700 pounds conditioned for the payment of 350 pounds with lawfull
interest on or before 10 Mar 1793, and whereas the said JOHN
YOUNG now is indebted unto the said JOHN SPARHAWK in the
further sum of 64 pounds 4 shillings 9 pence together with lawfull
interest ... in Broadkill Hund formerly the estate and inheritance of
BENJAMIN MIFFLIN, also 1/4 pt/o a 980 a. tr of land in Broadkiln
Hund, which trs are described in an indenture of mortgage bearing
date 1 Jan 1789 between JOHN YOUNG and ISAAC WIKOFF,
provided that if the said JOHN YOUNG or GUNNING BEDFORD
shall pay unto the said JOHN SPARHAWK the afsd debts, this
obligation shall become null void and of none effect. Wit: JAMES
HUMPHREYS, ASSHITON HUMPHREYS. Ackn 25 Jan 1793 before
WM BRADFORD judge. (B:pg 494)

30 Apr 1793. Articles of Agreement between JOHN RICCORDS and
JAMES RICCORDS, LEVIN RICCORDS and HAP RICCORDS
(RICORDS) all of Suss Co, whereas BENJAMIN RICCORDS late of
same co decd made his will bearing date 1 Mar 1793 and did devise
unto his wife ESTHER RICCORDS 3/4 of all his land and marsh during
her widowhood and the remaining 1/4 pt/o the land and marsh to his
son JOHN RICCORDS, and the whole of the land and marsh to his
said son JOHN RICCORDS after the death of or marriage of his wife
ESTHER and did by his will give to his said wife ESTHER all the
residue of his estate after payment of his just debts during her

widowhood and after her death or marriage to be divided among all his children, JOHN RICCORDS, JAMES RICCORDS, LEVIN RICCORDS and HAP RICCORDS have agreed that the said ESTHER shall enjoy the whole of the land & marsh, after her death or marriage the whole as afsd shall be equally divided among them and the residue of the estate devised to ESTHER RICCORDS shall at her decease be equally divided among the said JOHN RICCORDS, JAMES RICCORDS, LEVIN RICCORDS, ANN w/o JONATHAN STEVENSON and PRISCILLA RICCORDS, and to the performance hereof the parties bind themselves each to the other in the sum of 50 pounds. Wit: HESTER MOORE, WM HARRISON. (B:pg 495)

30 Apr 1792 at NY City NY. Power of Atty. EBENEZER GRACIE (GRACEY) (GRAICE) & THEOPHILUS BROWN of NY City NY have appointed NATHANIEL J. BURTON of CT and now residing at Pine Grove DEL our atty to sell and convey unto any purchaser pt/o the land belonging to us being several trs in Pine Grove .... Wit: JNO KEESE, RUSSELL EDWARDS. (B:pg 496)

30 Apr 1793 at NY City NY. JOHN KEESE a public notary for NY, before me personally appeared EBENEZER GRACIE and THEOPHILUS BROWN of NY City NY named in [above] letter of atty to NATHANIEL J. BURTON and severally ackn the same to be their deed. (B:pg 497)

9 May 1793. Bill of Sale. WILLIAM WROE of Suss Co farmer for 69 pounds 10 shillings sold to MORNING WROE of same co ... 2 horses, 8 head of horned cattle, 6 head of sheep, 2 sows, 10 shoats, 3 feather beds & furniture, 1 black walnut desk, 2 tables, 4 silver table spoons, 6 silver tea spoons, 1 sett of china, 12 pewter plates, 2 pewter dishes, 1 pewter bason, 1 sett of knives and forks, 2 ploughs, 2 harrows, 2 narrow axes, 2 grubbing hoes, 2 weeding hoes, 1 sett of iron wedges, 1 ox chain, 6 flag bottom chairs, 1 chest, 1 loom, 1 Bible, 1 book called "Josephus", 3 iron potts, 1 new man saddle, 1 tea cettle, 1 box iron & heater, and 1 canoe. Wit: PETER MOGEN, THOS ROBERTSON, RILEY BAKER, ELIJAH WOOTTEN. (B:pg 497)

11 May 1793. Bill of Sale. JOHN HAMBLIN of Suss Co for 28 pounds 7 shillings 6 pence sold to BENJAMIN HAMBLIN of Worcester Co MD ... 1 yoke of stears 7 pounds, 3 cows 7 pounds 10 shillings, 4 yearlings 2 pounds, 2 saws and 18 piggs 4 pounds, 2 beds and furniture 6 pounds and sundry household furniture 1 pound 17 shillings 6 pence. Wit: RICHARD SAMPSON, JESSE WEBB. (B:pg 498)

30 Nov 1792. Deed of Release. THOMAS STOCKLEY esqr of the town of Washington, Washington Co, PA and ELIZABETH his wife for 105 pounds release unto JOHN KING of same place ... a tr of land, whereas the said JOHN KING and MARGARET his wife on 12 Nov 1791 did convey a tr of land on Mill Cr about 1/2 mi above the Draw Bridge which is on Broadkill and is the passing direction from Lewes Town to Dover. Wit: ANDW WILSON, JAMES READ. (B:pg 498)

30 Nov 1792 at Washington Co (PA). Personally came before the Honorable ALEXANDER ADDISON esqr president of the court in said co, THOMAS STOCKLEY esqr of Washington Town and ELIZABETH his wife and did severally ackn the [above] deed for their act and deed. (B:pg 499)

30 Nov 1792 at Washington Co (PA). DAVID REDISH esqr prothonotory of the Court of Common Pleas for co afsd do certify that ALEXANDER ADDISON esqr [see above] was and still is president of the Court of Common Pleas in Washington Co and due faith and credit ought to be given to all his indices and acts. (B:pg 499)

Deed of Sale. WILLIAM WROE of Suss Co for 250 pounds sold to MORNING WROE of same co ... a tr of land called Manlove Grove n side of Broad Cr in Broad Cr Hund 250 a. adj Bakers Road and Old Ferry Road. Wit: THOS MOORE, ROBERT CREIGHTON, JOHN BACON. Ackn 9 May 1793. (B:pg 499)

1 May 1793. Bill of Sale. WILLIAM ROSS of Suss Co for 15 pounds 8 shillings 4 pence sold to JOSEPH TWILLEY of Somerset Co MD ... 2 feather beds & furniture, 1 cow and 2 earlings, 2 heifers, 1 sow & 4 pigs, 7 shotes and 1 barrow, 3 ewes and 1 lamb, 3 chests, 2 tables, 1 cubbord, 1 gun, 2 cow hides, 2 dishes and 3 bason, 9 plates, 2 pots, 1 frying pan, 1 dutch oven, 1 pear of cotten cards, 1 looking glass, 3 earthern bowls, 1 glass can, 1 small crop of corn, 1/2 dozen chears, 2 beehives, 1 saddle and bridle, 2 plowes and 1 harrow, 2 axes and 3 hoes, 1 spining whele, now remaining and being the possession of the said JOSEPH TWILLEY. Wit: ISRAEL WILLS, JOHN ROSS. (B:pg 500)

21 May 1793. Bill of Sale. WILLIAM ROSS of Suss Co for 22 pounds 10 shillings sold to ISRAEL WILLS ... 1 horse, 1 mare, 1 red cow and calf, 1 cart, 1 spining wheel, 1 ox yoke and chains, now remaining and being in the possession of the said ISRAEL WILLS. Wit: EDWARD CALLOWAY, SHELER MOORE. (B:pg 501)

1 Aug 1783. Agreement. SAMUEL DRAPER gardian to ELIZABETH DRAPER and SARAH DRAPER daus to HENRY DRAPER and now wives to JOSEPH STOCKLEY and JOHN WHEELTON doth agree with the said STOCKLEY and WHEELTON to give up all claims and demands of lands and marsh, negros or money as mentioned in my fathers will to my brother HENRY DRAPER and 1/5 of a 1/5 pt/o the remainder and residue of my fathers estate that is mentioned to be equally devided amongst his 5 children. Wit: COMFORT WEBB. (B:pg 501)

4 Sep 1792. Appeared before JOHN S. CAMPBELL, COMFORT CONNELLY formerly COMFORT WEBB, and being sworn deposeth & saith that she recollecteth to have been called upon by the parties [above] mentioned to wit the [above] instrument of writing. (B:pg 502)

1 Jun 1793. Deposition. NATHANIEL YOUNG aged 50 years saith

that himself with WILLIAM PERRY esqr and WILLIAM POLK esqr was appointed by order of court to settle a dispute between the above parties when this paper was produced and SAMUEL DRAPER was asked if he was in his proper senses when he signed the same, he answered yes or if any fraud was used by said STOCKLEY or WHEELTON to get him to sign the same and he answered no further this deponant saith not. Taken before RICHD HAYS. (B:pg 502)

9 May 1793. Bill of Sale. BENJAMIN RILEY and BETSEY RILEY of Suss Co do hereby sell a certain boy LEVIN a negro slave being about 12 years of age to JOHN WILLIS for 15 pounds. Wit: PERRY PRETTYMAN, JOHN MARTIN. (B:pg 502)

17 Apr 1793. Bill of Sale. PURNAL SHORT of Suss Co planter for 9 pounds 11 shillings 5 pence farthing sold to JOHN WILLIS Senr ... all my right unto 1 yoke of oxen aged about 7 or 8 years, the same which I now use in my work, together with the yoke belonging to be the property of said JOHN WILLIS Senr, PURNAL SHORT shall redeem the said oxen and yoke by 17 Sep next ensuing paying unto the said JOHN WILLIS Senr 9 pounds 11 shillings 5 pence farthing then the same to be mine as redeemed, otherwise to be the final property of the said JOHN WILLIS Senr. Wit: JAMES BURTELL, JOHN MARTIN. (B:pg 502)

4 Jun 1793. Petition of PETER ROBINSON of Suss Co esqr in behalf of WILLIAM DAVIDSON and ELIZABETH his wife humbly sheweth that on 2 Jan 1790 THOMAS EVANS late sheriff of Suss Co at public sale sold a tr of land in Indian River Hund, seized in execution as the property of the said WILLIAM DAVIDSON and ELIZABETH his wife at the suit of MARGARET KOLLOCK executrix of JACOB KOLLOCK late of Suss Co decd, to your petitioner for the use of the said WILLIAM DAVIDSON and ELIZABETH his wife for 10 pounds he being the highest bidder, your petitioner prays your honors to grant an order impowering THOMAS LAWS esqr the present sheriff to execute a deed, the said THOMAS EVANS being discharged from his office before he had executed a deed. 4 Jun 1793 read & allowed. (B:pg 503)

4 Jun 1793. Deed. THOMAS LAWS esqr high sheriff of Suss Co sold to WILLIAM DAVIDSON and ELIZABETH his wife ... a tr of land in Indian River Hund 50 a. [see petition above]. Wit: CHARLES POLK, NATHL MITCHELL. Ackn 4 Jun 1793. (B:pg 503)

26 Jan 1793. Deed. SARAH NEWBOLD dau to JOHN NEWBOLD (NEWBOULD) (NEWBOALD) and sister to PARNAL (PIRNAL) NEWBOLD of Suss Co for 25 pounds sold to CLOUDSBROUGHT WARRING of same place ... a peace of land in Great Neck in Nanticoke Hund on the County Road that leads from Johnstown to Deep Cr, the said land was the property of JOHN NEWBOLD father to said SARAH NEWBOLD and PARNAL NEWBOLD and was taken by an order of court at the complaint of CHARLES RICORDS adminr to JOHN NEWBOLD's estate and sold by said CHARLES RICORDS at public vandue to settle with WILLIAM NEWBOLD adminr to THOMAS

NEWBOULD's estate and the said SARAH NEWBOLD bid on said
land, bounded by land formerly belonging to THOMAS NEWBOULD
called Bashan, land called Addition to Fruitfull Plain, WILLIAM
LOFLAND's Forks Road Survey, THOMAS LAVERTY's new survey
and LEVIN WILLEY ... 92 a. Wit: GEORGE POLK, CHARLES POLK.
Ackn 5 Jun 1793. (B:pg 503)

31 Mar 1785. Bond of Conveyance. JOHN ABBOTT Senr bricklayer of
Suss Co am firmly bound unto RICHARD SHOCKLEY of same place
farmer in the sum of 600 pounds ... the condition of this obligation is
such that if JOHN ABBOTT shall convey 200 a. of land where the said
JOHN ABBOTT now lives in Seader Cr Hund then this obligation to
be void. Wit: NATHANIEL STOCKLEY, ELIAS SHOCKLEY. Proved 5
Jun 1793. (B:pg 506)

7 Apr 1785. Assignment. RICHARD SHOCKLEY assign over all my
right of the [above] bond unto CURTIS SHOCKLEY for value
received. Wit: ELIAS SHOCKLEY, ANNIAS HUTSON. (B:pg 506)

13 Jul 1792. Deed. JOHN CRAIG of the town of Lewis Suss Co
blacksmith for 8 pounds 12 shillings 6 pence paid by CORNELIUS
WILTBANK sold to ADAM HALL of same place taylor and
ELIZABETH his wife, RHOADS SHANKLAND of same co esqr and
MARY his wife and JAMES WILTBANK of the town and co afsd ... a
tr of land, whereas there is a parcel of land and marsh in Lewis and
Rehoboth Hund bounded by that pt/o the land allotted in the division
of the intestate lands of JOHN CRAIG decd unto CORNELIUS
PAYNTER and RUTH his wife and Hawks Nest Gut ... 5 1/2 a. being
the said JOHN CRAIG's pt/o larger parcel called Hawks Nest allotted
to him in the division of his said father's intestate lands on 7 Mar 1787,
and whereas JOHN WILTBANK late of this co esqr decd by his will
bearing date 21 Mar 1791 did devise unto his 3 children ELIZABETH
HALL, MARY SHANKLAND and JAMES WILTBANK afsd all the
remaining 3/5 pt/o his land, and whereas CORNELIUS WILTBANK
son of the said JOHN WILTBANK after publishing the will, purch of
the said JOHN CRAIG the 5 1/2 a., and JOHN WILTBANK on 3 Jul
1792 make a codicil to the afsd will which he did devise unto his son
CORNELIUS WILTBANK the remainder 3/5 part devised to his 3
children upon the special condition that his son should convey
emidiately after his decease unto his 3 children ELIZABETH HALL,
MARY SHANKLAND and JAMES WILTBANK as tenants in common
the said land to remain forever in common for the use of them and also
to pay to them 5 shillings. Wit: JNO RUSSEL, ELIZABETH RUSSEL.
Proved 5 Jun 1793. (B:pg 507)

13 Jul 1792. We the subscribers do hereby ackn to have received of our
brother CORNELIUS WILTBANK the sum of 5 pounds ordered to be
paid us by the said CORNELIUS WILTBANK by the will of our
honoured father JOHN WILTBANK esqr being the difference in value
between the lands & marsh conveyed to us by the [above] deed and
the lands and marsh devised to the afsd CORNELIUS WILTBANK in
the afsd will. Wit: [blank]. (B:pg 508)

21 Jan 1793. Deed. MARY WILTBANK and CORNELIUS WILTBANK of Suss Co exors of the will of JOHN WILTBANK late of Lewis same co esqr decd for 80 pounds sold to WILLIAM HARRIS of same co house carpenter ... pt/o a tr of land, whereas the said JOHN WILTBANK in his lifetime was seized of a parcel of land in Lewis and Rehoboth Hund binding upon the Deep Valley Br called Coopers Hall and being so seized, by his will bearing date 21 Mar 1791 he did order his exors to sell his land, n side of the road leading from Lewis to Saint Georges Chappel, whereas the said MARY WILTBANK and CORNELIUS WILTBANK in pursuance of the will on 22 Sep 1792 sold the land at public vendue to JOHN MAULL for 4 pounds per a. he being the highest bidder, and JOHN MAULL declared that 1/3 pt/o the land was for the use of the said WILLIAM HARRIS ... bounded by HUGH SMITH, Indian River Road and JOHN RUSSEL ... 20 a. 22 sq perches. Wit: JOHN MAULL, WILLIAM BRERETON. Ackn 5 Jun 1793. (B:pg 508)

5 Jun 1793. Deed of Release. RICHARD SHOCKLEY of Suss Co and REBECCA his wife for 30 pounds release unto ELIAS SHOCKLEY of the town of Milford Kent Co merchant ... a tr of land, whereas the said RICHARD SHOCKLEY by a deed of sale from BENJAMIN JOHNSON and a certain BRANTSON LOFLAND dated 5 May 1779 (Lib M Fol 254) became seized of a tr of land and marsh in Cedar Cr Hund n side of Slaughter Cr and sold 20 a. thereof to the said ELIAS SHOCKLEY bounded by the marsh late of JOHN DRAPER decd and marsh late of THOMAS HINDS decd ... RICHARD SHOCKLEY and REBECCA his wife hereby impower PHILLIP KOLLOCK and WILLIAM HARRISON to ackn this indenture in open court. Wit: CURTIS SHOCKLEY, NEHEMIAH TRUITT. Proved and Ackn 5 Jun 1793. (B:pg 510)

10 Jan 1793. Deed. ELIZABETH OAKEY of Suss Co for 70 pounds 4 shillings sold to ISAAC ATKINS of same place yeoman ... a percell of land nw side of Hairfields Br pt/o a tr laid out to WILLIAM COULTER ... 54 a. Wit: N WAPLES, STEPHEN COSTON, JONATHAN GORDON. Ackn 18 Jun 1793. (B:pg 511)

10 Jan 1793. Power of Atty. ELIZABETH OAKEY of Suss Co hereby appoint ISAAC WILSON, BENTON HARRIS & KENDLE BATSON gent my attys to ackn the [above] deed in open court. Wit: N WAPLES, JONATHAN GORDON, STEPHEN COSTON. Proved 18 June 1793. (B:pg 511)

5 Jun 1793. Deed. WILLIAM WHITE and ARCADA his wife of Suss Co for 37 pounds 10 shillings sold to PETER ROBINSON of same co esqr ... 1/2 of a tr of land in Angola Neck in Indian River Hund adj the lands of the said PETER ROBINSON, WILLIAM SHANKLAND and others which land by sundry conveyances became the right of a certain JOHN POTTER late of same co decd who by his will devised the same to his wife COMFORT POTTER, and COMFORT POTTER being seized of the tr died having first made her will bearing date 14 Jan 1789 and did devise unto her dau ARCADA WHITE and her 2 grandsons WILLIAM HOUSTON and JOSEPH HOUSTON all the

residue of her estate including the tr of land afsd, the 1/2 to ARCADA and 1/2 to WILLIAM HOUSTON and JOSEPH HOUSTON. Wit: ROBERT MARINER, CHARLES POLK. Ackn 5 Jun 1793. (B:pg 512)

22 May 1792. Deed. GEORGE MITCHELL, ROBERT HOUSTON, WILLIAM MOORE, JOHN COLLINS & RHOADS SHANKLAND commissioners in behalf of Suss Co for 21 pounds 15 shillings sold to NATHANIEL MITCHELL of same co ... 3 lotts of ground in George Town, #15 27 sq perches, #28 27 sq perches and #27 27 sq perches ... the commissioners appoint Colo DAVID HALL or THOMAS LAWS esqrs to ackn this deed in open court. Wit: ABRAM HARRIS, JOHN W. BATSON. Ackn 6 Jun 1793. (B:pg 513)

29 May 1793. Deed. HERCULAS KOLLOCK of Lewes Suss Co and ELIZABETH his wife for 100 pounds sold to DANIEL RODNEY of same place gent ... 2 parcels of land, whereas a tr of land n side of Pothooks Cr in Lewis and Rehoboth Hund which tr by sundry conveyances became the property of a certain JOHN HINMAN late of same co decd who by his will devised the same to his son JOHN HINMAN Junr and his dau ELIZABETH, whereas JOHN HINMAN the younger died intestate and adminr of his estate was committed to a certain JOHN NEILL, and JOHN NEILL by order of the Orphans Court to pay the just debts of the intestate sold the land at public sale to a certain WILLIAM GILL for 45 pounds 5 shillings he being the highest bidder, deed bearing date 15 Jan 1746, and whereas there is another parcel of land and marsh in the same hund adj the afsd tr which was formerly the property of SIMON KOLLOCK late of Suss Co decd by whose death the same descended to his son SHEPHERD KOLLOCK and his dau COMFORT KOLLOCK who intermarried with a certain JAMES TYBOUT, which said JAMES TYBOUT and COMFORT his wife conveyed unto the said SHEPHERD KOLLOCK her undivided right to the tr, which land the said SHEPHERD KOLLOCK by his will dated 24 Jun 1756 did devise to his wife MARY KOLLOCK, and whereas MARY KOLLOCK being seized of the tr died intestate and adminr of her estate was committed to a certain GEORGE KOLLOCK who by order of the Orphans Court held 8 Mary 1766 to discharge her debts sold at public sale the land to the afsd WILLIAM GILL for 84 pounds he being the highest bidder, deed dated 2 Aug 1768, and whereas WILLIAM GILL made his will bearing date 20 Apr 1775 and did devise unto his son WILLIAM GILL, after the death of MARGARET his wife, all his lands, whereas WILLIAM GILL the younger died before the death of his said father, and WILLIAM GILL the elder died without renewing his will, the same descended & became subject to division, after the death of the said MARGARET GILL, among the heirs of the said WILLIAM GILL namely to the representatives of PATIENCE JACOBS decd 1/6 part, to PRISCILLA PAYNTER 1/6 part, to ELIZABETH KOLLOCK 1/6 part, to SARAH LITTLE 1/6 part, to NAOMI ARNOLD 1/6 part and the remaining 1/6 part to MARGARET PERRY, and whereas in an Orphans Court HERCULAS KOLLOCK in behalf of ELIZABETH his wife and other representatives of the said WILLIAM GILL preferred a petition praying the court to make partition of the land, JAMES PATRIOT

WILSON, SAMUEL PAYNTER, JACOB HAZZARD, PETER MARSH
and ARTHUR HAZZARD gent freeholders of the co did make division
and among other allotments laid off to the said HERCULAS
KOLLOCK and ELIZABETH his wife a parcel bounded by land which
was allotted to JOHN LITTLE and SARAH his wife ... 26 1/2 a. also a
parcel of woodland adj land belonging to the heirs of DAVID HALL
decd 9 3/4 a. ... HERCULAS KOLLOCK and ELIZABETH his wife do
appoint PHILLIP KOLLOCK and KENDLE BATSON gent or either of
them to ackn this deed in open court. Wit: SIMON HALL, WILLIAM
HARRISON. ELIZABETH became party to this deed of her own free
will. Attest: PETER ROBINSON justice of the Orphans Court. Ackn 4
Jun 1793. (B:pg 514)

13 Oct 1792. Deed of Mortgage. Whereas CORNELIUS EVANS of
Suss Co stands bound unto SETH HUDSON of same place in an
execution bearing equal date with this indenture for 6 pounds 18
shillings 2 pence for securing the payment of said execution and
interest and 1 shilling whereof CORNELIUS EVANS sold to SETH
HUDSON 1 tr of land called Robinsons Chance 37 a. provided upon
this condition that CORNELIUS EVANS shall pay unto SETH
HUDSON the afsd execution then the land to be the property of
CORNELIUS EVANS if paid in 7 months otherwise to remain the
property of SETH HUDSON. Wit: STEPHEN STYER, JACOB
ROGERS. Proved 8 Aug 1793. (B:pg 516)

25 May 1793. Bill of Sale. LANGFORD BOYCE of Suss Co for 30
pounds sold to ABRAHAM (ABRAM) CALLAWAY of same place ... a
negro man called JACOB aged about 23 years which said negro
formerly belonged to a certain WILLIAM PRICE of said co & was by
him bequeath to my wife ELIZABETH. Wit: WM STAYTON, JANE
WARK. (B:pg 517)

1 Apr 1703. Deed. JAMES CARPENTER of Slaughter Cr Suss Co
planter for 38 pounds sold to JOHN HAGISTER of White Oak Neck
same co planter ... a tr of land in Kimballs Neck and front of WILLIAM
PILESes tr and given by the said WILLIAM PILES by his will unto
the afsd JAMES CARPENTER. Wit: THO FISHER, SAMUELL
BLONDELL. Ackn 4 May 1703. Attest: NEHEMIAH FIELD clerk.
(B:pg 517)

8 Oct 1760. Bond of Conveyance. JONATHAN DOLBEE of Worchester
Co MD planter am firmly bound unto NATHAN CULVER of same co
wheelright in the sum of 263 pounds ... the condition of this obligation
is such that if JONATHAN DOLBEE shall make over unto NATHAN
CULVER a tr of land & mills formerly belonging to a certain JOSEPH
MARSHOL thence conveyed unto a certain OBID OUTTEN then
conveyed unto the said JONATHAN DOLBEE then this obligation to
be void. Wit: JOHN SWAIN, WILLIAM SWAIN. Proved JBZ
JOHNSON clerk. (B:pg 518)

22 Oct 1760 at Worchester Co MD. Assignment. NATHAN CULVER of
Worchester Co MD do assign over all my rights of the [above] bond unto

RICHARD CROCKET of same place. Wit: JOHN SWAIN, WILLIAM SWAIN. (B:pg 518)

20 Mar 1793. Deed of Gift. MARY HAMILTON of Blockley Township Phila Co PA widow for natural love and affection and 5 shillings give to my son WILLIAM HAMILTON of the Woodlands in same co esqr ... several trs of land which I have in right of my late father WILLIAM TILL esqr & my mother MARY TILL both decd. Wit: JOHN CHILD, BENJN H. SMITH. Ackn 4 May 1793 at Phila before MATHEW CLARKSON esqr mayor of Phila. (B:pg 519)

28 Sep 1793. Power of Atty. SMITH & CANNON WINGATE of Suss Co do appoint PHILLIP WINGATE and JOSEPH COPES both of Suss Co to be our atty to recover and receive all sums of money due or payable to us. Wit: HENRY EDGER, EZEKIEL TIMMONS. (B:pg 519)

14 Oct 1793. Deposition. SAMUEL PAYNTER Junr of Broadkill Hund and JOSHUA HALL blacksmith of Lewis & Rehoboth Hund both of Suss Co say that on 1 instant Oct they were in a room at ISAAC WILSON's at George Town where only a certain GEORGE BACON and a certain JOSEPH COPES were present, and that they then and there heard the said JOSEPH COPES offer and request the said GEORGE to agree to divide a piece of vacant land that adj their pattent lands or else to call the commissioners at their joint request and let them determine the said division and all other their disputes, the said GEORGE BACON did refuse, JOSEPH COPES gave him warning not to pay any money to the State Treasurer on account of the said lands untill a hearing could be had before the commissioners on a caveat which JOSEPH was determined to enter against any resurvey the said GEORGE might pretend to have laid on the said land. Taken before CALEB RODNEY esqr justice of the peace. (B:pg 520)

15 Oct 1793. Arbitration Bond. JOHN HICKMAN, NUTTER LOFLAND and JACOB HICKMAN all of Suss Co are firmly bound each to the other the defaulter to pay to the other the penal sum of 500 pounds ... condition of this obligation is such that if the above bounders shall obey the award order [see below] of NATHANIEL YOUNG esqr, MARK DAVIS and JOHN S. CAMPBELL gent chosen to arbitrate the division of the thirds of the lands formerly in the possession of RACHEL HICKMAN decd and laying the same amongst the heirs of WILLIAM HICKMAN decd, upon 1 Nov next insuing, the above obligation to be void. Wit: ISAAC OSTON, THOMAS BROWN. (B:pg 520)

-- -- 1793. Award. Whereas by the death of RACHEL HICKMAN widow and relict of WILLIAM HICKMAN decd who died intestate leaving sundry lands which were divided amongst the heirs, the widows thirds being first aloted 38 a., whereas JOHN HICKMAN became intitled to 2 shares of said dower and NUTTER LOFLAND by purch of WILLIAM RICARDS Junr's share who intermarried with BETSEY dau of said intestate, and in right of his wife MARY dau of said intestate and

JACOB HICKMAN son of said intestate became intitled to 1/5 pt/o said dower and by mutual consent sold the building to JOHN HICKMAN one of said heirs, and said parties mutually agreed and bound themselves [see above] ... NATHANIEL YOUNG esqr, JOHN S. CAMPBELL and MARK DAVIS gent do make this our award, JOHN HICKMAN shall have 13 a. 58 perches, NUTTER LOFLAND shall have 14 a. 102 perches, JACOB HICKMAN shall have 10 a. and we do require each of the parties to execute a deed of release each unto the other ... . (B:pg 521)

11 Jan 1793. Deed of Mortgage. JOHN CAMMEL Senr and NANNY his wife for 50 pounds sold to GEORGE MITCHELL ... a tr of land in Baltimore Hund called Addition conveyed to him by a certain JAMES [?] on 2 Aug 1779, upon the condition that if JOHN CAMMEL Senr pay unto GEORGE MITCHELL a bond and judgment for 27 pounds 13 shillings 3 pence dated 3 Dec 1792 and one other bond for 19 pounds 19 shillings 6 pence dated 8 Dec 1792 together with interest then this indenture shall cease. Wit: BENJAMIN LONG, SEVERN? ROGERS (RODGERS). Proved 25 Dec 1793. (B:pg 522)

25 Mar 1769. Deed. SAMUEL BILES of Bucks Co PA gent, JOHN HINCHMAN of Gloucester Co NJ esqr and SAMUEL BLACKWOOD of same place esqr trustees of the estate of WILLIAM BROWN late of Gloucester Co for 175 pounds 7 shillings 3 pence sold to JOHN MIFFLIN of Phila merchant and REESE MEREDITH of same place merchant ... whereas JOHN JONES, JOHN CLOWES Junr and BENJAMIN MIFFLIN all of Suss Co did purch sundry trs of land in the whole 3630 a. and to effect a division of the said tr they did on 3 Oct 1765 confirm the division afsd and mutually released to each other the several allotments, whereas the allotment of the said JOHN JONES adj ANDREW COLLINS & PRETTYMAN DAY ... 1220 a. and JOHN JONES being so seized on 10 Nov 1767 did convey the same unto the said WILLIAM BROWN, and WILLIAM BROWN being so seized did convey 240 a. of the land unto one RICHARD HARTLEY, and RICHARD HARTLEY on 20 Nov year last afsd, and WILLIAM BROWN with REBECCA his wife did convey the residue of the tr 1000 a. to the said SAMUEL BILES, JOHN HINCHMAN and SAMUEL BLACKWOOD in trust that they should sell the land and the money to apply towards the payment of the just debts of said WILLIAM BROWN ... 980 a. Wit: MARY CLEMENT, ELIZABETH HINCHMAN, JOHN HINCHMAN Junr, WM HARTSHORN, JNO MIFFLIN. (B:pg 523)

9 Aug 1792 at NJ. Personally appeared before JOSEPH HUGG esqr one of the masters of the high court of Chancery and judge of the Court of Common Pleas for Gloucester Co, JOHN HINCHMAN one of the people called Quakers, wit to the [above] indenture and declared that he saw SAMUEL BLACKWOOD and JOHN HINCHMAN sign, seal and deliver the same as their respective acts and that ELIZABETH HINCHMAN and MARY CLEMENT subscribed their names as wits. (B:pg 524)

26 Sep 1792 at PA. PATTERSON HARTSHORNE of Phila merchant and one of the people called Quakers being duly affirmed declarith that he is well acquainted with the handwriting of his brother WILLIAM HARTSHORN and much accustomed to see him write and that he verily believes the signature of WILLIAM HARTSHORNE subscribed as a wit to the [above] deed is the hand writing of his brother WILLIAM HARTSHORNE. Taken before JAMES (M?)DDLE (B:pg 525)

13 Feb 1794. Affidvit. JOHN CLIFTON private soldier of the DEL Regiment came before ISAAC COOPER justice of the peace and made oath that he is the same JOHN CLIFTON to whom the original certificate was given and has it now in his possession [see below] and that he was disabled in the US service and that he resided in Broad Cr Hund before and since the war. (B:pg 525)

17 Feb 1792. Certificate. Doctr JOS HALL hereby certify that having examined JOHN CLIFTON late a private soldier in the DEL Regiment do find him still disabled from a wound he received in the service of the US and intitled to 1 pound 17 shillings 6 pence per month. (B:pg 525)

24 Oct 1771. Bond of Conveyance. JOSHUA CALLAWAY son of THOMAS CALLAWAY blksmith of Suss Co am firmly bound unto SAMUEL CALLAWAY of Summerset Co MD planter in the sum of 50 pounds ... the condition of this obligation is such that if JOSHUA CALLAWAY shall make over a tr of land called Cocland 50 a. in Summersett Co MD left to JOSHUA CALLAWAY son of PETER CALLAWAY [sic] by the said PETER CALLAWAY's will, then this obligation to be void. Wit: SAMUEL SHANKLAND, WILLIAM PRICE. (B:pg 525)

24 Feb 1772 at Worcester Co MD. Assignment. SAMUEL CALLAWAY for 5 pounds assign unto WILLIAM PRICE the [above] bond. Wit: G FARRINGTON. (B:pg 525)

14 Jan 177-. Assignment. WILLIAM PRICE of Suss Co for 35 pounds assigned unto THOMAS WALLER millwright the [above] bond. Wit: EBEN WALLAR. (B:pg 526)

6 Apr 1784. Assignment. THOS WALLER of Suss Co for 25 pounds assigned unto JONATHAN WALLER of same place the [above] bond. Wit: JOHN MORE, EBEN WALLER. (B:pg 526)

Agreement. NATHAN ADAMS, SARAH HITCH, ROBERT ELLEGOOD & WILLIAM ELLEGOOD have agreed with THOMAS ELLEGOOD & by these presents have sold unto the said THOMAS ELLEGOOD our right to a warrant of resurvey granted to WILLIAM ELLEGOOD Senr (now decd) dated at Phila 19 Mar 1776, and the said THOMAS ELLEGOOD have paid unto each of us 3 pounds. Attest: 8 Oct 1792 SETH GRIFFITH, 14 Oct WM E. HITCH, 4 Feb 1794 SETH GRIFFITH, 13 Oct 1792 WILLIAM E. HITCH, SETH GRIFFITH.

(B:pg 526)

22 Jan 1794. Deed. JOHN PARKER, JACOB HAZZARD and SARAH ROWLAND all of Suss Co for 57 pounds 6 pence 3 farthings sold to ESTHER RICKETS of same co ... a tr of marsh nw side of Coolspring Cr bounded by land late of BENJAMIN RICKETS decd, pt/o a patent called Greenfields formerly granted to a certain FRANCES CORNWELL which being once resurveyed became by sundry means the property of a certain ANDERSON PARKER decd who by his will directed the said piece of marsh to be sold by his executors the said JOHN PARKER, JACOB HAZZARD and SARAH ROWLAND ... 32 1/2 a. 13 perches. Wit: WILLIAM POLK, WM C. HAZZARD, LEVIN RICORDS. Ackn 25 Jan 1794 before DANIEL RODNEY judge. (B:pg 526)

18 Mar 1794. Deed. JOHN ANGE of Suss Co for 30 pounds sold to JOHN INSLEY of same co ... several trs of land, one called Curtisy and Tulls Addition that was the right of JOHN ANGE decd nw side of Nanticoke River with the saw mill and greece mill. Wit: JOHN ROBINSON, B.S., JACOB INSLEY. Ackn 18 Mar 1794 before GEO READ justice of the peace. (B:pg 527)

28 May 1793. JOHN CONNOWAY (son of PHILIP) do hearby relinquish all my wright of a tr of land sold by HALES SPICER to HANNAH CONNOWAY both of Suss Co 100 a. to SALLAH JONES (widdow). Wit: JEHU EVANS, CLEMENT JACKSON. (B:pg 528)

27 Feb 1793. Bill of Sale. JAMES BROOKS Senr for 40 pounds sold to JOSEPH BROOKS both of Suss Co ... 1 bay mair, 1 brindle cow, 1 three grass heifer, 1 reed yearling, 2 sows and 8 pigs, 1 horse cart, 2 beds & furniture, 2 pots, 1 skillet & sundry pieces of earthern ware, 1 grind stone, 1 axe, 4 old hoes, 1 grubbing hoe, 2 ploughs,, 2 harrows, some mean hanged up to dry, 60 bushels of indian corn, 2 stacks of fodder, 1 loom together with all residue of my estate. Wit: WILLIAM SWAIN, ROBERT SWAIN. (B:pg 528)

24 Aug 1793. Manumition. Then reserved of negro JOSEPH the sum of 30 pounds it being in full for his wife named NUBELS ROSE & her 2 children ELLECK & NELLY ... HENRY SAFFORD hereby declare the afsd negroes to be free ... . Wit: ABRAHAM CALLAWAY. (B:pg 529)

6 Apr 1794. Then came negro JOSEPH to my house to see if I knew the [above] hand writing which after viewing the same it appears very plainly to me to be the hand writing of HENRY SAFFORD and as the said negro JOSEPH is desirous to have the same recorded as the said HENRY SAFFORD and the wit have both left this state, I hereby certify that the [above] appears to be the handwriting afsd and no forgery in my opinion. (signed) ROBT ROBINSON. (B:pg 529)

18 Dec 179-. Bill of Sale. LEAH CANNON of Suss Co sold a certain negro boy by the name of TIMOTHY about 11 years of age unto CURTIS JACOBS. Wit: HENRY CANNON. (B:pg 529)

29 Apr 1794. Manumition. HENRY NEILL of Lewes Town Suss Co do sett free a negro wench named ALICE & 2 children her daus ALICE & NANCE. Wit: JNO RUSSEL, WM RUSSEL. (B:pg 529)

30 Apr 1794. Manumition. PHILIP HUGHES of Suss Co do set free a negro man named NEWTOWN. Wit: WM RUSSEL, JOHN FUTCHER Junr. (B:pg 529)

19 Jul 1795. Notice. To WILLIAM SKINNER, sir take notice that on 20 Aug next I shall take the deposition of CHARLES MANSHIP to perpetuate his testimony in a case of accidents in evidence at the trial of the case now depending between us, at the house of TRUSTIN LAWS POLK between the hours of 10 and 4 oclock. (signed) JOHN STEWART. (B:pg 530)

17 Aug 1795 at Dorchester Co. Then came COOK MOBERY before JNO STEVENS justice of the peace for co afsd & made oath that he did on 20 Jul 1795 deliver of copy of the [above] notice to WILLIAM SKINNER of this co. (B:pg 530)

17 Aug 1795 at Dorchester Co MD. H DICKINSON clerk hereby certify that JOHN STEVENS esqr whose name is subscribed [above] was at the time of taking and still is one of the justices of the peace for co afsd. (B:pg 530)

20 Aug 1795. Deposition. CHARLES MANSHIP aged 60 years or there abouts deposeth he sold JOHN TRAVILON STEWARD (STEWART) 1 negro girl called KIZ, and when this deponant sold the afsd negro girl JNO TRAVILON STEWARD said to the deponant he did not buy the negro girl for himself, he bought her for his son JOHN STEWARD and requested this deponant to deliver the said negro girl called KIZ to his son JNO STEWARD and this deponant did take the negro girl by the hand and deliver her to the afsd JNO STEWARD as his property forever, and after that the afsd JOHN TRIVALON STEWARD settled with this deponant for the afsd negro girl KIZ. Taken before TRUSTIN LAWS POLK justice of the peace. (B:pg 530)

20 Aug 1795. NATHL MITCHELL prothonotary do hereby certify that TRUSTIN LAWS POLK esqr before whom the above deposition was made is a justice of the peace for Suss Co and that full faith and credit is and ought to be given to him as such. (B:pg 530)

15 Sep 1795. Certificate. Doctr JOS HALL hereby certify that I have duly examined JOHN CLIFTON a private soldier in the DEL Regiment in 1792 and from the proof being made to me do believe him enable to attend from the bed situation he now is in arising from the wound he received in the service of the US, therefore thinks him intitled to 2 pounds - shillings per month. (B:pg 530)

17 May 1715. Deed. CHARLES BRIGHT now of Marshahope Kent Co planter for 18 pounds 10 shillings sold to WILLIAM ARY of Suss Co ... pt/o a tr of land, whereas 1 Jan 1682 there was granted unto

WILLIAM TRIPPIT by Suss Co Court a warrant to take up 300 a. of land and was on 2 Feb 1682/3 assigned over by the said TRIPPIT unto JOHN HILL late of this co decd, and JOHN HILL on 11 Jan 1689/90 did assign over all his right unto the warrant unto CHARLES BRIGHT afsd and on 10 Apr 1697 there was surveyed unto CHARLES BRIGHT by virtue of the warrant a 300 a. tr of land e & w sides of Beaverdam Br by THOMAS PEMBERTON then deputy surveyor adj land of one WILLIAM DURVALL and WILLIAM LIGHT'S 90 a. ... 202 a. Wit: RICHARD LAW, THO PEMBERTON. Ackn 2 Aug 1715. Attest: ROGER CORBETT clerk. (B:pg 531)

17 May --. Deed. CHARLES BRIGHT of Marshahope Kent Co planter for 11 pounds sold to WILLIAM LIGHT of Suss Co ... pt/o a tr of land [see above] ... 90 a. Wit: RICHARD LAW, THO PEMBERTON. (B:pg 532)

21 Jul 1715. Deed. WILLIAM ARY of Suss Co yeoman for 14 pounds sold to WILLIAM LIGHT of same co planter ... pt/o a tr of land [same as above] ... 120 a. Wit: STEPHEN KENNING, THOMAS BATE. (B:pg 533)

14 Sep 1789. Deed of Release. JAMES TOOLE of Baltimore Town and Co MD for 50 pounds release unto CONSTANTINE JACOBS of DEL ... a lot of ground, whereas the said JAMES TOOLE by a deed of lease bearing date 8 Sep 1784 did convey a lot of ground in Fells Point on Strabery Alley & Bank Street subject to the payment of the yearly rent of 6 pounds ... . Wit: JOHN GORDON, JNO REILY. Ackn 14 Sep 1789 at Baltimore Co before GEO GOULDN PRESBURY, JAS CALHOUN justices of the peace. (B:pg 534)

9 Apr 1796. Deed. WAITMAN GOSLIN (the elder) of Suss Co for 200 pounds sold to his son WAITMAN GOSLIN Junr of same co ... a tr of land, whereas the said WAITMAN GOSLIN Senr by virtue of sundry measures taken became seized in fee simple of a tr of land called Delight in N.W. Fork Hund including his dwelling plantation on the road leading from Marshyhope Bridge to Federalsburgh s side of Beach Br ... 495 1/2 a. ... but whereas the said WAITMAN GOSLIN Senr has lately laid off for his own use a certain pt/o the land including his mansion house with a competant parcel of cleared land and woods described in his will bearing date 5 Apr 1796 it is agreed by the parties that the said WAITMAN GOSLIN Senr and his wife MARY shall have quiet possession of all that pt/o the said land during their natural lives or the life of either of them, and WAITMAN GOSLIN the elder does hereby appoint JAMES WILSON & THOMAS LAWS esqrs of Suss Co or either of them his attys to ackn this indenture in open court. Wit: OLIVE JUMP, CLEMENT ROSS. Proved and Ackn 20 Apr 1796. (B:pg 536)

21 Oct 1794. Deed. WM WHALEY of Little Cr Hund Suss Co for 150 pounds sold to BENJAMIN VINSON of same place ... a tr of land called Maden Head which was originally granted unto a certain GEORGE HEARN on 23 Oct 1749 under the grant of MD on Head or

Broad Cr ... 50 a. ... WILLIAM WHALEY do appoint SETH GRIFFITH and WINGATE HALL both of this co or either of them to ackn this deed in open court. Wit: ELIJAH FREENY, SAML HEARN. Proved and Ackn 20 Apr 1796. (B:pg 537)

14 Feb 1793. Deed. EBENEZER WHALEY of Little Cr Hund Suss Co for 120 pounds sold to WILLIAM HEARNE DORMON ... a percel of land called Gosham ... 50 a. and also pt/o another tr called Goshans Addition ... 68 a. Wit: SOLOMON VINSON, JOSEPH VINSON. Proved and Ackn 20 Apr 1796. (B:pg 538)

6 May 1756. Bond. JAMES MUIR of Worcester Co MD gent am firmly bound unto RICHARD CROCKET of Somerset Co MD in the sum of 1000 pounds ... whereas the said RICHARD CROCKET executed a bond bearing even date with these presents in the penalty of 1000 pounds condition for the payment of 200,000 ft of inch pine plank to the said JAMES MUIR at or upon the expiration of 5 years, whereas in case the said RICHARD should fail in any of the payments the said JAMES should sue the said RICHARD for the same, the said JAMES would recover in curt money against the said RICHARD which would be of great prejudese to the said RICHARD, now the condition of this obligation is such that if the afsd RICHARD should fail to make payment of the afsd plank by the time in his bond to the afsd JAMES and JAMES should sue RICHARD for the same that then JAMES shall take and receive from RICHARD plank afsd at the rate of 5 shilings by the hundred in lew of any sum of money that shall be recovered against RICHARD, then this obligation to be void. Wit: MATHEW CANNON, THOS COLLIER Senr. (B:pg 540)

21 Apr 1796. GEORGE ADAMS made oath and declared that he was well acquainted with JAMES MUIR in his life time and his hand writing and verily believed his name as subscribed to [above] bond to be his hand writing, that he was also acquainted with THOMAS COLLIER Senr one of the wits and believed his name as hereto subscribed was his hand writing. (B:pg 540)

6 May 1756. Bond. JAMES MUIR of Worcester Co MD am firmly bound unto RICHARD CROCKET of Somerset Co MD in the sum of 1000 pounds ... the condition for this obligation is such that if JAMES MUIR shall convey all his right to the land in Worcester Co called Crockets Delight, Piny Marsh, [page torn] and Waltors Lott upon Gravely Br together with the water mill, unto RICHARD CROCKET upon the payment of 200,000 ft of inch pine plank the above mills and trs of land, that then this obligation to be void. Wit: THOS COLLIER Senr, MATTHEW CANNON. Proved 21 Apr 1796. (B:pg 540)

2 Apr 179-. WINDER CROCKETT for a valuable consideration hereby assign all my right to the [above] bond unto HUMPHRISS BROWN of Suss Co. Wit: THOS FISHER, WM STAYTON. (B:pg 541)

21 Apr 1796. Deed. JACOB HAZZARD of Suss Co esqr for 3 pounds 7 shilings 6 pence sold to ISAAC WILSON of same co innkeeper ... a lot

of ground #70 in George Town on Reece Street and Coopers Ally ... 25 sq perches. Wit: WM RUSSEL, WILLIAM HAZZARD. Ackn 21 Apr 1796. (B:pg 541)

29 Dec 1795. Deed. BARKLEY TOWNSEND of Suss Co yeoman for 37 pounds 10 shillings sold to EDWARD CREAGH (CREAH) of same co ... a lot of ground in Laurel Town #14 the lott where the said CREAGH now liveth on ... 99 ft sq. Wit: BENJAMIN RIGGIN, THOMAS FEENEY, SAMUEL WILLIAMS Junr. Ackn 21 Apr 1796. (B:pg 542)

29 Dec 1795. Power of Atty. BARLEY TOWNSEND appoint my trusty and well beloved NATHANIEL MITCHELL esqr my atty to convey the above deed in open court. Wit: THOMAS FEENY, SAMUEL WILLIAMS Junr. Proved 21 Apr 1796. (B:pg 543)

21 Apr 1796. Deed. WILLIAM SLAYTON of Suss Co for [page torn] money sold to JAMES BUCHANAN a minor son of JAMES BUCHANAN late of same place decd, paid by a certain JESSE GREEN, guardian to said minor ... whereas the said WILLIAM STAYTON in virtue of a pattent lately obtained hath become seized in a tr of land on Nanticoke River & Clear Brook Br in NW Fork & Nanticoke Hund ... adj land called Clear Brook, PHILIP HUGHES's land called Joppa, land called James's Lott, land called Mill Landing and land called Addition ... 76 1/2 a. ... WILLIAM SLAYTON doth appoint my trusty friend DAVID HALL esqr atty at law practising in said co to ackn this deed in open court. Wit: THO LAWS, ACAHEL PHELPS, JOHN LOFLAND. Ackn 21 Apr 179-. (B:pg 543)

5 Apr 1796. Deed. ISAAC KINDER of Suss Co for 16 pounds 12 shillings 6 pence sold to WILLIAM TWYFORD of same co ... pt/o a tr of land in N.W. Fork Hund called Browns Inclosure ... 9 a. 72 perches ... ISAAC KINDER do appoint JAMES PATRIOT WILSON & DAVID HALL esqrs attys at law to ackn this indenture in open court. Wit: JACOB KINDER, ABRAHAM CANNON. Proved and Ackn 21 Apr 1796. (B:pg 545)

1 Sep 1794. Deed. JOHN GOYAUX DE LA ROCHE of Phila gent and MARY his wife (late MARY HARPER widow and relict of THOMAS HARPER decd) for 65 pounds sold to JOHN MYERS of Phila ... a lot of land s side of Lewes in front 60 ft and 200 ft back towards the savannah which adj the lots late of RICHARD HINMAN decd & PETER HALL, being the same lot which the afsd THOMAS HARPER decd by his will bearing date 4 May 1790 in Phila devised unto his wife MARY. Wit: E ALINER, MA DAVIS. Ackn 24 May 1796 at Phila before ISAAC HOWELL associate justice. (B:pg 546)

20 Apr 1796. Deed. ISAAC KINDER of Suss Co for 150 pounds sold to JACOB KINDER of same co ... a tr of land in NW Fork Hund called First Choice near Clay Swamp adj land called Whites Industry ... 103 1/2 a. ... ISAAC KINDER do appoint JAMES P. WILSON & DAVID HALL esqrs attys at law to ackn this deed in open court. Wit: ARCHABEL TWYFORD, SOLOMON TWYFORD (TWIFORD). Proved

110

and Ackn 21 Apr 1796. (B:pg 547)

5 Nov 1795. Bond of Conveyance. SINDA RILEY PETTYJOHN of Suss
Co am firmly bound unto WILLIAM DICKERSON of same co in the
sum of [page torn] hundred pounds ... the condition of this obligation is
such that if SINDA RILEY PETTYJOHN conveys unto WILLIAM
DICKERSON all her right as one of the heirs of JOHN PETTYJOHN
decd in a tr of land in Broadkiln Hund where the said DICKINSON
now dwells called P.H. adj JAMES PETTYJOHN, JOSIAH ROTTEN,
BUTTLAR's line, BEAVINS's corner, JOHN CLOWS, BEDFORD's
land ... 154 a. then this obligation to be void. Wit: BETTEY MICHEL,
JAMES PETIJOHN. (B:pg 549)

6 Nov 1795. Bond of Conveyance. ANN ZEALEY PETTYJOHN of
Suss Co am firmly bound unto WILLIAM DICKERSON of same co in
the penal sum of 150 pounds ... this obligation is such that if ANN
ZEALEY PETTYJOHN conveys unto WILLIAM DICKERSON all her
right as one of the heirs of her father JOHN PETTYJOHN in a tr of
land in Broadkilln Hund [same as above] ... then this obligation to be
void. Wit: SARAH WEST, DAVID WEST. (B:pg 549)

5 Nov 1795. Bond of Conveyance. RICHARD PETTYJOHN of Suss Co
am firmly bound unto WILLIAM DICKERSON of same co in the penal
sum of 150 pounds ... the condition of this obligation is such that if
RICHARD PETTYJOHN conveys unto WILLIAM DICKERSON all his
right as one of the heirs of JOHN PETTYJOHN decd unto a tr of land
[same as above] ... then this obligation to be void. Wit: THOMAS
REYNOLDS, JOB RAYNOLDS. (B:pg 550)

10 Nov 1795. Bond of Conveyance. JAMES PETTYJOHN Junr of Suss
Co am firmly bound unto WILLIAM DICKERSON of same co in the
penal sum of 1-- [page torn] pounds ... the condition of this obligation is
such that if JAMES PETTYJOHN Junr conveys unto WILLIAM
DICKERSON all his right in a tr of land [same as above] ... then this
obligation to be void. Wit: WARRIN JEFFERSON, PRETTYMAN DAY.
(B:pg 551)

-- Nov 1795. Bond of Conveyance. JOHN PETTYJOHN of Suss Co am
firmly bound unto WILLIAM DICKERSON of same co in the penal
sum of 100 pounds ... the condition of this obligation is such that if
JOHN PETTYJOHN conveys unto WILLIAM DICKERSON all his
right in a tr of land [same as above] ... then this obligation to be void.
Wit: RICHARD FURMAN, JANEY STEEL. (B:pg 551)

14 Jan 1796. Power of Atty. WILLIAM DISHELD PRETTYMAN of
Suss Co have appointed my truly friend Capt ZADOCK BARKER of
same co to recover and receive all such debts as I have due and to
pursue all such lawful ways & means as may be nessary for the
recovery thereof ... . Wit: W WAPLES, JEHU BARKER. Proved 16 Jan
1796 at Dagsbury Suss Co before S KOLLOCK justice of the peace.
(B:pg 552)

[page badly torn] ... in the presence of GEO DAVIS.

29 Apr 1796. Personally appeared before S KOLLOCK justices of peace
& made oath that the names of LAMBERT CADWALADER &
PHILEMON DICKINSON on the within instrument are the respective
handwriting to be the best of his belief. (B:pg 553)

9 Mar 1797. Deed. WILLIAM DOD of Lewis merchant for 600 pounds
sold to WILLIAM PAYNTER of same place merchant ... a tr of land in
Rehoboth Neck on Lewes Cr [page torn] late of WILLIAM RIGNET?
and those of JOHN ELLIOT, RICHARD LITTLE and NATHANIEL
[page torn] 240? a. and 7 a. [page torn] to the said WILLIAM DOD by
patent bearing date 11 Dec 1795 ... . Wit: JAMES P. WILSON,
THOMAS COOPER. Ackn 9 Mar 1797 before DANL RODNEY judge.
(B:pg 553)

7 Nov 1796. Manumition. THOMAS [page torn] set at liberty my negro
man SAM ... and that he shall be free. (B:pg 554)

27 Mar 1797. Whereas a final settlement made between CURTIS
SHOCKLEY and ELENOR HUTSON (HUDSON), that ELENOR
[page torn] heirs of JONATHAN HILL late of Suss Co doth for 75
pounds due of my fathers estate left to me in the hands of the afsd
CURTIS SHOCKLEY do hereby discharge and acquit him of all [page
torn] of the estate of my father JONATHAN HILL. Wit: WILLIAM
KENDRICK, HESTER KENDRICK, RACHEL MORRIS. (B:pg 554)

LAMBERT CADWALADER and PHELEMINA DICKINS [page torn]
the will of MARTHA DAGWORTHY decd for 500 pounds paid by
WILLIAM HILL WELLS of Suss Co quit claim unto the said WM
[page torn] married ELIZABETH DAGWORTH AYDELOTT the
residuary devisee ... and unto LAMBERT CADWALADER and
GEORGE MITCHELL surviving executors of the will of the said JOHN
DAGWORTHY decd ... all the right of them LAMBERT
CADWALADER and PHILEMON DICKINSON as executors of the
said MARTHA DAGWORTHY decd against the said WILLIAM HILL
WELLS or ELIZABETH his wife ... made a full and final settlement ...
[the rest missing]. (B:pg ?)

Hancock Co, GA. Record of appointment of THOMAS ... [page torn] ...
CALLAWAY be appointed guardian to ANN CALLAWAY [page torn] ...
and ELISHA CALLAWY & POLLEY CALLAWAY and [page torn] ... to
amount of $500 ... [page torn]. (B:pg 555)

17 Oct 1767. Deposition of THOMAS [half the page is missing] ...
EDWARD STAPLEFORD ... JOHN RICHARDS ... sworn before
ISAAC WATTSON. (B:pg 555)

9 Apr 1798. Manumition. NANCY POLK hereby let absolutely free the
negro GRACE ... [page torn] free at the age of 27 years she being now
about 12 years ... . Wit: THO LAWS, THOS SORDEN. (B:pg 555)

25 Apr 1798. Deed. JESSE GREEN of Suss Co & BETSY his wife sold to WILLIAM MCDANIEL and JAMES MCDANIEL exors [page torn] both of Dorcester Co MD ... a tr of land called Knoxes Hazzard and another called [page torn] Neighbourhood? 10 a., and one called Long Swamp 100? a. ... in St. Johns Town in Nanticoke Hund which were purch by the afsd JESSE GREEN [page torn] property of JOHN MITCHELL late of Suss Co decd ... . Wit: THO FISHER, THO LAWS. Ackn -- -- 1798 [rest of page missing]. (B:pg ?)

End of Deed Record Vol B 2

LATE RECORDS OF LIBER A

Most of the records found in Deed Book A pertain to the period, 1681-1725 and have been published in an earlier book. The following records of Liber A pertain to the period, 1764 - 1805.

21 Jan 1769. Summons. ISAAC WATTSON and PARKER ROBINSON esqrs justices assigned to keep the peace, to BOAZ MANLOVE sherriff, whereas JOHN CIRWITHIN has represented unto us that he is seized in his own right of a tr of land n side of Primehook Cr suitable to erect a mill, yet cannot go onto compleat same (without) purchasing some pt/o the adj land on s side, these are therefore to command you to summons and cause to come before us 6 freeholders on 28 of this instant at the house of N [page torn] DAVIS Junr at ten oclock in order to assess the damages and value of 2 a. opposite to the land of JOHN CIRWITHIN, freeholders being summoned JOHN HEAVELO, ROBERT STEPHENSON, PARNAL JOHNSON, DORMON LOFLAND, JEHU CLAYPOOLE, HENRY SMITH. (A:pg 1)

28 Jan 1769. Verdict. Pursuant to a warrant JOHN HEAVELO, ROBERT STEPHENSON, PARNAL JOHNSON, DORMON LOFLAND, JEHU CLAYPOOLE and HENRY SMITH being hereby sumoned to appear before ISAAC WATTSON & PARKER ROBINSON esqrs justices of the peace for Suss Co to determine the true & intrinsick value of 2 a. of land s side of Primehook Cr and opposite to the land of JOHN CIRWITHIN who intends to build a mill and to assess the damages that may be to the owner of the said adj land, we therefore having viewed & considered the same, value the 2 a. to the sum of 3 pounds per a. and the damages to the sum of 1 penny sterling per a. to be paid to the owner of the said land, bounded to the n of STRINGER TILNEY's house. ISAAC WATTSON and PARKER ROBINSON justices of the peace for Suss Co do hereby certify to his majesty's justices of the Court of Common Pleas that the within instrument of writing was delivered to us by the freeholders thereunto subscribing as their virdict. (A:pg 2)

28 Jan 1769. Verdict. Pursuant to a warrant hereunto annexed JOHN HEAVELO, ROBERT STEPHENSON, DORMON LOFLAND, JEHU CLAYPOOL and HENRY SMITH summoned to appear before ISAAC WATTSON & PARKER ROBINSON justices of the peace of Suss Co to determine damage or loss that any person who has a mill either

above or below the place where JOHN CIRWITHIN hath or intends to build a mill near the head of Primehook Cr may receive by taking the water out of the river, cr or run above the mill and bringing it past the same in a race or by any other obstruction caused by the back water of the said JOHN CIRWITHIN ... we having viewed same do return and say that no person will receive any damage or loss. ISAAC WATTSON and PARKER ROBINSON justices of the peace for Suss Co do hereby certify that the within virdict was delivered to us by the freeholders. (A:pg 3)

2 May 1770. At a Court held at Lewes the [above] return was offered to the court for their acceptance and consideration whereupon the said court did order it to be filed and recorded. Attest: J RUSSELL d[ep] prothonotary. (A:pg 4)

18 Dec 1773. Summons. Whereas BENJAMIN BURTON esqr hath represented unto THOMAS ROBINSON & JOHN RODNEY esqrs justices of the peace of Suss Co that to built or repair a mill on Fishing Cr that he hath a real property in a tr of land, yet cannot go on to build or repair the same without obtaining and purchasing some pt/o the adj land, these are therefore to command PETER ROBINSON sheriff to summon 6 freeholders on 22 of this instant at the house of JOHN DEAN's at ten oclock in the morning, in order to assess the damages of any person who has a mill either above or below the place where BENJAMIN BURTON intends to build one ... summoned ISAAC SMITH, SAMUEL DARBY, PAYNTER STOCKLEY, WOODMAN STOCKLEY, LEATHERBURY BARKER & JAMES SHARPE. (A:pg 5)

22 Dec 1773. Verdict. ISAAC SMITH, SAMUEL DARBY, PAYNTER STOCKLEY, WOODMAN STOCKLEY, LEATHERBURY BARKER & JAMES SHARPE being summoned by the sherriff of Suss Co by virtue of a precept from THOMAS ROBINSON & JOHN RODNEY esqrs in order to assess the damage or loss that any person who has a mill either above or below the place where BENJAMIN BURTON esqr intends to build one and determine the value of 2 a. of land laying opposite to the lands of the said BENJAMIN and the damage and loss that may be to the owners ... we do make a return and say 1st that no person hath or have a mill either above or below the place where said BENJAMIN intends to build one except an old mill which the said BENJAMIN lately purch and therefore no damage or loss can be assessed, seondly we do determine the true and intrinsick value of 2 a. opposite to the lands of said BENJAMIN BURTON to the sum of 1 pound 3 shillings 9 pence per a. which said 2 a. is the property of JACOB STOCKLEY ... damages we do assess 7 shillings 6 pence per a. the mill pond shall overflow to the owner thereof. [bottom of page blurred and torn] (A:pg 5)

7 Jun 1765 at Phila. Apppointment. To JOHN VINING, JACOB VANBEBBER, RICHARD MCWILLIAM and JOHN CLOWES esqrs our justices of our supreme court, reposing special trust and confidence in your loyalty, integrity and ability, we have assigned you our justices ... . (signed) JOHN PENN esqr by virtue of a commission from

THOMAS PENN and RICHARD PENN esqrs true and absolute proprietaries of PA. 10 Aug 1765 recorded CASAR RODNEY recorder. (A:pg 322)

2 Nov 1764 at New Castle. Appointment. To JOHN CLOWES of Suss Co esqr, reposing special trust and confidence in your loyalty integrity and ability we have appointed you one of the justices of our supreme court ... . (signed) JOHN PENN esqr by virtue of a commission from THOMAS PENN and RICHARD PENN esqrs true and absolute proprietaries of PA. (A:pg 323)

1 Nov 1764 at New Castle. Appointments. To JAMES HAMILTON, WILLIAM TILL, BENJAMAN SHOEMAKER, LARRANCE GROWDEN, JOSEPH TURNER, WILLIAM LOGAN, RICHARD PETERS, LYNFORDS LANDNER, BENJAMAN CHEW, THOMAS CADWALADER and RICHARD PENN esqrs members of the proprietary and governors council and to JACOB KOLLOCK Senr, BENJAMAN STOCKLEY, DAVID HALL, BENJAMAN BURTON, NEHEMIAH DRAPER, THOMAS PRETTYMAN, JACOB KOLLOCK Junr, JOHN SPENCER, ISAAC WATTSON, WRIXAM LEWIS, GILBELSHER PARKER, LEVEN CRAPPER and THOMAS ROBINSON all of Suss Co esqrs, reposing special trust and confidence in your loyalty integrety and ability, know ye that we have assigned you jointly and severally our justices our peace in co afsd ... . (signed) JOHN PENN esqr by vertue of a commission from THOMAS PENN and RICHARD PENN esqrs true and absolute proprietaries of PA. (A:pg 325)

1 Jul 1765 at Phila. To WILLIAM CONWELL of Suss Co esqr, reposing special trust and confidence in your loyalty integrity and ability know that we have assigned you one of our justices of Suss Co ... (signed) JOHN PENN esqr by virtue of a commission from THOMAS PENN and RICHARD PENN esqrs true and abolute proprietaries of PA. (A:pg 326)

1 Nov 1764 at New Castle. Appointment. To DAVID HALL and JACOB KOLLOCK Junr of Suss Co esqrs, reposing special trust and confidence in your loyalty and integrety I authorise and empower you or either of you to administer to all judges, justices, sheriffs, coroners & all other officers civil and military and all other persons the oath of office and oath of allegiance ... . (signed) JOHN PENN esqr lieutenant governor and commander in chief. (A:pg 327)

29 Oct 1765 at Phila. Whereas the justices of the co Court of Common Pleas of New Castle Co have recommended JOSEPH EARLE esqr atty at law in MD for my licence to practice the law in Newcastle, Kent and Suss Cos, I do hereby grant my permission and licence to practice as atty at law in said courts. (signed) JOHN PENN esqr lieutenant governor and commander in cheaf of PA. (A:pg 328)

10 Apr 1773 at New Castle. Appointments. To JAMES HAMILTON, JOSEPH TURNER, WILLIAM LOGAN, RICHARD PETERS,

LYNFORD LARDNER, BENJAMIN CHEW, THOMAS
CADWALADER, JAMES TILGHMAN, ANDREW ALLEN and
EDWARD SHIPPEN Junr esqrs members of the proprietaries and
governors councill and to BENJAMIN BURTON, JACOB KOLLOCK,
WRIXAM LEWIS, GILBELSHER PARKER, LEVIN CRAPPER,
THOMAS ROBINSON, WILLIAM CONWELL, JOHN RODNEY,
ANDERSON PARKER, PARKER ROBINSON, BOAZ MANLOVE,
JOHN WILTBANK, DANIEL NUNEZ and NEHEMIAH DAVIS of
Suss Co, reposing special trust and confidence in your loyalty, integrity
and ability, know ye that we have assigned you jointly and severally
our justices .... (signed) RICHARD PENN esqr by virtue of a
commission from THOMAS PENN and JOHN PENN esqrs true and
absolute proprietaries, lieutenant governor and commander in chief of
PA. (A:pg 337&338)

10 Apr 1772 at New Castle. Appointment. To DAVID HALL and
JACOB KOLLOCK of Suss Co esqrs, reposing special trust and
confidence in your loyalty and integrity I authorize and impower you or
either of you to administer to all judges, justices, sheriffs, coroners and
all other officers civil and military and all other persons, the oath of
office and the oath of allegiance .... (signed) RICHARD PENN esqr
lieutenant governor and commander in chief of PA. (A:pg 338)

The court granted to JOHN TRUMAN [page torn] a. of land. (A2:pg 1)

JOHN ROADES hath this day demanded of Capt JOHN AVERY the
patten of a tr of land called Blackwallnut [page torn] which the said
AVERY had purch from HENRY STRETCHER, which demand the said
AVERY replyed would not deliver the said patten without ye order
form the governor. (A2:pg 1)

By the Governer: whereas I did in 1675 among other regulations made
for incouragement remitt the quitt rent for the first 3 years of all new
land to be taken and seated in Delaware which having proved
inconvenant by not taking up land and not seating att all, I do
therefore repeall and recall the same except for such as have seated
and improved upon said order, but all such as have taken up lands and
not seated and improved and made due return thereof as by law to
forfeit the same and the land not seated and improved to dispose of as
warrant lands .... This is a true copy of the governore order taken out
of Newcastle Court per EPH HARMAN clerk. (A2:pg 1&2)

1773 THOS ROBINSON, JNO RODNEY

3 Feb 1774. the return of 6 freeholders on the condemnation of lands
for the use of a mill at the instance of BENJAMIN BURTON esqr was
offered to the court for their acceptance and confirmation, whereupon
the said court after said return being read and heard, did accept and
confirm the same and ordered it to be filed and recorded. Attest: JNO
RUSSEL dep prothonotary. (A2pg: 5)

Commission from the Court of Common Pleas upon the petition of
JOHN MARTIN, RICHARD GREEN and SACKAR WYATT for the
marking and bounding a tr of land called White Meadow together with
the return plot thereof. (A2pg: 5)

14 Nov 1797. The State of DEL to JACOB HAZZARD, JOHN
COLLINS, CORNELIUS WILTBANK, THOMAS MARSH and
STEPHEN WARRINGTON gent, whereas JOHN MARTIN, RICHARD
GREEN and SACKAR WYATT of Suss Co pursuant to a petetion to
the Court of Common Pleas held at George Town 16 Nov 1797 setting
forth that they are seised of estates of a tr of land part in Lewes Hund
and part in Indian River Hund called White Meadow granted by patent
to ALEXANDER MOLLESTON and JOHN KIPSHAVEN for 1000 a.
the bounds whereof have and are in danger of decaying or becoming
obsolete and humbly praying the said court to appoint a commission to
mark the lines and establish the boundaries ... the court appoints you
to be commissioners for the purpose afsd .... (signed) RICHARD
BASSET esqr chief justice. Issued 10 Jan 1798 NATHL MITCHELL
prothonotary. (A2pg: 5&6)

6 Mar 1798. JACOB HAZZARD, JOHN COLLINS, CORNELIUS
WILTBANK, THOMAS MARSH and STEPHEN WARRINGTON do
hereby certify that we met at the house of JOHN LANK in Broadkiln
Hund on 25 Jan last past, after publick advertisement, we met on the
said land on 20 & 21 Feb and caused the lines of the said land to be
run in our presence by WILLIAM STAYTON by us appointed to
survey, we do settle adjust and determine the original location of the
said tr of land to be ... to plantation now in the possession of JOSIAH
HOPKINS, near s side of Coolspring Br, s side of road to Lewis and
between that road and the state road from George Town to Lewis, to
Dugans Swamp .... WILLIAM STAYTON surveyor and JOHN
MUSTARD and JAMES HUDSON chain carriers were solemnly sworn
on 21 Feb 1798 that they would execute their respective duties
faithfully and impartially according to the best of their skill before
JACOB HAZZARD. JACOB HAZZARD was solemnly sworn 6 Mar
1798 before GEO HAZZARD. [survey drawing shown]. At a court 26
Apr 1798 the commissioners did make their return which was read and
approved by the court. NATHL MITCHELL prothonotary. (A2pg: 6-8)

Commission from the Court of Common Pleas upon the
petetion of BENJAMIN BURTON for marking & boundering a
tr of land called Indian Tr together with the return plott
thereof. (A2pg: 9)

21 Apr 1802 at George Town. The State of DEL to JOSEPH HASLET,
JOHN COLLINS Senr, NATHL MITCHELL, KINDLE BATSON &
PAYNTER FRAME gent, whereas BENJAMIN BURTON of Suss Co
prefered a petition on 23 Apr 1802 setting forth that he is seized of an
estate of a tr of land in Dagsborough Hund called Indian Tr the bounds
of which are in danger of becoming absolute and unknown and humbly
praying the said court to appoint a commission to mark and establish
the lines and boundaries of the afsd tr ... the court has appointed you

to be commissioners for the purpose afsd ... . (signed) JAMES BOOTH
esqr chief justice. Issued 30 Aug 1802 NATHL MITCHELL proth.
JAMES BLAYIS surveyor and JOHN PHILLIPS & PURNEL
PHILLIPS chain carriers were solemnly swown that they could execute
their respective duties faithfull and inpartially according to the best of
their skill 1 Sep 1802 before EDW DINGLE. (A2pg: 9-11)

24 Nov 1802. NATHANIEL MITCHELL, KINDAL BATSON &
PAYNTER FRAME hereby certify we met at the house of WOOLSEY
BURTON in Dagsborough Hund 1 Sep 1802 after public advertisement
and caused the lines to be run by JAMES F. BAYLIS by us appointed
to survey the said land ... we do settle adjust and determine the
original location of Indian Tr renewed to be ... . [survey drawing
shown]. Return made 7 Nov 1802 NATHL MITCHELL proth. (A2pg:
11-13)

1 Sep 1802. Deposition. EDWARD DINGLE Junr deposeth and says
that sometime in 1794 he was called upon by JOB INGRAM, late decd,
to lay a land warrant on the land that formerly was granted to him by
a certain JOSHUA BURTON off a tr called Indian Land and that
accordingly he whent with the said JOB INGRAM to the beginning
bounder and was informed by the said JOB INGRAM that the said
beginning bounder of the said deed was a corner tree of the tr of land
called Indian Land a side of Askakison Br on an island between a
Quackerion House and the INGRAM's mills and the said DINGLE
layed the warrant for the same. (A2pg: 14)

1 Sep 1802. Deposition. JACOB BURTON showed a [page torn] pine
standing on the s side of the Askakison Br on an island which he says
the year 1796 he whent with WOLSEY BURTON and WM
B(UTCHER) in a surveyer to the said pine in order to begin to [page
torn] a warrant for BENJAMIN BURTON the said WOOLSEY's son,
at which time this deponant says he was informed by the said [page
torn] and the said BUTCHER that the above described pine was a
corner of the Indian Land. (A2pg: 15)

2 May 1803. NATHL MITCHELL esqr from motives of justice and
humanity hereby manumit and set free from me all the negroes that
have been born as my property, to wit a negro boy named HARRY to
be free on 1 May 1820, a negro girl named JENNEY to be free 1 May
1828 & a negro girl named CLARISSA to be free 1 May 1830. Wit:
THOMAS EVANS, PETER ROBINSON. Ackn: 2 May 1803 before
ISAAC COOPER judge. (A2pg: 15&16)

26 Feb 1805. To THOMAS COOPER, JAMES ANDERSON,
FRANCES BROWN, WILLIAM RUSSELL and SIMON KOLLOCK
esqrs of Suss Co, know you that reposing especial trust and confidence
in your knowledge, conduct and integrety, we impower you or either of
you to administer to all officers civil and military and to all other
persons the oaths of office and the oaths required to the US and the
Constitution of DEL ... . (signed) NATHANIEL MITCHELL governor
of DEL. By order of the governor PETER ROBINSON secretary of the

118

State of DEL. (A2pg: 16&17)

26 Jan 1805. Bond. PETER ROBINSON, JAMES ANDERSON and
GEORGE ROBINSON are firmly bound unto the State of DEL in the
sum of $4000, to wit PETER ROBINSON $2000, JAMES ANDERSON
and GEORGE ROBINSON $1000 ... the condition of this obligation is
such that the afsd PETER ROBINSON do well and faithfully and duly
discharge and perform the trust to him committed as Secretary of
DEL, then this obligation to be void otherwise to be and remain in
force of law. Wit: JOSEPH RUSSEL. I do approve of JAMES
ANDERSON and GEORGE ROBINSON securityes as above. NATHL
MITCHELL. (A2pg: 17)

25 Feb 1805. Deed. CANNON LANK for 146 pounds 10 shillings sold
unto GEORGE PRICE both of Suss Co all his right unto a tr of land
called Virginia and Calloways Invention that he recved by deed of sale
from JOHN TUZOL of VA in Little Cr Hund ... . Wit: ISAAC
COOPER, WM B COOPER. Ackn 8 Mar 1805. (A2pg: 18&19)

20 Jul 1804. Deed. JEHU (JEHEW) STOCKLEY of Broad Cr Hund
Suss Co husbandman for the purpose of indeminifying and keeping
harmless from the consequences of their becoming surities sold to
EDWARD SHORT Senr & WINGATE SHORT both of Dagsborough
Hund same co ... a tr of land, whereas EDWARD SHORT Senr and
WINGATE SHORT as suritys of the said JEHU STOCKLEY together
with the said JEHU STOCKLEY became bound to the State of DEL in
the penal sum of $436 on this date conditional for the payment of
$136.25 with interest ... . Wit: PETER ROBINSON, GEO ROBINSON.
Ackn 7 Feb 1805 before ISAAC COOPER judge. (A2pg: 19-21)

22 Jun 1804. Deed. ISAAC COOPER of Suss Co for $16 sold to
JARRED (JARED) WILEY of same place ... a parcel of land beginning
at the second line of the deed of conveyance from the afsd ISAAC
COOPER to the afsd JARRED WILEY dated 14 Nov 1799 ... . Wit:
JACKSON GORDY, STEPHEN PUSEY, WILLIAM B COOPER. Ackn
8 Nov 1804 before HENSEY JOHNS chief justice. (A2pg: 21&22)

25 Feb 1805. Deed. WILLIAM TOWNSEND, THOMAS TOWNSEND,
THOMAS SKINNER and ELLEANOR his wife, JOHN TOWNSEND
and SALLEY his wife heirs of BARKLEY TOWNSEND of Little Cr
Hund late decd for 140 pounds sold to NANCY TOWNSEND and
BETSEY BAYLEY TOWNSEND heirs of WILLIAM TOWNSEND late
of Laurell Town decd ... 1 lott of ground in Laurell Town on Front and
Wheal Streets ... provided that BETSEY BRITTINGHAM late
BETSEY TOWNSEND widow of the said WILLIAM TOWNSEND may
possess the lott during the term of her natural life and to hold the lot
of ground unto NANCY TOWNSEND and BETSEY B. TOWNSEND as
tenants in common. Wit: JOHN POLK, ISAAC COOPER. Ackn 25 Feb
1805 before ISAAC COOPER esqr. (A2pg: 22&23)

18 Jun 1804. Quit Claim. ZEBEDEE JAMES and SOPHIA his wife of
Little Cr Hund Suss Co for $90 quit claim unto JOHN MORRIS of

same place ... all their right unto 1 undivided 1/8 pt/o of the saw mill near the mouth of Bold Cypress Br in Little Cr Hund called Treshams Mill together with 1/4 pt/o the pond ... . Wit: NELLY HALL, JOS COPES. Ackn 15 Mar 1805 before ISAAC COOPER judge. (A2pg: 24&25)

18 Mar 1805. Deed. WILLIAM WRIGHT and CHARLOTTEE his wife of Suss Co for $265 sold to MARVEL KNOWLS of same place ... a parcel of ground called Callaways Venture which my wife CHARLOTTEE fell heir to by the death of her father in Little Cr Hund adj land called Puzzle Wit ... 61 1/2 a. Wit: ISAAC COOPER, WILLIAM SKILLEY. Ackn 18 Mar 1805 before ISAAC COOPER judge. (A2pg: 25-27)

1 Mar 1805. Deed. THOMAS MOORE and CHARLES WALSTON of Suss Co for $100 sold to OBADIAH HASTINGS (HASTON) of same co ... a tr of land called Moores Previledge in Little Cr Hund n side of HASTING's own land ... 15 a. Wit: ISAAC COOPER, JNO POLK. Ackn 1 Mar 1805 before ISAAC COOPER judge. (A2pg: 27&28)

14 Jun 1804. Deed. HENRY FIELDER and wife CHESIRE (CHESIARE) (KESIER) of Suss Co for $40 sold to JESSE PASWATERS of same co ... a parcel of land in Nanticoke Hund adj land belonging to SMART HARDY and ELI LYNCH, land called Fork Road Tr it being the land that SOLOMON WILLIAMS live on taken up by JACOB COVERDALE and secured by him for WILLIAMS ares and HENRY FIELDER marrying CHESAIRE BELOME an are with hur for 1/6 of the land 70 or 80 a. Wit: WILLIAM PASWATERS, JOHN MCCOLLISTER. Ackn 17 Jul 1804 before NICHOLAS RIDGLY chancillor. CHESIRE declared she signed deed willingly. (A2pg: 29&30)

23 Jul 1804. Assignment. JESSE PASWATERS (PASSWATERS) assign over all my right of the [above] deed unto SMART HARDY ... SMART HARDY clear him of all damages in the penalty of $500. Wit: JOHN PASSWATERS. (A2pg: 30)

17 Mar 1803. Deed. THOMAS JOINS and BRIDGET his wife, HENRY FIELDER and KESIER his wife, OWEN ODAY and ELIZABETH his wife all of Suss Co sold to SMART HARDY of same co ... a tr of land in Nanticoke Hund e side of Gravelly Br adjacent to land belonging to the afsd HARDY, ELI LINCH, SAMUEL LAVERTY and others taken up and surveyed for a certain SOLOMON WILLIAMS by virtue of a warrant dated 29 Nov 1793 73 1/2 a. called His Right it being a tr of land whereof the said SOLOMON WILLIAMS late of said co died seized and not leaving a written will the said BRIDGET JOINS, KESIER FIELDER and ELIZABETH ODAY being heirs of the afsd SOLOMON WILLIAMS for 41 pounds sell 1/2 the afsd tr, their part, unto SMART HARDY. Wit: JOHN COLLINS Junr, HENRY H. TRAVERN. Ackn 17 Mar 1803 before ISAAC COOPER judge. (A2pg: 31&32)

16 Feb 1805. Deed. THOMAS MOORE of Suss Co for 835 pounds sold

to CHARLES WALSTON of same co ... several trs of land in Little Cr
Hund, the one tr called Moores Previledge and one tr called Moores
Previledge Enlarged adj 303 a. and another tr called Liberty Field 60 a.
near the saw mill of MOORE and WRIDER, also one tr called Moores
Liberty near Liberty Field also 1/2 of the saw mill and grist mill on
Tusaka Br .... Wit: LEVIN LANK, THOS RIDER. Ackn 1 Mar 1805
before ISAAC COOPER judge. (A2pg: 32-34)

14 Mar 1805. Deed. WILLIAM RICKARDS and ABIGAIL his wife and
WILLIAM LOFLAND shoemaker and SARAH his wife of Suss Co for
50 pounds sold to NEHEMIAH BENNETT shoemaker ... their pt/o a
parcel of land in Slaughter Neck s side of Ceedar Cr and ne side of
Milners Br 38 a. 11 perches it being their pt/o a large tr devised to
them by AARON OLIVER decd whos land adj WILLIAM HICKMAN's
land 76 a. 22 perches. Wit: SMITH FARCIT, JOSEPH ARGO. Ackn 19
Mar 1805 before KENSEY JOHNS esqr chief justice. (A2pg: 34-37)

4 Jan 1804. Deed. WILLIAM JONES of Somerset Co MD for $75 sold
to JOSEPH S. COLLINS of Suss Co ... 1 undivided 1/3 pt/o a tr of land
in Broad Cr Hund in Parsons Neck adj land late of JONATHAN
BOYCE decd being originally granted unto a certain Revd
ALEXANDER ADAMS from MD called Barrow Field from whom it
descended to LEAH JONES lately LEAH ADAMS the mother of the
afsd WILLIAM JONES. Wit: JAMES CANNON, THOMAS
ELLYGOOD. Ackn 6 Jan 1804 before ISAAC COOPER judge. (A2pg:
37&38)

20 Nov 1803 at Dorchester Co. CLEMENT BROWN, JAMES BROWN,
JOSEPH S. COLLINS, DANIEL BROWN and PEGGY BROWN did on
26 Jul 1803 mutily appoint CHARLES ADAMS of co afsd to divide the
land that CHARLES BROWN late of Dorchester Co died possest with
and on same day did enter into a bond with the penalty of 500 pounds
binding themselves to stand and abide by the division to be made ...
the land being part in Dorchester Co part in Caroline Co MD and part
in Suss Co, CHARLES ADAMS do certify that the land was carefully
surveyed by MATTHEW SMITH of Dorchester Co MD and JOSEPH
VICKERS of Suss Co, and have divided them in the form as follows,
first for CLEMENT BROWN and MARY his wife all that tr called Iron
Mind Neck 108 a. and also pt/o a tr called Shoolership Improved and
pt/o a tr called Crooked Ridge ... 57 a. ... laid out for JAMES BROWN
pt/o a tr called Laytons Chance pt/o a tr called Scholarship Improved
and pt/o a tr called Crooked Ridge adj Duns Purch, also 1 tr called
Venture Running 171 a. ... I lay out for DANIEL BROWN a tr adj
where FRANCIS BROWN now lives and where JOHN GRAYHAM now
lives and the tr called Smiths Adventure, a tr called What You Please,
land called Batchelors Quarters & land called Hickory Ridge ... 162 a.,
lay out for JOSEPH S. COLLINS and REBECCA his wife a lot adj
land called Addition to Hazzard, land called Browns Chance & land
called Hopkins Lott ... 140 3/4 a. also a small a parcel adj land called
Hazzard ... 2 1/2 a., lay out for PEGGY BROWN adj land called Lister
... 162 3/4 a. A true copy taken from the land record books of
Dorchester Co MD. Attest: 8 Mar 1805 H DICKINSON. (A2pg: 38-44)

21 Mar 1805. Deed. WILLIAM RODNEY Junr of Dagsborough Hund
Suss Co and MARY his wife for $560 sold to ROBERT PRITTYMAN
(of THOS) of same place ... all thos trs and pts/o trs of land in
Dagsborough Hund adj the lands of the afsd ROBERT PRITTYMAN,
AARON MARVEL, ADAM MARVEL & others, called What You
Please, Rodneys Lot, Liberty and Caution and pt/o a tr called Division
which is not sold to ARON MARVEL afsd. Wit: FRANCIS BROWN,
HENRY EVANS. Ackn 23 Mar 1805 before HENSEY JOHNS chief
justice. (A2pg: 44&45)

21 Mar 1805. Deed. WILLIAM MORGAN and TAMMEY his wife of
Suss Co for $165 sold to JESSE GREEN of same place esqr ... several
trs of land, whereas a writ dated 19 Nov 1803 directed sherriff
GEORGE ROBINSON esqr to seize in execution 2 trs of land of
THOMAS SMITH in the possession of RACHEL SMITH and HENRY
SMITH executors of THOMAS SMITH late of said co decd for a debt
of 89 pounds 7 pence 1/2 penny which HENRY SMITH & SIDNEY
BOWNESS late SIDNEY LOWERY executors of JAMES LOWERY
decd lately in our Court of Common Pleas has recovered against them
and $20.69 damages ... in Broad Cr Hund called Smiths Contrivance
and Smiths Venture in the whole 150 a. ... sold and conveyed same to
WILLIAM MORGAN joiner for $151 (Lib Z No 24 fol 314). Wit: ISAAC
COOPER, POLLY MESSICK. Ackn 21 Mar 1805 before ISAAC
COOPER judge. (A2pg: 45-47)

12 Mar 1805. Deed. PHILIP MARVEL the elder of Nanticoke Hund
Suss Co and BETSEY his wife for $360 sold to WARREN
PRETTYMAN of same co farmer ... a tr of land in Dagsborough Hund
50 a. originally granted by patent from the proprietary of MD bearing
date 2 Jul 1754 unto a certain JOHN BEVINS called Bevens Peace
also all the land granted by DEL bearing date 12 Oct 1797 unto the
afsd PHILIP MARVEL called Marvels Luck 145 a. 84 sq perches, s side
of road from Indian River to Deep Cr and w side of ZACKIRIAH
JONES resurvey and e side of land called Bevens Peace to bounder
lately made by ROWLAND BEVENS, to lands of WILLIAM RODNEY
Senr ... surveyed 20 Nov 1793 by JESSE SAUNDERS for RHEAD
SHANKLAND esqr surveyor of Suss in pursuance of a warrant dated
18 Oct year afsd granted to THOMAS MARVEL (son of ROBERT)
who by his will devised the same to PHILIP MARVEL party to these
presents. Wit: JOSIAH MARVEL, THOMAS PRETTYMAN. Ackn 6
Mar 1805 before ISAAC COOPER judge. (A2pg: 48-50)

9 Mar 1805. Deed. ABRAHAM HARGESS (HARGIS) and ELIZABETH
his wife for $710 sold to THOMAS RODNEY all of Suss Co ... a tr of
land in Pilot Town on Lewes Cr pt/o a larger tr which THOMAS
EVANS esqr high sheriff of Suss Co sold as the property of JACOB
KOLLOCK decd and conveyed by deed pole unto RICHARD BASSETT
esqr (Lib O N14 fol 328) and in a deed from WILLIAM COLEMAN
and wife (Lib H N7 fol 245) the title is particularly recited and by the
said RICHARD BASSETT and ELIZABETH his wife conveyed unto
ABRAHAM HARGESS party to these presents, beginning at JOHN
SMITH's land, to ARMWELL LONG's land, to DANIEL CLIFTON's

122

line, to JOHN SMITH's land ... 35 1/2 a. Wit: DANL RODNEY, MARY
BEELE. Ackn 9 Mar 1805 before DANL RODNEY judge. (A2pg: 50-52)

8 Sep 1804. Deed. THOMAS ROWLAND Senr of Pilot Town Suss Co
pilot and HANNAH his wife for $87 sold to COOK CLAMPET pilot ...
a lott of land which DAVID JOHNSON lately purch of THOMAS
EDDONFIELD and wife on the bank of Lewes Cr beginning at DAVID
JOHNSON's lott along Pilot Town Road to SAML EDWARDS decd
lott, to other land of THOMAS ROWLAND. Wit: SARAH RODNEY,
SARAH F. TREGLOHAN, DANL RODNEY. Ackn 10 Sep 1804 before
DANL RODNEY judge. (A2pg: 52&53)

14 Mar 1805. Deed. COOK CLAMPET (CLAMPITT) of Lewes pilot
and POLLEY his wife for $87 sold to DAVID JOHNSON of same place
pilot ... a lott of land [same as above]. Wit: DANL RODNEY, SARAH
RODNEY, WM MARSHEY. Ackn 14 Mar 1805 before DANL RODNEY
judge. (A2pg: 53&54)

16 Mar 1805. By advertisement 8 Mar 1805 giving notice to the
congregation of St. Matthews Episcopal Church in Cedar Cr Hund met
at the church to elect trustees ... nominate to wit, BETHUEL
WATTSON, ISAAC WATTSON, RATLIFF POINTER, NATHANIEL
POINTER, WILLIAM DAVIS, JOHN BENNETT and LAWRENCE
RILEY to be trustees. Wit: JOHN ROBINSON Junr, JOHN
TOWNSEND, TILMAN GRAY. (A2pg: 54&55)

17 Jun 1803. Deed. JAMES DONAVAN and MARY his wife of
Broadkiln Hund Suss Co for $175 sold to BAKER DUTTON of same
place ... a tr of land formerly the property of FOSTER DONAVAN
father of the said JAMES DONAVAN which after the death of the said
FOSTER DONAVAN of Broadkiln Hund his landed estate being
divided, the said JAMES inherited 98 1/2 a. adj the lands of JOB
DONOVAN, WILLIAM DONAVAN, FOSTER DONAVAN, AVERY
CORNWELL, JAMES REDDEN, JACOB DONOVAN, ABRAHAM
DONOVAN & JAMES REED. Wit: LAURENCE RILEY Senr,
ABRAHAM DONOVAN. Ackn 18 Jul 1804 before DANL RODNEY
judge. (A2pg: 55-57)

9 Aug 1804. Deed. NUTTER LOFLAND and MARY his wife of Suss Co
for 137 pounds sold to DANIEL GODWIN of same place ... a tr of land
in Slaughter Neck Ceedar Cr Hund pt/o a larger tr taken up by a
certain DAVID SMITH of co afsd by a patent called Lebinon and the
said DAVID SMITH by his will devised the said tr to his 3 grandsons
JOHN SMITH, DAVID SMITH and JOHN HICKMAN and this being a
pt/o JOHN HICKMAN's divident after sundry transferences became
the property of the said NUTTER LOFLAND and by his aleination
bond bearing date 20 Nov 1800 sold the same to a certain WILLIAM
DRYDON Senr and he by his assignment bearing date 14 Feb 1804
sold his right to the land unto the afsd DANIEL GODWIN beginning at
LEMUEL WILLIAMS land ... 60 1/4 a. Wit: DANL RODNEY,
RACHEL MOORE. Ackn 9 Aug 1804 before DANL RODNEY judge.
(A2pg: 57-59)

18 Jul 1804. Deed. NEHEMIAH CAREY of Suss Co yeoman in obedience with a decree for 500 pounds sold to DENNIS MORRIS of same co ... a tr of land, whereas by a decree by the honorable NICHOLAS RIDGLY esqr chancellor of DEL passed 27 Jul 1802 DENNIS MORRIS was complainant and the said NEHEMIAH CAREY defendent, it is ordered that the said NEHEMIAH CAREY on or before 1 Sep next shall assure to the said DENNIS MORRIS a good and sufficient deed of a tr of land mentioned in the bill of complaint, on Herring Br formerly taken up by one JAMES EATON esqr called Richland and that 500 pounds be the consideration. Wit: DAVID ROBBINS, ISAAC WILSON. Ackn 18 Jul 1804 before DANL RODNEY judge. (A2pg: 59-61)

1 Mar 1805. Deed. WHITE B. SMITH and his wife ARAIT of Suss Co for $1000 sold to ISAAC FISHER of same co ... a parcel of land that was laid off to WHITE B. SMITH and his wife by an order from the Orphans Court out of the lands of HUMPHRIESS BROWN decd late of Suss Co beginning at Thomas's Lott and Browns Manner to JOHN HINSON's line, to Cypress Swamp, to line of Sharps Chance, to Walters Lot, to Shanklands Descovery ... 165 a. Wit: ISAAC COOPER, JESSE FISHER. Ackn 1 Mar 1805 before ISAAC COOPER judge. (A2pg: 61-64)

3 Dec 1802. Deed. GARRET LOOKUS of Kent Co cordwainer and MARGARET (MARGIT) his wife for 40 pounds sold to MARGARET WILLEY of Monongohalia Co VA widow ... all their right in 2 trs of land, whereas ABSALOM WILLEY of Suss Co was formerly seized of certain lands and being so seized departed this life intestate leaving sundry issue to whom the said lands descended, 2 trs one called Beaverdam Neck and the other Croneys Folly whereof the said MARGARET LOOKUS, the present w/o said GARRFET LOOKUS as dau and heriess to the said ABSALOM WILLEY decd, became intitled to 1/11 pt/o the intestate lands. Wit: JOHN LEWES, JAMES JOHNSON. Ackn 17 May 1804 before RICHARD COOPER justice. (A2pg: 64&65)

17 May 1804 Receipt. GARRET LEWES received of MARGARETT WILLEY by the hand of JAMES JOHNSON 40 pounds with interest it being the full purch money for the [above] land. Wit: JOHN EATON. (A2pg: 66)

20 Mar 1805. Writ of Execution. By writ dated 20 Apr 1802 KENDAL BATSON high shirriff of Suss Co seized in execution a tr of land of JAMES POLK decd in the possession of DAVID POLK adminr in Nanticoke Hund called Polks Conclusion 200 a. for a certain debt and damages and sold same at publick vendue to JOHN CLARKE esqr state treasurer for $500 he being the highest bidder ... KENDAL BATSON conveys the land unto JOHN CLARKE. Wit: JOHN ROBINSON, WM TATMAN. Ackn 20 Mar 1805 before JNO RUSSEL clerk. (A2pg: 66-68)

20 Mar 1805. Deed. JOHN CLARKE state treasurer esqr of Kent Co

for $500 sold to WILLIAM GRAYHAM of Suss Co ... [same as above].
Wit: JOHN ROBINSON, WM TATMAN. Ackn 20 Mar 1805. (A2pg: 68&69)

21 Mar 1805. Deed of Mortgage. LAZARUS (LARARUS) TURNER of
Suss Co for 300 pounds sold to WILLIAM PEERY (son of JOHN) of
New Castle ... a tr of land being the same land which the said
LAZARUS purch of a certain JOHN PEERY of New Castle ... if the
said LAZARUS truly pay to the said WILLIAM PEERY 300 pounds
with interest, 37 pounds 10 shillings before 21 Sep next ensuing and
262 pounds 10 shillings the residue in full with interest before 21 Mar
1807 then this indenture shall be utterly null and void. Wit: THO
COULLER, WM RUSSEL. Ackn 21 Mar 1805 before JOHN RUSSEL
clerk. (A2pg: 69-71)

21 Mar 1805. Deed. JOHN PEERY of New Castle Co for 600 pounds
sold to LAZALRUS TURNER of same co ... all his right in the lands
which descended to him by the death of his brother WILLIAM PEERY
which was laid off to MARGARET PEERY widow of WILLIAM for her
dower ... . Wit: THO COULTER, WM RUSSEL. Ackn 21 Mar 1805
before JNO RUSSEL clerk. (A2pg: 71&72)

20 Apr 1790. Power of Atty. JOHN STEPHEN HILL of Suss Co
appoint my trusty friend BENJAMIN HOLLAND of same co my atty
to ask and demand, sue for, levy, recover and receive all such sums of
money as are contained in a list of unsettled accounts due me ... . Wit:
WILLIAM RICKARDS, JAMES WHARTON. Proved 20 Mar 1805
before JNO RUSSEL clerk. (A2pg: 72-74)

30 Jan 1805. Deed. ISAAC BEACHAMP esqr and MARY his wife of
Suss Co for 305 pounds 2 shillings 3 pence sold to WILLIAM DAVIS of
same place carpenter ... a tr of land in Ceder Cr Hund that the said
WILLIAM DAVIS now liveth on it being 1/2 of a tr I purch of PHEBE
VINING of the Borough of Wilmington beginning at JOHN DEPUTY's
land lately WM HINDS land, to ROBERT HILL's land, to Ceder Town
Tr ... 137 a. 118 sq perches surveyed 23 Jan 1794 by JAMES
JOHNSON pt/o a tr called Ceder Town and pt/o a tr called Coverdill
which BENJAMIN WYNCOOP and SARAH his wife by indenture
dated 11 Sept 1790 (Book O No 14 pg 322) conveyed to PHEBE
VINING and the said PHEBE VINING by indenture dated 12 Aug
1791 (Book W No 21 pg 763) conveyed to the said ISAAC BEACHAMP
... ISAAC BEACHAMP and MARY his wife appoint WILLIAM
RUSSEL and WILLIAM HAZZARD of George Town co afsd to ackn
this deed in open court. Wit: ROBERT HILL, JOHN DEPUTY. 19 Mar
1805 ROBERT HILL made oath that he saw ISAAC BEACHAMP esqr
decd and MARY his wife sign seal as their act and deed the within
deed. Ackn 10 Apr 1805 before JNO RUSSEL clerk. (A2pg: 74-77)

13 Apr 1805. Deed GEORGE PARKER of Lewes Suss Co merchant
and HANNAH his wife whose maiden name is HANNAH PAYNTER
for 5 shillings sold to JOHN PARKER of same place yeoman ... all
those lotts of ground in the town of Lewes which the said HANNAH

received from her father by inheritance gift on Second, Third & Fourth Streets between Market and South Streets. Wit: DANL RODNEY, JOSEPH MILBY. Ackn 13 Apr 1805. (A2pg: 77&78)

13 Apr 1805. Deed. JOHN PARKER of the town of Lewes Suss Co yeoman for 5 shillings sold to GEORGE PARKER of same place merchant ... [same as above]. Wit: DANL RODNEY, JOSEPH MILBY. Ackn 13 Apr 1805. (A2pg: 78&79)

19 Apr 1805. Deed. THOMAS RUST and ANN his wife of Indian River Hund Suss Co for $447 sold to WILLIAM HARRIS of same place yeoman ... the residue of a tr of land in the hund afsd called Laws Tr that the said ANN inherited from her father SOLOMON STOCKLY near Braceys Br beginning at the land the said WILLIAM HARRIS purch of PETER PARKER to land of WILLIAM HOPKINS on Chappel Road ... 139 1/2 a. Wit: DANL RODNEY, JOSEPH MILBY. Ackn 19 Apr 1805. (A2pg: 80&81)

18 Apr 1805. Quit Claim. THOMAS RUST of Suss Co farmer and ANN his wife for 50 pounds quit claim unto WILLIAM HOPKINS of same co planter ... a parcel of land pt/o a tr granted to RICHD LAWES n side of Braceys Br or Lawses Pond n side of Chappel Road in the line of JOHN MCILVAIN's land ... 20 a. Wit: BAILEY WEST, ABSALOM RUST. Ackn 19 Apr 1805 before DANIEL RODNEY judge. (A2pg: 81-83)

19 Apr 1805. Deed. Revd JAMES P. WILSON of Suss Co and MARY his wife for 150 pounds and also 5 shillings sold to FREDRICK ROE of same place ... a parcel of land between Indian River & Geo Town Road 2 miles from Lewes beginning at land formerly laid off to Col. HALL & PETER HALL to CALEB RODNEY's land, toward Quaker Town ... 32. a. ... 3/4's of the land the said JAMES purch of the heirs of DAVID HALL Senr and the other part was the maiden property of the said MARY [see #1916]. Wit: DANL RODNEY, NANCY RECARDS. Ackn 19 Apr 1805. (A2pg: 83-85)

18 Apr 1805. Deed. JOSEPH MILBY of Suss Co for $562.50 sold to ABSALOM RUST of same place ... 1/2 pt/o a 225 a. tr of land conveyed from a certain WILLIAM WELCH to LEVIN MILBY father to the afsd JOSEPH MILBY ... 112 1/2 a. in Indian River Hund. Wit: DANL RODNEY, W HARRIS. Ackn 19 Apr 1805. (A2pg: 85-87)

22 Nov 1803. Deed. WILLIAM DICKERSON of Suss Co house carpenter for 53 pounds sold to JONATHAN CALHOON of same place yeoman ... a tr of land in Broadkiln Hund on Long Bridge Br being the intestate land of EDMOND DICKERSON late decd, beginning at EDMOND DICKERSON's land, to land of JOHN PETTYJOHN ... 53 a. Wit: WM HAZZARD, THOS L. CALHOON. Ackn 24 Nov 1803 before DANL RODNEY judge. (A2pg: 87-89)

22 Apr 1805. Deed. WILLIAM DANIELS & wife ZIPORAH (ZIPOIAH) of Suss Co yeoman for $383 sold to PURNELL (PURNEL) TATMAN

of same place yeoman ... a tr of land pt/o a larger tr in Nanticoke Hund called Turkey Swamp surveyed by virtue of a warrant bearing date at Phila [blank] and by her sold to a certain NATHANIEL HAYS and by several trammutations became the property of the said WILLIAM DANIELS and wife ZIPORAH ... 127 a. 20 perches. Wit: JOSEPH TRUITT Junr, ZADOC RICKARDS. Ackn 22 Apr 1805 before ANDREW BARRETT judge. (A2pg: 89-91)

18 Apr 1805. Deed. JOSEPH MILBY of Suss Co for $562.50 sold to THOMAS RUST and his wife ANN of same place ... 1/2 pt/o a 225 a. tr of land conveyed from a certain WILLIAM WELCH to LEVIN MILBY father to the afsd JOSEPH MILBY ... 112 1/2 a. in Indian River Hund. Wit: DANL RODNEY, W HARRIS. Ackn 19 Apr 1805. (A2pg: 91-93)

25 Nov 1804. Deed. COMFORT MORRIS of Suss Co for 100 pounds sold to NEHEMIAH HAND of same co ... a tr of land in Broadkiln Hund pt/o a larger tr formerly the property of JOSEPH MORRIS surveyed by LAWRENCE RILEY 19 Nov 1802 ... 52 a. 12 perches. Wit: NATHAN READ, JOHN REILEY. Ackn 25 Apr 1805 before DANL RODNEY judge. (A2pg: 93&94)

25 Apr 1805. Deed. MICAJAH TURNER and HANNAH his wife of Suss Co for 65 pounds sold to WILLIAM WAPLES Junr of same co ... 1/4 pt/o a tr of land in Baltimore Hund pt/o a tr called Diggs Point 57 a., also 1/4 pt/o another tr in same hund adj afsd land and pt/o Diggs Point 37 a., also 1/4 pt/o 12 a. in same hund called Seder Neck, also 1/4 pt/o 7 a. in same hund in Muddy Neck. Wit: ARMWELL LONG, ISAAC TUNNELL. Ackn 25 Apr 1805 before DANL RODNEY judge. (A2pg: 95&96)

23 Jan 1802. Deed. PARKER NICHOLDSON of Kent Co for 140 pounds sold to JACKSON ROGERS of Suss Co ... pt/o 2 trs of land one called Dumfries and the other called Brotherhood on sea board side on Assawamon Bay called Rumbley Marsh 175 a. it being the said PARKER NICKOLDSON's great grandmother TABITHA PARKER's maiden land. Wit: DANIEL ROGERS, GEORGE WALLER. Ackn 23 Jan 1802 before HENSEY JOHNS esqr chief justice. (A2pg: 96-98)

24 Apr 1805. Deed. JOHN ROBINSON farmer of Suss Co and BETSEY his wife for $372 sold to LEVIN TODD of same co yeoman ... pt/o 2 trs of land in Northwest Fork Hund one called Hog Range and the other called Wildgoose Chase that JOHN ROBINSON became seized in on 30 Dec 1798 (Lib X No 22 fol 249) ... beginning near WILLIAM ROSS's dwelling plantation and EBENEZAR LEDENUM's land, to FRANCES WRIGHT's land ... 124 a. Wit: WATTSON PEPPER, THO LAWS. Ackn 24 Apr 1805 before DANL RODNEY judge. (A2pg: 98-100)

5 Jun 1804. Deed. THOMAS HART Senr of Suss Co for 49 pounds sold to THOMAS L. CALHOON of same co ... w pt/o a tr of land in Broadkiln Hund pt/o a larger tr called Parmocas Struggle adj RICHARD HART's old place, CHASE's land, to ELISHA JOSEPH's

127

fence, to Waples Swamp ... 50 a. Wit: THOMAS HART Junr,
JONATHAN CAHOON Senr. Ackn 26 Apr 1805 before JAMES
BOOTH chief justice. (A2pg: 100-103)

19 Apr 1805. Deed of Mortgage. FREDRICK ROE of Suss Co and
ELIZABETH his wife for 150 pounds which Revd JAMES P. WILSON
hath released to them being the purch money due him from them for
certain lands & also 5 shillings sold to JAMES P. WILSON a parcel of
land [same as #1906] ... if the said FREDERICK ROE shall pay unto
the said JAMES P. WILSON the sum of 150 pounds with interest
before 2 years then this deed to be of no effect & the land & premises
to remain the inheritance & right of the said FREDRICK ROE &
ELIZA ROE. Wit: DANL RODNEY, JOHN ROGERS. Ackn 19 Apr
1805. (A2pg: 103&104)

12 Mar 1805. Deed. SHADRACK POSTLES of Cedar Cr Hund Suss Co
yeoman and ANASTASIA (ANNASTACIA) his wife in discharge of
their alienation bond and 600 pounds sold to DAVID SMITH of same
place yeoman ... a tr of land, whereas a certain THOMAS POSTLES
late of said co decd did in his lifetime obtain a warrant bearing date 1
Mar 1742 for 300 a. of land, 1/2 of the land the said THOMAS
POSTLES son JOHN POSTLES conveyed to the said SHADRACK
POSTLES 7 May 1788 (Lib N No 13 fol 501) and SHADRACK
POSTLES obtained a patent on the land 190 a. called Talberts Plott
dated 7 Dec 1796 (Lib T No 19 fol 283), also one other tr adj the
former called Security patent to the said SHADRACK POSTLES
bearing equal date and same book surveyed 20 Mar 1794 by order of
RHOADS SHANKLAND surveyor of Suss Co in pursuance of a
warrant bearing date 19 Mar 1794, together the trs begin at Mannor of
Warminghurst to Browns Choice, to land now of THOMAS POSTLES,
to Townsend Road and SOLOMON DEPUTY's land, to JOSEPH
HUDSON's land ... 254 a. 115 sq perches, 40 a. which lyes within the
lines of Browns Choice is reserved and excepted. Wit: GOVE CASE,
GEORGE BARRATT. Ackn 12 Mar 1805. (A2pg: 104-108)

-- Apr 1805. Deed. ELISHA JOSEPH of Suss Co yeoman for 60 pounds
sold to STEPHEN BLIZZARD of same place ... a parcell of land in
Indian River Hund pt/o a larger tr surveyed and laid out to BENJA
STOCKLEY ... 25 a. Wit: RHOAD SHANKLAND, JAMES
ANDERSON. Ackn 30 Apr 1805 before DANL RODNER judge. (A2pg:
108-110)

1 May 1805 at George Town. Appointment. To JAMES F. BAYLIS of
Suss Co esqr, know you that reposing special trust and confidence in
your integrity and ability we appoint you and by the authority of the
governor of DEL NATHL MITCHELL to be escheator of Suss Co ... .
PETER ROBINSON secretary of DEL. 2 May 1805 By virtue of a
commission I do hereby certyify that the oath of office was taken by
JAMES F. BAYLIS. Attest: FRANCIS BROWN. (A2pg: 110)

20 Jun 1801. WOOLSEY BURTON guardian of AZARIAH
BROOKFIELD a miner, grandson of URIAH BROOKFIELD late of

128

Suss Co decd, and URIAH THOMAS of lawful age likewise a grandson of the said URIAH decd, by virtue of the power given them by the will of said URIAH decd bearing date 15 Dec 1788 appoint JAMES F. BAYLIS, MILLER THOROUGHGOOD and ISAAC WAPLES freeholders of said co, to lay off and divide the lands of the said testator agreeably to the true intent, sperit and meaning of his will. Attest: JACOB HAZZARD justice. (A2pg: 111)

26 Nov 1801. JAMES F. BAYLIS, MILLER THOUGROUGHGOOD and ISAAC WAPLES in pursuance of the authority given us [see above] having gone upon and viewed the lands and premises, divide the said lands, all that pt/o the said testators Cypress Swamp in Dagsborough Hund ... 86 a. 23 perches, all that tr in Indian River Hund ... 74 a. 120 perches to AZARIAH BROOKFIELD and 113 a. 137 perches and ... 252 a. 59 perches to URIAH THOMAS. [drawing shown] (A2pg: 112-114)

21 Nov 1804 at Jessamine Co KY. Quit Claim. JONATHAN V. WOODGATE of Jessemine Co KY and NANCY his wife for 100 pounds quit claim unto ROBERT GRIFFITH of Scott Co KY ... all the estate both real and personal which I am entitled to by the will of my father and mother late of Suss Co now decd or in case they died without will my proportion which I am entitled to of their estate as one of their joint heirs, 150 a. called the Balance of Venture, 136 1/4 a. Flowers Chance, 125 1/2 a. Hickory Ridge, 143 a. Bounds Lot and Danl Security, 330 a. Addition, 50 a. Tidles Venture, 5 a. bought of JOSEPH BOYCE Senr, which I am entitled to by the will of my uncle EDWARD VAUGHAN late of same co now decd in the hands of THOMAS LAWS my uncle and late guardian. Ackn 21 Nov 1804 before SAML H. WOODSON clerk. (A2pg: 115&116)

18 Dec 1804 at Jessamine Co KY. JOHN METCALF chief justice of the peace hereby certify that SAML H. WOODSON is clerk and that his certificate [above] is in due form. (A2pg: 116)

6 May 1805. Deed. JOSEPH MORRIS late of Suss Co now of Kent Co for 50 pounds sold to SOLOMON MORRIS of Kent Co ... a tr of land s side of Pembertons Br in Broadkiln Hund which said land by warrant bearing date at Phila 7 Jun 1737 granted unto a certain JOHN HALL and JOHN READ which land being divided between them, the said JOHN READ did convey his share unto a certain JOHN CLOTHERS 150 a. and JOHN CLOTHERS did by his letter of atty to LAWRENCE RILEY impower him to ackn a deed on 7 Aug 1770 unto a certain JOSEPH MORRIS, and JOSEPH MORRIS on 3 Nov 1789 conveyed the afsd land unto the afsd JOSEPH MORRIS party to this indenture ... adj ROBERT CALE's land and land formerly laid out for PETER LUCUS now in possession of WILLIAM MILTON ... 150 a. Wit: SUSANNA WELLS, GEORGE CUMMINS. Ackn 8 May 1805 before DANL RODNEY judge. (A2pg: 117-119)

INDEX

BRERETON, William, 99
BREWEN, Jacob, 91
BRICE, John, 76; Rebecah, 76
BRIDGE, John, 8
BRIGHT, Charles, 20, 106, 107
BRIGS, John, 8, 10, 11; Mary,
10
BRINCKLOE, ---, 11; John, 6
BRINKLOE, John, 11
BRITTINGHAM, Betsey, 118
BROOKFIELD, Azariah, 127, 128;
Uriah, 127
BROOKS, James, 105; Joseph, 105
BROTHERER, Joseph, 41
Brotherhood, 126
Brothers Adventure, 55
Brothers Adventure, 55
Brothers Portion, 1
BROWN, Betsey, 71, 72; Charles,
120; Clement, 120; Curtis,
67; Daniel, 8, 9, 14, 15,
120; Edward, 56; Ezekiel, 42;
Frances, 117; Francis, 92,
120, 121, 127; Humphress, 32;
Humphries, 56; Humphriess,
123; Humphriss, 108; Israel,
50; James, 43, 56, 120; John,
71, 72; Mary, 71, 72, 120;
Peggy, 120; Rebecca, 103;
Theophilus, 95; Thomas, 102;
White, 32, 56; William, 71,
103
Browns Inclosure, 109
Browns Chance, 120
BRUEN, Jacob, 91; John, 91
BUCHANAN, James, 109
BUCHER, William, 76
BULL, Manaen, 63
BUNDICK, Richard, 16, 33, 34;
Suanna, 33
BUNDOCK, Richard, 33; Suanna,
33
BUNDUCK, Richard, 33, 34;
Suanna, 33, 34
BURCH, Adam, 20
BURDGE, William, 7
BURK, John, 79
BURTELL, James, 97
BURTON, Benjaman, 114;
Benjamin, 113, 115, 116, 117;
Jacob, 52, 53, 117; John, 52,
67; Joseph, 71; Joshua, 72,
85, 117; Martha, 71; Mary,
72; Nathanial J., 95;
Nathaniel, 95; Robert, 6;
William, 1, 32, 84; Wolsey,
117; Woolsey, 117, 127
BUSH, George, 26, 82
BUTCHER, William, 40, 117
BUTLAR, William, 9
BUTLER, Israel, 45; Samuel, 45;

William, 9

-C-
CADE, Robert, 17, 18, 20;
Thomas, 29, 54
CADWALADER, John, 46; Lambert,
111; Thomas, 114, 115
CAHOON, Jonathan, 127; Mary,
52, 53; William, 52, 53
CAINE, William, 13
CALDWELL, James, 35
CALE, Esther, 71; Robert, 128
CALHOON, Jonathan, 125; Thomas
L., 126; Thos. L., 125
CALHOUN, James, 107
CALLANDE, Samuel, 34
CALLAWAY, Abraham, 105; Abraham
(Abram), 101; Ann, 47, 111;
Ebenezar, 36; Ebenezer, 36;
Edward, 92; Elenor, 92;
Elisha, 111; Isaac, 92;
Joshua, 104; Mathew, 47;
Peter, 104; Polley, 111;
Samuel, 104; Thomas, 104, 111
Callaways Venture, 119
Callis Land, 6
CALLOWAY, Edward, 96; Lowder,
92
CAMMEL, John, 103; Nanny, 103
CAMPBELL, John S., 48, 96, 102,
103; John Simpson, 46
CAMPTON, Jacob, 74
Canaan Improved, 32, 56
CANNON, Abraham, 109; Constant,
93; Elijah, 49, 50, 74;
Hayward, 76; Henry, 105;
James, 120; Jeremiah, 58, 74;
Leah, 105; Mary, 76; Mathew,
108; Matthew, 108; Rebecah,
76; Richard, 56; Wingate, 49,
50
Cannons Regulation, 26, 58
CANTWELL, Ed., 9; Edmond, 9, 12
CAREY, Nehemiah, 65, 66, 123;
Thomas, 31
CARLETON, Joseph, 44, 45
CARLILE, Rebeckah, 50; Thomas,
76
CARPENTER, Elizabeth, 72;
Esther, 72; George, 65;
James, 22, 72, 101; John, 72;
Luke, 72, 84, 85; Mary, 72;
Phebe, 72; Samuel, 85; Sarah,
72, 79
Carpenters Field, 22
CARTER, William, 6, 15, 19
CARTOR, William, 15
CARY, Nehemiah, 80
CASE, Gove, 127
Cattle Delight, 5
Ceder Town, 124

132

Ceder Neck, 10
CHAMBERS, John, 34; Michall,
  18, 19
CHANCE, John, 54, 55; Sarah,
  54; Spencer, 54, 55; William,
  54
Chance, 41
CHEW, Benjaman, 114; Benjamin,
  115
CHILD, John, 102
CHIPMAN, Hannah, 35; John, 35;
  Mary, 35, 90; Paris, 35;
  Pariz, 90
CIRWITHIN, Caleb, 7, 8, 42, 62,
  68, 73, 75; John, 73, 112,
  113; Nanny, 73
CLAMPET, Cook, 122; Polley, 122
Clare, 79
CLAMPETT, William, 20
CLAMPITT, Cook, 122; Polley,
  122; William, 21
CLARK, Charles, 87; Elizabeth,
  39; Honnor, 12; Honour, 12;
  John, 90; Jonathan Deare, 74;
  William, 1, 2, 3, 4, 5, 6, 7,
  8, 9, 10, 11, 12, 13, 14, 16,
  17, 18, 19, 20, 21, 22, 23,
  28, 29, 30, 39, 43, 52, 69
CLARKE, John, 123
CLARKSON, Benniah, 87; Mary,
  87; Mathew, 102; Wiliss, 87;
  Williss, 87
Clarksons Lott, 58
Clarksons Meadow, 58
CLAYPOOL, Jehu, 112; Norton, 29
CLAYPOOLE, James, 3, 4, 7, 18,
  19, 23, 29; Jehu, 112;
  Norton, 6, 14, 16
CLAYTON, Joshua, 86
CLAYWELL, Shadrach, 27
Clear Brook, 109
CLEMENT, Abraham, 12, 20; Mary,
  103
CLEMENTS, Abraham, 12
CLEMMENT, Abraham, 6
CLIFTON, Daniel, 121; John, 24,
  25, 27, 44, 81, 104, 106;
  Robert, 5, 32; Thomas, 5, 18,
  29
CLINDANIELS, John, 62
CLOTHERS, John, 128
CLOWE, ---, 52, 53
CLOWES, Catharine, 63; David,
  63; Gerhardus, 63; Isaac, 90;
  John, 31, 35, 40, 52, 53, 55,
  57, 59, 62, 63, 64, 68, 70,
  71, 72, 74, 75, 76, 90, 103,
  113, 114; Lydia, 63; Mary,
  55, 63, 90; William, 63
CLOWS, John, 110
Cocland, 104

COE, Daniel, 43; John, 32;
  Timothy, 43, 46
COGGESHALL, Preserved, 7
COGGSHALL, Preservd, 34, 52;
  Preserved, 46
COLE, Cornelius, 64; Coverdale,
  62
COLEMAN, William, 60, 79, 121
COLLIER, Thomas, 108
COLLING, John, 41
COLLINGS, Charles, 56; Elijah,
  40; Hencock, 65; John, 41,
  47; Josiah, 93; Leven, 65;
  Levin, 65; Lovey, 75; Thomas,
  48
COLLINS, Andrew, 103; George,
  47; John, 47, 87, 88, 89, 90,
  100, 116, 119; Joseph, 47,
  73, 79; Joseph S., 120;
  Levin, 66; Lovey, 75; Noah,
  81; Rebecca, 120; Robert, 47;
  Thomas, 48, 51, 52, 53, 73
CONNELLY, Comfort, 96
CONNER, Elizabeth, 87;
  Rackliff, 68, 69
CONNOLLY, Bridget, 62; Frances,
  62
CONNOWAY, Hannah, 105; John,
  105; Philip, 105
Content, 41
CONWAY, William, 83
CONWEL, William, 86
CONWELL, George, 89, 90; Jehu,
  51; William, 114, 115; Yeats,
  28
COOK, Arther, 29
COOKE, George, 87
Cool Spring, 56
COOMBE, Benjamin, 79
COOPER, Isaac, 93, 104, 117,
  118, 119, 120, 121, 123; John
  Richards, 16; Richard, 123;
  Thomas, 111, 117; William B.,
  118; Wm. B., 118
Coopers Hall, 37, 71, 99
COPE, Thomas, 28
COPES, Joseph, 102, 119
CORBETT, ---, 23; Roger, 1, 2,
  7, 17, 20, 22, 30, 32, 33,
  43, 46, 107
CORD, ---, 90; William, 50
Cornbury, 16, 21
CORNELISON, Harmon, 14
CORNWELL, Avery, 122; Frances,
  105; Francis, 30, 76, 84
COSTON, Joshua, 40, 87;
  Sommerset Dickerson, 83;
  Stephen, 99
COUCH, Meshach, 54
COULLER, Tho., 124
COULTER, James, 50; Joseph, 69,

140

87, 88, 89, 90, 93, 94, 100
Moores Liberty, 120
Moores Previledge, 119, 120
Moores Previledge Enlarged, 119
Moores Lott, 93
MORE, John, 104; Thomas, 14
MORGAN, Jemima, 43; John, 40,
   43; Sarah, 40; Solomon, 40;
   Tammey, 121; Thomas, 11;
   William, 121
Morgans Timber Land, 40
Morgans Chance, 34
MORRIS, Antoney, 20; Bevins,
   70, 76; Comfort, 126; Dennis,
   76, 123; Edward, 43, 46;
   John, 42, 118; Joseph, 70,
   126, 128; Rachel, 111; Sarah,
   43, 46; Solomon, 128;
   William, 76, 92
MORRISS, Beavins, 75
MORROGH, John, 28
MUIR, James, 108
MUMFORD, Elizabeth, 56
MURDOCK, Robert, 15, 20
MURPHEY, Daniel, 77
MURRAY, Isaac, 92; James, 38,
   69
MUSTARD, John, 116
MYERS, John, 109
My Fortune, 27

-N-
NAIGHT, James W., 70
Narrow Chance, 39
Neighbourhood? [page torn], 112
NEILL, Charles, 46; Henry, 24,
   25, 58, 106; John, 46, 47,
   56, 100; Joseph, 47
NELSON, Robert, 56
NEWALL, John, 6
NEWBLE, William, 76
NEWBOALD, John, 97
NEWBOLD, James, 78; John, 97;
   Parnal (Pirnal), 97; Sarah,
   97, 98; William, 41, 97
NEWBOULD, John, 97; Thomas, 98
NEWCOMB, Ann, 30; Baptist, 30,
   62; Betty, 39; Hester, 62;
   Thomas, 39, 62
NEWCOMBE, Ann, 19; Baptist, 19
Newcombs Barrons, 62
New England:
   Boston, 13
   Piscattaway, 1
New Port, 76
NICHOLDSON, Parker, 126
NICHOLLS, Mathias, 12
NICHOLS, Mathias, 10, 12;
   Nehemiah, 85
NICOLLS, Mathias, 9; Matthias,
   46; Nehemiah, 56; William, 78

NOBLE, William, 76
NOGE, John, 52
NOGLE, John, 52
NORMAN, Elijah, 72; Elizabeth,
   72
NOTTINGHAM, Jonathan, 38
NUNCZ, Hannah, 92
NUNEZ, Daniel, 115; Hannah, 52
NUTTER, Christopher, 30, 32;
   John, 22, 30, 32
Nutters Farme, 22, 30

-O-
OAKEY, Elizabeth, 39, 99; John,
   6, 7, 13, 14; Thomas, 39
OBEIER, Joshua, 88
OBUR, Joshua, 26
ODAY, Elizabeth, 119; Owen, 119
OLDHAM, Thomas, 5
OLDMAN, ---, 23; Tho., 19, 30;
   Thomas, 3, 5, 15, 22
OLIVER, Aaron, 120
O'NEILL, Hamilton, 25, 48
ONIONS, Hoday, 65; John, 82;
   Pearson, 81, 82
ORR, William, 2, 20, 22
OSTON, Isaac, 102
OUTHAM, John, 27
OUTON, John, 6; Obid, 27
OUTTEN, Obid, 101
Outtens Mistake, 85
OUTTIN, Obid, 27
OWENS, Robert, 93; Sarah, 54
OWINGS, Beal, 56; Nicholas, 56
OZBORNE, Mathew, 23
OZBURN, John Jenefor, 33;
   Thomas, 62

-P-
PAGE, Edward, 20
PAIRMORE, Alexander, 50; Mary,
   50
PARAMORE, Solomon, 70
PARIMORE, Matthew, 90; Solomon,
   69
PARKER, Anderson, 44, 52, 74,
   83, 105, 115; Edw., 33; Eli,
   33; George, 124, 125;
   Gilbelsher, 59, 114, 115;
   Hannah, 124; John, 105, 124,
   125; Mathew, 30; Matthew, 30;
   Peter, 44, 59, 125; Tabitha,
   126
PARKS, Catharine, 77
Parmocas Struggle, 126
PARMORE, Job, 76; Solomon, 69
PARR, Richard, 4
PARRAMER, Solomon, 70
PARRAMOR, Solomon, 70
PARROMORE, Stephen, 70;
   William, 70

WOOTTEN, Elijah, 95
Worcester Co., Maryland, 27,
  37, 44, 55, 58, 64, 66, 69,
  79, 95, 101, 104, 108
WORTON, Reavel, 72; Thomas, 72
WRIDER, ---, 120
WRIGHT, Charlottee, 119; David,
  40; Frances, 126; Francis,
  67, 68; Keziah, 58; Peter F.,
  44, 60; Peter Fretwell, 52,
  53, 55, 57, 58, 59, 60, 61,
  62, 67, 68, 72, 73; William,
  119
WROE, Morning, 95, 96; William,
  95, 96

WYATT, Sackar, 116
WYNCOOP, Benjamin, 124; Sarah,
  124
WYNKOOP, Benjamin, 62, 65;
  Woodrop, 65
WYNNE, Elizabeth, 21, 22;
  Jonathan, 16, 17

-Y-

Yoark, 55
YOUNG, Charles, 82; George, 1,
  12, 14; John, 18, 19, 82, 94;
  Mary, 48; Nathaniel, 44, 81,
  82, 96, 102, 103
Youngs Hope, 12, 13

www.ingramcontent.com/pod-product-compliance
Lightning Source LLC
Chambersburg PA
CBHW072057090426
42739CB00012B/2802